TOXIC BURN

TOXIC BURN

The Grassroots
Struggle against
the WTI Incinerator

Thomas Shevory

UNIVERSITY OF MINNESOTA PRESS
MINNEAPOLIS
LONDON

Published by the University of Minnesota Press
111 Third Avenue South, Suite 290
Minneapolis, MN 55401-2520
http://www.upress.umn.edu

Library of Congress Cataloging-in-Publication Data

Shevory, Thomas C.
   Toxic burn : the grassroots struggle against the WTI
incinerator / Thomas Shevory.
      p. cm.
   Includes bibliographical references and index.
   ISBN 978-0-8166-4852-8 (hc : alk. paper)—ISBN 978-0-
8166-4853-5 (pb : alk. paper)
   1. WTI incinerator (East Liverpool, Ohio).
   2. Environmental protection—Citizen participation.
   3. Hazardous wastes—Incineration—Government policy—
Ohio—East Liverpool. 4. United States. Environmental
Protection Agency—Public relations. I. Title.
   TD1062.S54 2007
   363.738'46—dc22
                                              2006039641

Printed in the United States of America on acid-free paper

The University of Minnesota is an equal-opportunity
educator and employer.

15 14 13 12 11 10 09 08 07   10 9 8 7 6 5 4 3 2 1

Contents

Preface

In early November 2005, I watched with keen interest as Bill Clinton gave a eulogy at Rosa Parks's funeral. The former president can still give speeches that are eloquent, moving, and perfectly in pitch with the occasion. The rhetorical disabilities of the current occupant of the Oval Office made Clinton's skills all the more apparent. The speech was organized around the theme of standing (or in this case sitting) against injustice. Rosa Parks, Clinton said, personified the idea that one person, challenging power, could change the world. He recounted how, as a nine-year-old boy, he was so inspired by Rosa Parks's action that he and a couple of his white friends tried to emulate her by sitting in the *back* of a local segregated bus, a small act of solidarity with the newly emerging civil rights movement. The audience was moved to applause at many points during the speech, and understandably so. As I admired the former president's eloquence, however, I couldn't help but think of the impact of his administration's decisions to validate the U.S. Environmental Protection Agency's actions in the case of the WTI incinerator. It seems pretty clear that the president took an active, if behind-the-scenes, role in protecting the permit. As I listened to the televised address, then, I noted the contrast between a fine speech about a woman who stood against injustice and the actions of a man who, as president, protected a permit to build and operate a hazardous waste incinerator within one hundred yards of an elementary school, the students of which were disproportionately African American. At that school, the emergency response plan to an accident involving a chemical explosion was to put tape over the windows.

At one time, the WTI incinerator in East Liverpool, Ohio, was slated to be "the world's largest." Depending on your point of view, such a designation could be considered an accolade or a threat. Such high aspirations were never reached, however, because a second proposed incineration unit, or kiln, was not constructed for complicated reasons that I address in *Toxic Burn*. That there is only one kiln, rather than two, is a tangible fact within which is contained thirty years of political, legal, and environmental history. This history involves a town whose residents have had a complicated and often contested relationship to the facility. This history implicates the trajectories of globalization and the evolution of the advanced nation-state from environmental regulator to facilitator of global capital. In the case of WTI, there is a mountain of evidence that state and federal agencies bent to the will of a corporate entity. This is a history that is still unfolding. It is a history that matters.

The following facts about the WTI incinerator are undeniable: It burns sixty thousand pounds of hazardous waste a year. The actual content of the burned waste can be kept secret under Ohio law. The incinerator emits a panoply of toxic substances, including dioxins, furans, and heavy metals, all implicated in a variety of health problems. It sits in a natural bowl that is part of the Ohio River valley, in an area that is subject to frequent temperature inversions. The name of the company that owns the plant has changed at least forty-four times, but whether this indicates an actual change in ownership is difficult, if not impossible, to determine. Two EPA-mandated risk assessments have been made of the plant's operations, one of which was discredited by an internal EPA memo, the other of which cost about four million dollars. Both suggested that human life is worth sacrificing for the sake of burning hazardous waste. For much of WTI's operating history, state monitoring efforts were undermined by some combination of corruption, mismanagement, incompetence, and human error. The plant has experienced dozens of accidents, some relatively small but others undeniably severe. Most recently, in August 2005, a drum exploded as it was being loaded into the incinerator's kiln. The explosion blew a hole through the wall of the building, and the force of the blast was strong enough to carry debris outside the facility's grounds. A worker was seriously injured and airlifted to a hospital in Pittsburgh.

Opposition to the plant has been determined and imaginative from the start. It has continued on and off for more than thirty years. One anti-WTI demonstration in East Liverpool resulted in arrests and subsequent jury acquittals under the "necessity defense" (which posits that a defendant be acquitted of a crime if it can be shown that she or he believed that no other recourse was possible), the only time such a criminal defense has been successful in the history of the state of Ohio. Opponents traveled to Washington, where on one occasion they were arrested for occupying the EPA building. On another they blocked traffic in front of the White House. Anti-WTI activists significantly undermined the credibility of *Earth in the Balance* author Al Gore. Gore, after all, had acquiesced to the Clinton administration's determination to keep the plant open and operating in spite of legitimate concerns about its safety. The WTI incinerator may never have become "the world's largest," but its political implications have been huge.

Power is most intimidating when it colonizes territories close to home. Challenging the powerful is never easy. It is especially difficult when the powerful not only come from distant places such as Washington, D.C., or Little Rock, Arkansas, but have close connections to the folks that you might see at the grocery store, or walking along the street in your hometown. The anti-WTI activists challenged power in distant and not-so-distant places. They were smart, stubborn, and relentless, while, as far as I can tell, never losing a sense of perspective, decency, or balance. Power has infrastructure: physical, financial, human. The infrastructures of power provide layers of protection. When you challenge power, you have to create your own infrastructures, and you are always vulnerable. Anti-WTI activists created complex, multilayered infrastructures of support, in effect a national movement against WTI. In the process they, along with other environmental justice activists, helped to foster a new environmental politics that still resonates in communities across the country and around the world. In the days before flash mobs and Deaniacs, anti-WTI activists challenged a system of power in the streets, over bridges, in courtrooms, and in the concrete buildings that house the administrative apparatus for our supposed environmental protection.

The Rust Belt continues to rust. No one seems capable of dealing with its multifaceted problems. The vaunted equilibrium of market forces doesn't have much impact on places like East Liverpool, Ohio, or its neighbor across the river, Chester, West Virginia. If it did, then low costs of living and an eager workforce would attract businesses and residents who would revive these areas left behind by the global economy. It turns out, however, unsurprisingly, that large numbers of people are not interested in moving into a formerly industrial landscape, even one that is in a still-beautiful river valley. Part of the reason is the industrial detritus that has been deposited there. At one point, someone had the bright idea that you could replace industries that fashioned the goods of U.S. consumer society with industries that handled the waste of the consumer economy, and that this would somehow be a worthy and respectful substitute. It's hard to organize a productive economy simply on the destruction of waste. Not only is it not productive; it's the antithesis of being productive.

Recently there has been much talk about the "death of environmentalism." If environmentalism is dying, it is, partly at least, because its focus has changed toward rethinking business practices as "sustainable" rather than challenging the broad networks of power that support and sustain global capital. Environmentalists must continue to interrogate the concrete realities of how power functions to disrupt and disfigure the lives of ordinary people. Perhaps the white middle-class environmentalism of the 1970s is dead, and perhaps that is a good thing. But in dozens, if not hundreds, of communities around the United States and across the globe, environmentalism is not a matter of choice; it is a necessity, and to signal its death is simply an indication of privilege. For those who confront the applications of power on a daily basis by opposing unseen and unknowable risks, such privileges cannot be taken up or put down after further consideration. They are real necessities. This book attempts to illuminate and explain those necessities and to show how ordinary people from an ordinary place did and continue to do extraordinary things. That is, of course, entirely consistent with the actual legacy of Rosa Parks.

Introduction:
East Liverpool and
the Politics of Power

The exercise of power is determined by thousands
of interactions between the world of the powerful
and that of the powerless, all the more so because
these worlds are never divided by a sharp line.
—*Václav Havel*, Disturbing the Peace

I traveled across the southern tier of New York. Just west of Erie,
Pennsylvania, I turned straight south, down the eastern edge of Ohio.
It was a pleasant enough drive, which took me past farms and small towns
and around Youngstown, where congressman James Traficant had recently
been tried and convicted on federal charges of accepting bribes, demand-
ing kickbacks from his staff members, obstructing justice, and racketeering. He hadn't yet decided whether to run for reelection. While he would
undoubtedly be challenged in the Democratic primary, he threatened to
run as an independent, potentially throwing the district to a Republican in
a three-way race. Traficant seemed to be viewed as something of a lovable
rogue, not unlike perhaps Louisiana governor Edwin Edwards, or even
former president Bill Clinton. East Liverpool is about an hour south of
Youngstown. Terri Swearingen had given me clear directions to her house,
across the Ohio River from East Liverpool, in Chester, West Virginia.

Highway 11 into East Liverpool announced that the town was the
birthplace of Lou Holtz, the former football coach of Notre Dame.
Southern Ohio is indeed football country. The Pro Football Hall of Fame
is in Canton. Columbus, 150 miles to the west, is where Woody Hayes
reigned supreme at Ohio State until 1978, when, on national television,

he attacked a Clemson player who strayed across the Ohio State sideline after intercepting a pass. Hayes was soon thereafter forced to resign.

I traveled through and around East Liverpool along Highway 30 and headed over the Jennings Randolph Bridge into West Virginia. Jennings Randolph had been a longtime senator from West Virginia. Not unlike the stentorian Robert Byrd, Randolph served for many years and made certain that the state benefited as much as possible from federal largesse, which, while welcomed, never seemed quite enough to pull West Virginia from the bottom of the nation's socioeconomic rankings. As one pays homage to Senator Randolph by crossing his namesake, it is difficult not to notice that below lies a deep river valley, as the river bends just north of East Liverpool, before it opens up to a straighter path just a few miles south. As I crossed the bridge, I could see the WTI incinerator to my left, at a crook in the river. No smoke or steam was rising from the stack. Apparently the facility was not at that moment burning any of the sixty thousand tons of hazardous waste per year that it was permitted to incinerate. I climbed a steep hill out of the natural bowl where East Liverpool and Chester were located. Just on the other side, I found Terri's driveway and turned into it.

I had talked to Terri on the phone about a week earlier. I had begun the project by surveying old newspaper and magazine articles and other published accounts. My interest in the incinerator had been provoked by an article in the *New York Times* that I had encountered during the 2000 elections. It had been a short piece, buried in the middle of the paper, about protests in New Hampshire that were being organized by opponents of the southern Ohio incinerator in response to Al Gore's run for the presidency. I had remembered the incinerator controversy and recalled that it had tarnished Gore's green credentials. I couldn't remember much more than that. I was surprised to learn that there was still resistance against something that seemed to have occurred such a long time ago. I cut out the article and made a mental note to look into it further.

I followed up with a more detailed investigation in spring 2002. The complexity of the story, all the twists and turns that it had taken since first being proposed in 1980, was astounding. Not only had there been several legal attempts to stop the incinerator, but an active, clever, and in some respects very successful grassroots movement had been organized against it. Several members of Congress and two senators, Howard

Metzenbaum and Jay Rockefeller, had actively opposed it. Congressional hearings, chaired by Massachusetts congressman Barney Frank, had been held to examine the U.S. EPA's actions in the case. The Ohio attorney general had issued a lengthy analysis of the legality of the plant's permit. Gore had gotten involved during the 1992 campaign, when he made what turned out to be an infamous, and politically misguided, promise to stop the incinerator from being permitted—misguided because there appeared to be forces stronger than the vice presidential candidate's good intentions that were determined to move the plant forward toward permitting and operations. The Clinton administration decided not to intervene in the permit, though a Government Accountability Office (GAO) report eventually confirmed many of the opponents' claims about the health and environmental hazards posed by the facility. The Gore presidential campaign, on the verge of the New Hampshire primary, not wanting to have a victory tarnished by bad publicity, reached an agreement with the WTI opponents to have a U.S. EPA ombudsman conduct a full investigation of the plant. In October 2001, ombudsman Robert Martin recommended that the plant be shut down for at least six months. In January, George W. Bush was sworn in as president of the United States. Martin was soon forced from his EPA post after the ombudsman's power was gutted by the new administration. Needless to say, the incinerator remains open and operational.

"East Whirlpool" is how Terri said she liked to refer to the area, with specific reference to the incinerator controversy, because it "just sucks everybody in." I had called Terri after doing some preliminary research on the project. She did not know me, nor I her. I was just another person interested in the incinerator. Terri turned out to be smart, interesting, energetic, and generous. After talking to her on the phone, I became even more certain that this was indeed an issue worth investigating more fully. I suggested that I might make a trip to East Liverpool, and she told me that she would be very open to spending some time with me. She also informed me that she had dozens of banker's boxes full of documents on the incinerator's troubled history.

Terri Swearingen was born in the city of East Liverpool. She is the daughter of a steelworker and was trained as a nurse. She had lived a relatively ordinary life in Chester after her marriage to a local dentist. Terri was peripherally involved with local opposition groups in 1982, pregnant with her daughter, and concerned about the health impacts of the proposed facility. Her leadership position in the movement began in 1990 after her husband Lee took the Greenpeace video *Rush to Burn* to a Sunday school class on environmental stewardship. After seeing the video, a woman in the class asked Terri to speak about it at a public forum, so she began to research the issue in some detail. Then she was invited by a local neurosurgeon to speak to the county medical society. She delved deeper into her research, finding an Office of Technology Assessment (OTA) document on neurotoxicity particularly helpful and particularly disturbing. The more she learned, the more concerned she became. She began to meet regularly with other local activists who had been working against the incinerator's siting. As a leader, she brought great energy to the movement, and she had a knack for creating clever public spectacles, as well as an obsessive devotion to gathering and organizing information. She was persistent and successful in garnering support from potential allies, such a EPA whistle-blower Hugh Kaufman.[1] Her entry into activism transformed her life in many ways. She is now on the board of directors of Greenpeace, and in 1997 she won the Goldman Environmental Award. At one point, she was named one of *Time* magazine's fifty most interesting young people. She is on a first-name basis with Ralph Nader and Jerry Brown. She has delivered dozens of talks around the country, with a slide show, giving advice to grassroots activists on how to organize against the environmental depredation of their communities.

Terri talked practically nonstop from the moment I met her, regaling me with stories about the incinerator and the attempts to stop it, including the events of 1992, when Al Gore made his promise. After the 1992 election, activists met with U.S. EPA officials and members of the Gore staff. They seemed to indicate that the plant's permit would be invalidated. For a few days, she thought that the incinerator's opponents had won, and she broke down in tears from exhaustion and happiness. What happened has never been entirely clear, but the ground shifted rapidly. Carol Browner, the newly appointed EPA director, recused herself from the case.[2] A decision about the permit was turned over to EPA deputy Robert Sussman. Sussman had been a law school classmate of the Clintons. He was a former legal counsel to the Chemical Manufacturers Association and at one point had negotiated contracts between several chemical companies and WTI. Within the EPA, support for the incinerator's permit returned. Terri was told by the *New York Times* reporter Keith Schneider that "your man (Gore) has had his legs cut out from under him." Terri compared this experience to Terry Anderson's stories of being held hostage in Lebanon in the 1970s. The worst times, Anderson had recounted, were when his captors told him to ready himself because he was going to be released, only later to retract the offer. The strategy was to demoralize him. It constituted a form of psychological torture. Al Gore's intentions might not have been as abhorrent as those of the Lebanese kidnappers, but the impact of his actions struck Terri as having the same effect.

The information that she had collected was overwhelming. Boxes and boxes of materials lined one basement wall. Each was labeled with a different aspect of the incinerator's history. One was marked "Risk Assessment," another "Rose Law Firm," another "WTI Ownership." As I began to learn more about the history of the matter, these phrases began to take on meaning. Not only did the boxes contain the raw materials that told the WTI story in its many aspects and phases, but in each case, Terri had put together detailed chronologies of the various issues. The chronologies were in turn stapled or paper clipped to the original documents. The chronologies were generated to organize press releases, as well as to provide background information for various interested parties, such as public officials, organizers, and academics who were helping with the resistance. I spent the better part of three days in Terri's basement as she talked about various aspects of the incinerator's history. I was fascinated by her accounts. Occasionally she would reach into a box and pull out a document. "Here's an interesting story," she would tell me, and then take off on a lengthy disquisition on a particular subject. She was right. The stories were compelling. I found myself being pulled deeper into the swirl of East Whirlpool.

On my second day in East Liverpool, Terri offered to give me a tour of the surrounding area. We hopped into her minivan and headed back toward the Ohio River. She showed me how close the incinerator was to the West Virginia side of the river. From the parking lot of an elementary school, you had an unobstructed view of the facility sitting right on the opposite river bank. She also took me on a road through the hills into the West Virginia countryside to show me something else, another environmental problem that was not directly related to the incinerator. About two miles outside Chester, in an area that was still very residential, she showed me a small lake consisting of a substance that was nothing like I had ever seen before. It was not a color that appears in nature. It was yellowish green, almost Day-Glo, like an overchlorinated and gelatinous swimming pool. You could see through to the bottom. Whether it was liquid or some kind of gel was not entirely obvious, and I didn't want to get close enough to find out. I found it to be more frightening than the incinerator. Dead tree trunks were sticking up through the middle and seemed to surround it on the edges as well. From where I was standing, I couldn't tell how far into the distance it reached, but it looked about a half mile wide and at least a mile or two long. There wasn't even a fence around it. Terri told me that her daughter had told her that some of the local kids would ride their ATVs around it. There were lots of dead animals near it. And when kids would get the substance on their clothes, it would stain them badly. Even more disturbing to me was that small, well-kept suburban bunga-lows stretched along the tops of its banks. Terri said that some local people were starting to get more interested in what this was. She thought that something was being dumped there from the Shippensburg nuclear power plant in Pennsylvania. It looked like chlorine to me. In any case, it was evidence that deindustrialized cities such as East Liverpool had become a primary dumping ground for the detritus of industrial civilization.

We then drove over to the other side of the river and into Ohio. East Liverpool stretches along the Ohio River, but in some respects it is more like two towns than one. If you cross from West Virginia and turn left, you will end up in the southern end of the city, the larger section of East Liverpool proper, where the city's center is located. This part of the city has seen better days. It has the faded look of dozens of other former industrial centers in the Northeast and Midwest. Downtown has some storefronts, a burger joint, some office spaces, a few antique stores. There was some activity, but the town seemed neither cheerful nor especially prosperous. Still, the city was functioning, and there were people on the streets en-gaged in productive activities. But if you cross the Jennings Randolph Bridge and turn right to go north toward the incinerator, you end up in what is known as the East End. The East End is removed both physi-cally and psychologically from the rest of East Liverpool. And when the Jennings Randolph Bridge was built, it, like so many federal highway proj-ects, reinforced the separation between the two already divided parts of town. The East End is where most of the city's black residents live. While East Liverpool proper appears a bit worn, the East End looks worse. While there are nice residential homes in parts of the East End, there are other parts where the traces of poverty are clearly apparent. Part of the East End encompasses an industrial warehouse district, where modest housing was no doubt once provided for the lower-paid employees of the potteries that once provided the economic basis of the community.

The East End is where the incinerator is located. Terri and I drove down to take a look. She advised me that there was a court order keeping her from the facility's property, but we could walk up along the railroad tracks behind it. A building in front had a sign for the Columbiana County Port Authority (CCPA). As the name implies, the CCPA was originally set up to develop the riverfront into a working port. No port was ever constructed, however, and none now exists, so precisely what the CCPA's function was is not clear to me. The CCPA was given title to the land on which the incinerator was built by the state of Ohio through eminent domain. Because of its ownership, the CCPA was supposed to sign WTI's initial permit application. Eventually, however, opponents were able to determine that no one from the CCPA had signed it, presumably invalidating the permit. Managers at the CCPA had apparently not wanted to accept liability for bad things that might happen as a result of the plant's operation. Who could blame them? This was an early and clear violation of state and federal regulations on hazardous waste permitting, one of many that would follow. Not only had the EPA overlooked it, but an EPA official even signed the permit for the CCPA. CCPA officials, however, wisely refused to recognize the validity of the signature. Instead the CCPA sold the property to WTI for a very modest price.

The incinerator itself looked pretty nondescript, just another industrial facility on the Ohio River with a smokestack. The workers milling around outside paid us little attention. Terri told me that on Fridays the facility would sometimes have picnics in the parking lot for the local residents. Schoolchildren would be encouraged to visit, take a free balloon, a hotdog, and maybe an ice cream cone. These regular events are even spotlighted on the Web page of Von Roll, the corporation that owns the plant. No doubt the kids of the East End were delighted with these treats. It reminded me of the fairs put on by the district noblemen in medieval Europe, designed to reinforce the loyalty of local peasants. I had to wonder about this noblesse oblige, however, since, in this case, the seemingly benevolent master was releasing toxic chemicals into the environment where many of these children lived.

We drove by Alonzo Spencer's place, a small, neatly kept frame house on the East End's main drag. Alonzo was one of the early and very vocal critics of WTI. A steelworker by trade, now retired, Alonzo had placed a large poster on his front door with the words "WTI Equals Death." Later I would meet him at the home of Sandy Estell, who was also a longtime activist. Sandy and Bob Estell's home is also in the East End and sits on the high bank overlooking the river. If you were to travel straight out of their backyard and continue toward the river, there is a good chance that you might end up right in the large rotary kiln into which is dumped some of the thousands of tons of hazardous materials that are burned up by the plant each year.

Next Terri took me up into the East Liverpool hills. This residential area sits far above the incinerator's smokestack, and to the west, and thus not in the path of the prevailing winds that sweep across those hills to carry the stack's effluent toward West Virginia or trap it in the East End in one of the inversions that blanket that unfortunate part of town two out of every three days a year. Every city in America has a class divide, and it always overlaps race and ethnicity in complicated patterns. In East Liverpool, the class differences are perhaps more striking than most. Touring the East End or the downtown area, one would think that the city has very little affluence. But the hills of East Liverpool are obviously the repository of large amounts of wealth. Here sit some of the most impressive-looking homes that I have encountered in a city of this relatively modest size. These houses are not McMansions—large, characterless boxes, thrown up according to prefabricated specs in the newly sprawling suburbs of Dallas or Chevy Chase, whose only architectural principle is that "size matters." These are houses of a different sort, similar to the stately mansions that can be found in parts of Pittsburgh and Buffalo, built during a period when American industrial might was still reaching toward its possibilities. These homes are, in other words, simply beautiful. It was almost impossible to imagine that this was the same city, or perhaps even the same planet, as the area that we had just left at the bottom of the hill.

I asked Terri how these folks had achieved their wealth. She said that much of it had been accumulated from the pottery works that had once been the foundation of East Liverpool's economy. As I later learned from a tour of the local pottery museum, East Liverpool had once produced 60 percent of American pottery. Not unlike the city that I had grown up in, Jamestown, New York, 150 miles to the north, the industrial activity that had once sustained East Liverpool had either disappeared or fled. Here the wealth that it generated was still being held by a few families that had once managed and owned it. In Jamestown, a fair amount of such capital was placed into foundations and is sometimes used for economic development projects. There seemed little evidence that this was occurring in East Liverpool. Yet while the evidence of private wealth was impressive, and while the residents of this part of town were removed from direct contact with the incinerator's steam plume, it was difficult for me to imagine why the people of means living here didn't move someplace that didn't have a hazardous waste incinerator in such close proximity, or at least didn't work with the grassroots efforts to try to have it shut down. Terri said that few of the folks that worked with them had come from this part of town. It seems altogether not unlikely that wealth encourages one to adopt the dominant ideology. And, in this case, the business class may have believed the promises of the plant's managers and public officials regarding its safety.

The final leg of my tour was a drive down the Ohio side of the Ohio River. Here the terrain flattens out, and the river seems to straighten. Here you will find link after link of a long chain of industrial facilities, including many chemical plants and oil refineries, along with coal-burning power plants, whose huge stacks emit sulfurous emissions that travel into northern New York and New England, wreaking havoc on upper-elevation forests. These power plants service the needs of what remains of the steel industry. But they also generate power that is used for residential purposes throughout the American Midwest and even the Northeast. While it is impossible to definitively locate the center of the nation's mythic "power grid," if you wanted to take a stab at it, the Ohio River valley is probably as good a place as any to start.

The residents of this area, then, are used to living with an industrial infrastructure. It has been a central aspect of the area's ecology for more than a century. But while they look on industrial activity as crucial to their employment and general prosperity, there are limits to what they are willing to absorb in its name. The hazardous waste facility at East Liverpool was a place where many of them were prepared to draw the line.

Two nights later I attended a meeting of the city council's incinerator "liaison" committee with Alonzo Spencer. The committee's main purpose,

Alonzo told me, was to act as a public relations front for the plant. Origi-nally, plant officials had promised to meet once a month with the public so that members of the community could be alerted to incinerator activi-ties and have their questions about its operations answered. Alonzo said that residents would attend the meetings and ask hard questions, based on research that they had undertaken. WTI officials weren't apparently interested in an actual dialogue, so as questions became more substan-tive and difficult for them to spin, fewer meetings were held. Now they appeared to happen only sporadically. On the occasion that I attended, two of the committee's three members didn't even bother to show up. That didn't stop Alonzo, however, from approaching the podium to ask a series of questions. His most important concern at that moment had to do with ownership of the facility. One might think that the ownership of a large industrial facility that burns hazardous waste would be easy to determine. But questions of ownership had been uncertain from the beginning of the permitting process.

Terri and a diverse group of researchers had uncovered more than forty-four possible owners through the mid-1990s. The obvious shell game had been designed, it seemed, to make the determination of liability an almost impossible pursuit, should a lawsuit be filed as a result of harms done from the facility's operations. The game was still being played. At the previous meeting, Alonzo had asked the committee's chair to talk to the managers of the plant, to determine who the owners were. Alonzo had information that Von Roll, the previous owner, had recently sold the plant to Heritage Environmental Services. The council member was vague and said that the managers had told him about Heritage something-or-the-other, but he couldn't be sure about it. While under ordinary circum-stances one might chalk the difference in names up to an oversight or a glitch in communication, opponents of the plant knew that even the smallest name differences were potentially significant. At one point, one of the partners had evolved from Waste Technologies Inc. to Waste Tech-nologies, Inc. The comma indicated a different legal owner.

The council member who attempted to respond to Alonzo's questions seemed rather clueless. He exhibited a notable lack of curiosity about the ownership issue and had apparently taken at face value what the plant managers had told him. Also at issue was the fee that the incinerator's owners, whoever they were, were paying to the city for every ton of hazardous waste brought into the plant. The plant's owners considered the fee to be a "gift" to the city, and one that they could conceivably withdraw at their discretion. The city's budget was now, however, highly dependent on these funds. Alonzo thought that some kind of formal contract ought to be negotiated with the plant. The council member didn't necessarily disagree, but he didn't seem interested in pursuing it.

My impression from attending this meeting was that the city's political power structure, such as it is, was unwilling to challenge the incinerator operators in any significant way. Partway through the meeting, Alonzo turned to me and said, "See what we have to put up with?" The way the meeting unfolded was almost comical. Alonzo could see the humor in it as well, although it was a rather bleak kind of humor. Too much was at stake for one not to take the ridiculousness of what was occurring seriously.

The two of us walked out of the building together and stood and chatted for a while out front. Alonzo said that a fight such as this becomes "your whole life." "You organize your vacations around it." He was on his way to Detroit for a July 4 get-together, but he had put off leaving so that he could attend the meeting. He also told me that there were many problems at the plant that weren't public. He knew people who worked there. They had talked to him about their experiences. Alonzo did not begrudge local folks working at the plant. One needed to make a living. Yet what he'd heard worried him. The incinerator had been built on a floodplain; essentially it was resting on fill. Because of this, pilings were driven into the bedrock to support the facility's weight, especially the weight of the stack. But as workers drove the pilings through, the builders broke into an aquifer. This had previously been contaminated by an old oil-refining facility that had at one time been on the property. Workers continued through the aquifer and back into the bedrock underneath. But there was another aquifer underneath the first, one of apparently immense size, stretching all the way to Pittsburgh. They broke through this one as well as the piling continued to the bedrock underneath it. As a result, the plant was resting on footers that were nearly 1,700 feet long. Because of the instability that this created, the smokestack was of a relatively modest height, making it more difficult for its effluvia to escape the deep and narrow river valley. Even more disconcerting, Alonzo said that people who worked at the plant had told him that cracks were starting to appear in its floor.

Before I left East Liverpool, I made one last stop at Terri Swearingen's

place, and we had a final talk about some of her experiences with the
movement to stop the incinerator. She showed me a videotape made by
Greenpeace in the early 1990s, when opposition against the incinerator
was starting to peak. Terri was interviewed in the video, as was another
young woman, also very articulate, whom Terri said she had not known
before or met since. She talked with great intensity about the dangers that
she felt the plant posed to children and others in the community. Several
times in the video, which was shot in autumn after the leaves had fallen,
the camera turned to the incinerator behind Terri and the other woman.
You could see the steam rising out of the plant, but rather than blowing
out of the valley, as you might hope, it circulated back and around in an
almost perfect circle as many of its ambient effluents certainly settled back
into the neighborhoods that lined the Ohio River on both the Ohio and
West Virginia sides. The image was disturbing. Despite Von Roll's claims
that virtually all the toxins were burned to the point of harmlessness,
there was still a percentage of PICs (products of incomplete combustion)
and other materials that, even if only in traces, were consistently being
funneled into the environment. These included dioxins, furans, and heavy
metals, such as lead, chromium, and mercury, all known to have damaging
health effects. EPA officials themselves admitted that they had conducted
no studies on the effects of the vast majority of PICs being released, and
did not even know the chemical constitution of many of them. Moreover,
unseen were the various "fugitive emissions," a known part of the operations of this and other hazardous waste facilities, which could include an
entire palette of toxic substances. When an accident occurred—and many
already had—significant amounts of known toxins were released into the
air. (On one occasion, for example, a smell of cat urine permeated the
entire East End.) If a Bhopal-type accident were to happen, an event not
entirely ruled out by the EPA's own "risk assessment" of the plant's operations, the results would be catastrophic.

What follows is a multidimensional study of the politics of the WTI
incinerator. As such, it is a study of the operations of power and resistance to it, a fundamental dynamic operating within democratic societies.
The siting, building, and protection of WTI occurred with the support of
powerful economic and political forces. The study of WTI is a study of
how democratic forces resist the incursions of the powerful. Power itself

is, however, a slippery concept. Some attention to its meanings is necessary as a context for understanding the concrete realities of waste disposal in deindustrialized America. Understanding power is essential for
viewing WTI's genesis and trajectory.

Power: Individual Acquisition

In American society, bookstores and cybershelves are replete with popular
works that guide individuals toward gaining individual power for themselves, often at the expense of others. Part of the reason for this, ironically,
is that so many people feel powerless. Many, perhaps most, feel as though
their lives are governed by economic, political, and cultural forces beyond not only their control but even their understanding. While there are
cultural forms that can help people understand and even challenge the
powerful forces that seem to govern their lives, others appeal to the sense
that power can be acquired and used.

A quick search of books at Amazon.com under the term "power"
(ranked, as they are, by sales) reveals numerous manuals on how to
achieve power. The message is that by learning certain techniques, one
can gain control over others for one's own benefit, pleasure, or financial
gain. Robert Greene's *The 48 Laws of Power* is a good example. Touted
as a book that distills the thinking of the greatest thinkers about power
in human history—Nicolo Machiavelli, Sun Tzu, Casanova, and Carl von
Clausewitz—it takes an entirely unsentimental view of human relationships. According to the authors, everyone wants and is in fact seeking
power. Each is trying to gain control over others for his or her own particular purposes. Even the seemingly innocent are engaged in such activities.[3] By learning, practicing, and applying Greene's carefully considered
rules, any person can soon be on the road to a successful life. That the
book consistently ranks around 200 on the Amazon.com sales list is an
indication that there is a large audience looking for help on how to achieve
this kind of power.

A slightly different take on the theme of accumulating personal power
can be found in *Power v. Force,* in which Dr. David R. Hawkins exposes the
secrets of "kinesiology," a practice that exposes "the intimate connections
between mind and body, revealing that the mind 'thinks' with the body

itself." By applying its principles, a person can, according to Hawkins, take control of his or her own life and achieve power in the financial markets, politics, health, and even the creative arts. Success, not only material but spiritual, is touted as the reward to Hawkins's imminently masterable methodology.[4] Again, as with Greene, Hawkins associates power with individual success and the capacity to shape the behavior of others.

In fact, success and power are virtually interchangeable concepts in the how-to presentation of power. Individuals achieve power via financial success, and financial success is an indicator of one's position and power. The capacity to present oneself as successful in turn reinforces others' perceptions of accumulated power and success. Success generates access to power and to the illusion of power. The latter, if properly cultivated, can be synonymous with the former. It is no accident that there is a subgenre of the how-to approach to power that focuses primarily on achieving success in the corporate ranks.

Hawkins and Greene are recent expressions of popular thinking that has a relatively long historical reach. Norman Vincent Peale[5] and Dale Carnegie both revealed the secrets of financial and social success as the capacity to gain influence over others.[6] Neither was as openly Machiavellian as Greene, but both taught that success was primarily an individual accomplishment and a reward for persistence, a positive outlook, and energetic spirituality. For the most part, the authors operating in this genre are uninterested in thinking about power as "political." They do not teach or encourage readers to challenge political authorities, given that such challenges might undermine an individual's capacity for success. Moreover, to focus one's attention on social forces would belie the belief that individuals have complete control over their own destinies if only they can master the proper techniques. In the how-to approach to power, structural forces are either malleable or irrelevant to the ambitious individual seeking to start the long and laborious climb "to the top." Moreover, the audience for books aimed at ambitious seekers of power no doubt tends to be those who accept the legitimacy of power systems as currently organized. Ambitious power seekers do not seek to challenge structural systems of power; they seek to find prominence within those systems. Given what we know about the distribution of power and income in the United States and globally, however, the odds are probably slim at best.[7]

Power : Pluralism and Power Elite Theory

Social scientists, political theorists, and cultural critics are less likely to think (or at least write) about power in such narrowly instrumental terms. Social scientists are more likely to think in terms of the distribution of power. The classical distinction here is between "pluralism" and "power elite theory." While the very terms may seem to have an anachronistic quality, undergraduate students are still exposed to them in introductory political science texts, and they offer as good a place to start as any when thinking about how power is organized in American and perhaps global contexts. Pluralists contend that power is fairly evenly distributed in American society. Accordingly, interest groups are able to bargain on relatively equal terms through institutional forms such as state and national legislatures, administrative agencies, the courts, electoral participation, and even the media.[8] Pluralism was partly an intellectual response to very low voting rates that existed (and still exist) in the American electoral system. Some social scientists have argued that the specific act of voting or other overt forms of political participation are essentially unnecessary, because various American publics are adequately represented through interest groups. Pluralism was the product of a particular historical moment: the postwar "consensus," when American power and prosperity seemed nearly limitless, and the sharing of generated wealth would make the United States a capitalist utopia that would serve the interests of all working as well as owning classes.[9]

Power elite theory was developed partly in response to pluralism as a non-Marxist (or perhaps quasi-Marxist) approach to analyzing how power is distributed and exercised in the American political context. C. Wright Mills's classic text starts with a rebuke of liberal individualism: "The powers of ordinary men are circumscribed by the everyday worlds in which they live, yet even in these rounds of job, family, and neighborhood they often seem driven by forces they can neither understand nor govern. . . . The very framework of modern society confines them to projects not their own [and they accordingly] feel that they are without purpose in an epoch in which they are without power."[10] Mills's stark depiction of the powerlessness of ordinary Americans was part of a set of intellectual responses to global economic and political forces undergoing consolidation in the post–World War II era. For example, the French sociologist Jacques

Ellul lamented the loss of human autonomy in the face of encroaching "technique."[11] Lewis Mumford feared the influence of the "pentagon of power."[12] A variety of social critics warned that individuals were being overwhelmed by impersonal bureaucratic forces and "mass society."[13] The rugged individual was being replaced by the "organization man."[14]

Mills's contribution to this set of intellectual trends was to focus on a specific group of individuals and to consider their role in controlling economic and political life. The "power elite" was composed of roughly five hundred people, who were connected through elite schools, business relationships, military service, and political office. This tiny collection of people was, Mills contended, responsible for shaping domestic and foreign policy in the United States. Members of it knew each other. They traveled in the same circles. They had similar ideological predispositions. They had a strong sense of class privilege and interest.

There are respects in which Mills's work now seems dated. When he wrote, American corporations still had a distinctively national character. Absent, necessarily, are any references to "new economy" elites such as Bill Gates or Rupert Murdoch. Yet there is much in Mills's writing that seems relevant to how power operates in the United States, especially in terms of "local power." "Local society" is still, in most places, "a structure of power as well as a hierarchy of status." It is still organized around "a set of cliques or 'crowds' whose members judge and decide the important community issues, as well as the many larger issues of state and nation in which 'the community' is involved."[15] These cliques often represent different sectors of the local economy: industrial, retail, and banking.

Yet even within local economies, important changes have occurred. In 1958 Mills was correct to remind his readers that "we could not understand" the pattern of local upper-level society "were we to forget that cities are all very much a part of the national system."[16] Local elites may still have power, but they are less "local" than they were. Even during Mills's time, older elites, organized around complex social hierarchies, for whom participation in civic affairs was an obligation, were being displaced by corporate elites, often from suburban areas, who had little loyalty toward, or interest in, strictly local affairs.[17] Since Mills wrote, local power has become ever more interconnected with, and constrained by, national and global forces. Local elites have less autonomy than ever. They are at the mercy of globalization's reach, and they are often painfully aware of that fact. Corporate managers have few, if any, local loyalties.

East Liverpool, like other deindustrialized areas of the United States, provides fertile ground for studying these power shifts. In the 1970s, as East Liverpool elites looked nationally and internationally for investment, expertise, and support, the Arkansas investment banker Jackson Stephens connected to East Liverpool through "local boy" Don Brown. The partnership was complicated from the start and included a prominent place for the Swiss multinational Von Roll AG. The building of the incinerator at East Liverpool could be seen as a determination to reconnect the local elites with national and global ones, to reassert their presence and importance in the face of the changing features of global capital. The pottery industry in East Liverpool was in decline. Local elites that managed and owned it were looking for new investments that might return them to power, prominence, and prestige.

Power elite theory has been criticized from both the left and the right. Left criticism of Mills focused on the lack of a conventionally Marxist class analysis. Mills, in this view, focused too much on what amounted to "superstructure" and placed too much emphasis on individual action, to the neglect of broader dialectics operating through history. Mills, Paul Sweezey contended, misunderstood the distinction between a "power elite" and a "ruling class."[18]

Liberal critics such as Robert Dahl questioned the level of concentration and the degree of coordination within the power elite. Dahl attempted to deal Mills's concept of power death by a thousand cuts. How do we know when A has power over B? Is it possible that B will have some power in relation to A? What were B's preferences when the interaction began? Are the alternatives mutually exclusive? Is A always a member of the power elite? Do all of the A's exercising power over all of the B's constitute less than a majority? The imponderables, according to Dahl, made power elite theory virtually impossible to either verify or falsify. It became, in Dahl's hands, "a type of quasi-metaphysical theory made up of what might be called an infinite regress of explanations."[19] In a word, it was "unscientific."[20] Dahl had a point. Discerning and revealing how power operates does not easily lend itself to scientific investigation. Power is elusive and difficult to specify in concrete terms.

Mills may also have been hurt by an unfair association of power elite theory with a conspiratorial view of political life. Mills was not a conspiracy theorist. He focused on loose associations that existed within the upper class and the institutions that fostered them. He was interested in broad policy trends. His ideas about the operations of power are clearly distinct from the narrow conspiratorialism that we might associate with JFK assassination aficionados or John Birchers. Still, because of Mills's willingness to document and expose a power structure, the existence of which is inconsistent with American liberal democratic mythology, he could be cast as having a narrow, and indeed somewhat conspiratorial, view of power's operations, and thus as working at the fringes of respectable political analysis. Mills's ideas were also superseded in some ways by Michel Foucault's writings on power, which, as they become more widely disseminated and known, had an extraordinarily important influence in a wide range of academic fields. Foucault's analysis of the "microprocesses" of power seemed more in tune with the antistructuralism of the post-Vietnam era and more relevant to a variety of then emerging left social movements organized on issues of race, gender, and sexual identity. I argue later that there are important compatibilities between Mills's and Foucault's analyses of power. Nevertheless, as Foucault's work on power drew increasing attention, it may have come partly at Mills's expense, as it shifted emphasis toward power as a set of widespread and deeply embedded social practices.

This is not to say, however, that power elite theory has not continued to be influential. William Domhoff, for example, has carried on in rather close ways to the work that Mills started, tracking the elite relationships and the patterns of movement between business, politics, and the military. Domhoff has done this over the course of many years through the publication of various editions of *Who Rules America?*[21] A genre of political exposé that tracks high-profile scandals also owes a debt to Mills. James Ring Adams is a leading practitioner of this form of investigative journalism. He has written books on the American savings-and-loan scandal of the 1980s, on the BCCI banking scandal, and on "supergun" inventor Gerald Bull (and his connections to the international arms trade).[22] Adams follows the trail of key principals in these cases, leading readers behind the scenes to glimpse the personal ambitions and conflicts at stake, allowing them to believe that they are getting a peek at how the worlds of politics

and finance operate at a kind of "street" level. The stories are complicated, often mind-numbingly so; but whether an attentive reader can keep
track of where all the trails lead, she or he is left with a sense that corruption, greed, and betrayal are not uncommon practices within the halls of
many powerful public and private institutions. The Bush administration
has spawned a renewed interest in this sort of investigative analysis.
Kevin Phillips's *American Dynasty* and Craig Unger's *House of Bush,
House of Saud* reveal the intricate, but real and important, connections
between global business and political leaders at the center of which is the
administration of George W. Bush.[23] Both find the Bush family to be at the
heart of a corrupt set of global networks. Michael Moore's film *Farenheit
911* borrowed generously from these works.[24] There is also an overlapping
series of investigations dealing specifically with the Enron and Halliburton
scandals.[25]

Public Information Research Inc. probably also owes something of
a conceptual debt to Mills. Founded and directed by the Vietnam War
resister Daniel Brandt, the nonprofit research foundation is dedicated to
revealing elite linkages. Brandt founded PIR (which began as Micro Associates) in the early 1970s. By the late 1980s, he had collected a database
of 30,000 names, most of whom had some relation to the CIA and other
intelligence services. According to Brandt, the work was "a continua-
tion of what I started as an undergraduate protesting U.S. policy in Vietnam."[26] PIR's NameBase Web site has 125,000 names and 280,000 cita-
tions,[27] all drawn from Brandt's singular research pursuits, which attempt
to track the activities of the intelligence community and economic and
political elites. The research is based on published sources and information compiled from Freedom of Information Act requests. All a visitor to
the PIR Web site has to do is to type in a person's name. After a few sec-
onds, a grid appears, at the center of which is the name queried. Radiating
spokes connect to other names, with colors indicating the strength of the
relationships.

Brandt claims an intimate knowledge of elite activities. As he noted in
an interview, "I've read all the books in NameBase, which is how they got
indexed. After reading and indexing 700 investigative books, there aren't
too many surprises about what the ruling class is up to. I know when something is new and interesting, or is more of the same old useless spin."[28]
Brandt, a highly respected figure even within the intelligence community

that he frequently criticizes, attempts to make knowledge about elite activities intuitively accessible by organizing it visually.[29] Brandt transforms power elite analysis into an aesthetically appealing visual game.[30]

To get a sense of why this perspective on power has relevance to WTI, I would encourage a curious reader to access NameBase and type in the name "Jackson Stephens."[31] Stephens, son of an Arkansas businessman who gained national prominence, was one of the early investors in the facility. NameBase shows his connections with an array of familiar names: Jimmy Carter, Bill and Hillary Clinton, Mochtar Riady, and Clark Clifford. Stephens epitomizes the sort of figure that Mills had in mind with the term "power elite." His importance to WTI, especially early on, cannot be overstated. The NameBase network for Stephens is a visual summary of much that follows in this book.

Stanley Aronowitz has argued that Mills has been an "absent presence" in social science theorizing. Cultural theory and postmodernist deconstructions of social life have supplanted the cultural anthropologies, case studies, and social realism of the 1940s and 1950s, helping to account for the "absence." Yet "although Mills's work rarely appears on the reading lists of fashionable graduate courses in social and cultural theory," there has been something of a revival in interest in Mills's thought.[32] Several of his most important works have been republished with introductions by respected contemporary scholars. The renewed interest in Mills has been reinforced by the recent spate of corporate scandals that once again cast a light on the activities of the powerful in ways that a Mills reader would find unsurprisingly familiar. In Halliburton's case, for example, military, political, and corporate power seems to have been tightly bound into a set of networks that appear at their core to be almost entirely corrupt. During the same period, two presidential candidates emerged, each of whom was the product of elite prep schools, each of whom graduated from Yale, each of whom came from a very old and established family, and each of whom represented a somewhat different faction of the upper class.

Power: Foucault

Michel Foucault's impact on thinking about the meanings and applications of political power cannot be overstated. While the primary emphasis of his most important works was on power's historical transformations, he was very much aware of, and sensitive to, the continuing political relevance of those transformations. Foucault argued that the character of power had shifted in the West with the decline of monarchical authority and the rise of the modern democratic state. In one oft-quoted passage, he asserted that "in a society like that of the seventeenth century, the King's body wasn't a metaphor, but a political reality. Its physical presence was necessary for the functioning of the monarchy." In the famous opening scene of *Discipline and Punish*, the reader is introduced in graphic detail to the consequences of challenging the seventeenth-century French legal order. A parricide is subjected to horrifying public torture and then death. The exercise of power is deliberately spectacular. Such spectacles are eventually replaced by more impersonal and bureaucratic interventions, exemplified by Jeremy Bentham's "panopticon," a means by which a prison guard could stand at a central point and survey the activities, and the bodies, of several hundred prisoners, even as they were all confined to separate individual cells.[33]

With the full emergence of modernity, the king's body was supplanted, according to Foucault, by the "social body." Power was dispersed, but it did not disappear. The social body organizes and protects itself through the development and application of the "disciplines" of the human sciences. "It is this social body which needs to be protected in a quasi-medical sense. In place of the rituals that served to restore the corporal integrity of the monarch, remedies and therapeutic devices are employed such as the segregation of the sick, the monitoring of contagions, the exclusion of delinquents."[34] Power is thus constituted in scientific methodologies and their applications via the practices of medicine, psychiatry, and penology. These practices are circumscribed and reinforced, but not controlled, by legality and administrative rule making. Their success hinges on their internalization. Power is, in effect, written onto and into physical bodies. As Foucault says, "The phenomenon of the social body is the effect not of a consensus but of the materiality of power operating on the very bodies of individuals."[35] In John Caputo's words, "Where sovereignty had held lord over the land and its bounty, disciplines now directed the eyes of power to bodies, allowing meticulous control over their operations by a strategy distinct from repression."[36]

Under a monarchical regime, power was deliberately made tangible and obvious. Violations were punished swiftly and severely. Within current regimes of power, its presence is often difficult to locate, even though, or perhaps because, it is utterly pervasive. Power's reach has expanded as its centers have proliferated. Power is everywhere and invisible, legitimized by scientific practices, reinforced by experts, and imposed unremittingly via countless instances of social exchange and interaction.[37] This constitutes an important and nearly complete historical reversal. Whereas power was once clearly embodied, and the subjects of its actions went largely unnoticed, now, as Todd May notes, "it is power that resides in the shadows while its object is put under the scrutiny of the psychological case."[38]

Foucault's understanding of power is both highly attractive and deeply unsettling. Its attraction partly lies in a commonsense recognition that everyday social practices are indeed organized according to systems of power—work regimens, family relations, friendships, romance. Such practices are continuously evaluated and redefined by psychiatrists, sociologists, and medical professionals. By locating power in everyday practices, Foucault seemed to offer the promise, or at least the hope, that power could again be made visible, tangible, or "material." Moreover, Foucault hoped to reveal not only power's operations but also strategies of resistance against it. Resistance to power, in fact, provided one mechanism for further revealing power's operations. Foucault hoped to investigate "this resistance as a chemical catalyst so as to bring to light power relations, locate their position, and find out their point of application and methods used." Power would be analyzed not in terms of "its internal rationality" but via "the antagonism of strategies."[39] Foucault's writing is unsettling because it can be interpreted to suggest that power is "all there is," and that no meanings exist beyond it. And if this is the case, then resistance is ultimately futile, because all acts of resistance are simply new forms of collusion in power's operations.

Unsettling as it may be, Foucault's suggestion in a 1978 interview that the question of who exercises power is "fundamental" in Western industrialized societies is still valid. He asks, "Who makes decisions for me? Who is preventing me from doing this and telling me to do that? Who is programming my movements and activities? Who is forcing me to live in a particular place when I work in another? How are these decisions on which my life is completely articulated taken?"[40] Such questions are, however, maddeningly difficult to answer in the terms by which they are proposed, precisely because power is no longer embodied entirely within

a sovereign. Individuals can be located in positions of political or administrative authority, but locating them and revealing their activities do not
answer the questions of how or why power is exercised, much less acceded
to. As Foucault states, "Of course we have to show who those in charge
are, we know that we have to turn, let us say, to deputies, ministers, principal private secretaries, etc., etc. But this is not the important issue, for
we know perfectly well that even if we reach the point of designating exactly all those people, all those 'decision-makers,' we will still not really
know why and how the decision was made, how it came to be accepted
by everybody, and how it is that it hurts a particular category of persons,
etc."[41] Foucault's "geneaological" investigations of the transformation and
application of institutional power are notoriously difficult to decode,[42] and
whether they give tangible or material answers to the fundamental question of how power operates is, I would suggest, an open question.

Mills's focus on hierarchies of power—"naming names," so to speak—
thus seems incomplete in Foucault's terms, because it does not interrogate the historical or epistemological sources of power's transformations.
Foucault contended that it is naive and perhaps even dangerous to focus
exclusively on the power of what he referred to as the "ruling class," partly
because this could lead to the false conclusion that the transference of
power out of the hands of the ruling class could resolve the problem of
power. This error was promulgated by the Marxist theories of the state
and applied in revolutionary practice with unfortunate consequences.
In traditional European Marxism, "the State apparatus must be undermined, but not completely undermined, since the class struggle will not
be brought to an immediate end without the establishment of the dic-
tatorship of the proletariat. Hence the state apparatus must be kept suf-
ficiently intact for it to be employed against the class enemy." But for the
state to continue to function, "technicians" and "specialists" must be employed, and for that to occur, "one has to call upon the old class which is
acquainted with the apparatus, namely the bourgeoisie." Any revolutionary movement that places its primary emphasis on the state while neglect-
ing "the mechanisms of power that function outside, below and alongside
the state apparatuses, on a much more minute and everyday level," cannot, in the end, succeed. But while Foucault may not have been interested
in mapping the contours of public administrative authorities, he did not
deny the importance of state power.

If a focus on power's "official story" is inadequate, incomplete, and even somewhat naive, it is still, I would argue, important. Certainly power is dispersed, and Foucault's contributions have done much to transform thinking about power as sets of "microprocesses." His writing spawned a drastic rethinking of power's meanings throughout the social sciences and humanities, with incredibly rich and varied results. Yet while Foucault nodded to the continuing importance of the state apparatus, he did little to reveal the vast and intricate networks of power that were and are associated with it. In truth, power is dispersed and concentrated. Technicians, specialists, and experts generate, reinvent, and reinforce systems of power that create meanings, shape bodies, and organize the postmodern soul. Yet there are some individuals, call them "elites," who exercise more control over political and economic life than do most others. These elites benefit from the operations of advanced systems of capital accumulation and bureaucratic organization. They are subjected to the "normalizing" aspects of power and the "psy" disciplines as are the rest of "us," but that does not mean that they are subjected to power in quite the same way. Elites exercise a kind of "sovereignty," but it is not the deliberately spectacular sovereignty of the seventeenth-century French monarchy. Rather, it remains largely hidden, deliberately so, seeking to maintain invisibility and perhaps mystique.

Environmental Politics, Power, and Film Noir

Film noir provides artistic maps of real and imaginary terrains of power. Attention to the myriad plots, characters, themes, subgenres, and atmospheres that constitute film noir is useful for thinking about the multiple hierarchies and microprocesses that constitute political power's meanings and applications. It might seem strange to draw on noir as a pathway into discussions of environmental politics, as I seek to do here. Environmental politics is, after all, usually organized by "greens." It is about protecting the lushness and ecological diversity of rain forests and rivers. Environmentalism is usually associated with the defense of what is pure and pristine. Noir, on the other hand, is black and white. Noir filmmakers deliberately rejected the color tools that were available to them during noir's genesis. Noir is about the "trashiness" of postwar American culture. It's about desiccated cityscapes, crime, sexuality, and corruption. Noir is a modern narrative that evolved into neo-noir, a form of postmodern pastiche and irony. Environmentalism often celebrates the premodern, perhaps the medieval, as in the work of Murray Bookchin, or even the prehistoric, as in some versions of deep ecology.[43] Noir antiheroes drive cars and wander through large Hollywood mansions. Noir is, as John Nelson has stated, "politics as if Hollywood were everywhere."[44]

Noir plots usually unfold in cities, not the green, sustainable cities that glitter in the dreams of environmentalist planners, but the dark and decaying cities that littered the landscape of postwar America and Europe. Noir cities are not bright, alluring, and attractive. They may have their attractions, but those attractions are grounded in the fascination that many have toward darkness, greed, and evil. Cities are defined by mayhem. They are threatened with disease outbreaks, as in *Panic in the Streets* and *Frightened City*.[45] Cities are an "asphalt jungle."[46] They are populated by prostitutes, crooks, and losers, all on the hustle for their own little slice of postwar prosperity, as in the deranged London underground of *Night and the City*.[47]

Paula Rabinowitz sees in noir a critique of postwar urbanism and suburbanism, stating: "The development of Levittown and other cheap suburbs as well as the visions of urban planners, such as New York's Robert Moses, doomed most U.S. cities, crisscrossing neighborhoods with thruways, tearing down tenements for high rises. Film noirs reveal what happened both within those evacuated, blackening cities and behind the doors of the well-kept, bleached suburbs."[48] The cities of noir are, as Eddie Muller has coined them, "dark cities."[49] Noir characters "will carom through a storyline in which the structure resembles the city itself. Unexpected intersections. Twisted corridors. Secrets hidden in locked rooms. Lives dangling from dangerous heights. Abrupt dead ends. The blueprint for noir scripts seemed to have been drafted by a demented urban planner."[50] Noir characters are sending "postcards from the ruins."[51]

Noir's definition remains notoriously elusive. As James Naremore notes: "It has always been easier to recognize a film noir than to define the term. . . . Nobody is sure whether the films in question constitute a period, a genre, a cycle, a style, or simply a 'phenomenon.'" In fact, "nothing links together all the things described as noir."[52] Noir, in Nelson's words, is

"a family of artistic conventions that figure in films, as in television programs, and popular novels."[53] Noir is a "feel," an "aesthetic," a "sensibility,"
a pastiche, the product, as Naremore says, "of a postmodern culture."[54]

I want to suggest that a noir *sensibility* can help us understand the
meanings and workings of political power in shaping the deindustrialized
ruins of contemporary America, those places left behind in the wake of
global capital's ongoing waves of transformation. Naremore is correct that
noir, whether we are aware of it or not, "is one of the dominant intellectual
categories of the late twentieth century."[55] Most important for my purposes, noir tells us something important about political power. Power's
motivations and actions can be complex and multifaceted in film noirs,
but it is safe to say that in general, noir characters without it want it. Those
who have it enjoy it, are corrupted by it, and are seldom willing to relin-
quish it, even at the cost of their own destruction. Yet noir is not simply
a liberal critique of power's corrupting aspects. Noir teaches lessons of
where to look for and how to "feel" the operations of power. Noir exposes
the facades presented by the conventional institutional structures of business and political life to reveal the underside of things: sometimes the
back room, at other times the boardroom. Noir enters a terrain where "the
boundary between crime and legitimate enterprise blurs." Here "the cop
and the criminal, the gangster and the tycoon, become interchangeable,
and the crime that is socially acceptable, behind its succession of veils,
may be responsible for more deaths in real numbers than violent street
crime."[56]

Many have noted the connection between noir and European Marxisms.
Nelson refers to this as the "hardboiled detection" side of noir, grounded
in a "sense of a realistic, historically productive attack on the corrupt institutions of a late-capitalist order in America."[57] As such, I would also
suggest that noir has an affinity with the Americanized Marxism represented by the power elite theory of C. Wright Mills. Noir, like power elite
theory, was the product of postwar America. Noir and power elite theory
explore the labyrinths of power, searching for an elusive center that may
or may not exist. Both attempt to develop an *aesthetic* of power, an artistic
representation of power's motivations, meanings, and operations.

Some passages from C. Wright Mills thus read like a noir text. Take
the following from *The Power Elite*:

Somewhere in Maryland people in red coats are riding to hounds; in a
Park Avenue Apartment, a coal miner's daughter, having lived in a married state for twenty months, has just decided to accept a five-and-one-
half million dollar settlement. At Kelly Field, a General walks carelessly
between rows of painfully rigid men; on Fifty-Seventh Street, expensive
women inspect taut manikins. Between Las Vegas and Los Angeles,
an American-born Countess is found dead in her railway compart-
ment, lying full-length in a long mink coat alongside a quarter million
dollars worth of jewelry. Seated in Boston, a board of directors orders
three industrial plants moved, without employees, to Nashville. And in
Washington, D.C., a sober politician, surrounded by high military aides
and scientific advisers, orders a team of American airmen to fly toward
Hiroshima. . . . All over the world, like lords of creation, are those who,
by travel, command the seasons and, by many houses, the very landscape
they will see each morning or afternoon they are awakened. Here is
the old whiskey and the new vice; the blond girl with the moist mouth,
always ready to go around the world; the silver Mercedes climbing the
mountain bend, going where it wants to go for so long as it wants to
stay. . . . On a yacht, with its crew of ten, somewhere off the Keys, a man
of distinction lies on his bed and worries about the report from his New
York office that the agents of the Bureau of Internal Revenue are busy
again.[58]

At the heart of Mills's noir sensibility was his suspicion that crime was
at the center of an advanced system of capital accumulation. "Perhaps,"
as he noted, "there is no straightforward economic way to accumulate
$100 million for private use; although, of course, along the way the un-
straightforward ways can be delegated and the appropriator's hands kept
clean. If all the big money is not easy money, all the easy money that is
safe is big. It is better, so the image runs, to take one dime from each of
ten million people at the point of a corporation then $100,000 from each
of ten banks at the point of a gun. It is also safer" (95). If crime is an essential element in the creation of vast wealth, then those with power will
have little compunction in bending systems of administration and law
to protect their interests. As Mills says, "The general facts, however, are
clear: the very rich have used existing laws, they have circumvented and
violated existing laws, and they have had laws created and enforced for
their direct benefit" (99).

Mills was concerned with the corruptions and immoralities generated by the impersonality of the large business corporation, the separation of actions from consequences. As he put it: "There may be corrupt men in sound institutions, but when institutions are corrupting many of the men who live and work in them are necessarily corrupted. In the corporate era, economic relations become impersonal—and the executive feels less personal responsibility. Within the corporate worlds of business, war-making, and politics, the private conscience is attenuated—and the high immorality is institutionalized" (343). In the era of Kenneth Lay and Bernie Ebbers, Mills's critique continues to be fresh. "Many of the problems," he notes, "of 'white-collar crime' and relaxed public morality, of high priced vice and of fading personal integrity, are problems of *structural* immorality" (343). Inevitably, according to Mills, "raising money to the plane of absolute value, will produce the sharp operator and the shady deal" (347). Crime is thus not an aberration within the U.S. system. Nor is it simply an unfortunate external cost. A noir aesthetic encourages one to perceive corrupt and "clean"—legal and criminal—exercises of power as intertwined to the point of indistinguishability.

Foucault's name has also been raised in connection with film noir.[59] Camile Paglia's quip that Foucault's "police state is a third rate film noir" is hardly complimentary, but it correctly draws attention to a noir sensibility that pervades much of Foucault's work. His writings have been used to make sense of noir's representations of sexuality, violence, and power.[60] And at least one noirish film, *Foucault Who?*, makes direct references to the philosopher's life and work within the context of a hard-boiled crime drama involving patrons of a gay bar. Foucault was undoubtedly influenced by noir films, given not only the style and substance of his writings but also his position as a postwar French intellectual.

The critical writings that invented and defined film noir first appeared in French film journals in 1946. The French, according to Naremore, "invented the American film noir." And the earliest film noirs, *The Maltese Falcon, Double Indemnity, Laura,* and *Murder My Sweet,* "would have an unusual influence on French thinking for over a decade."[61] The French, in effect, created the category of noir and helped to turn it into a self-conscious artifice of filmmaking. Especially important to the French intellectuals' attraction to noir was its subversion of the ordinary—in effect, bourgeois—system of values. The French critics Raymond Borde and Etienne Chaumeton celebrated the "incoherent brutality" of film noir and its capacity to "disorient the spectator" by undermining Hollywood conventions: "a logical action, an evident distinction between good and evil, well-defined characters with clear motives, scenes that are more spectacular than brutal, a heroine who is exquisitely feminine and a hero who is honest."[62] In disrupting the conventions of morality and legality, noir strips away artifice and reveals the social power grid undergirding bourgeois capitalist society. Noir is all exposé. It is gritty realism grounded in surrealist fantasy.

Noir, then, provides a popular cultural reading of power's meanings that contrasts with the "how-to" approach discussed previously. Noir's take on power is realistic, as it interrogates the structural features of power's terrain while never losing sight of the value, if not outright necessity, of character, plot, and narrative. Noir, in fact, has drawn on and informed power's most influential academic thinkers. East Whirlpool is a noir text. As such it teaches lessons on how to think about power's meanings and applications. While what follows, then, is a case study of a set of policy problems related to environmental protection, the intention is somewhat more audacious than that. I offer an analytical narrative that someone might encounter in a noir film or novel as well as critical judgments about its meanings.

CHAPTER 1.

Past as Prelude:
History and Hazardous Waste

Who can foretell the destiny of the
future greatness of this wonderful valley?
—*Judge G. L. Cranmer,* History of the Upper Ohio Valley

East Liverpool, Ohio, like other older and economically challenged cities of the northeastern and midwestern United States, has striking contrasts. On one side of town, you can find a commercial strip with numerous fast food joints and a huge Wal-Mart. This section of the city has the depressing feel that mass consumerism elicits in nearly every community where it is found, which includes any city of any size in the United States at this time. Commerce seems to have abandoned much of the downtown area, no doubt in proportion to the rate at which the shopping strip expanded. Yet, like many smaller communities in this part of the country, East Liverpool has a beautiful Carnegie library, a classic nineteenth-century structure that sits in the center of town. There are 1,946 such libraries in the United States and nearly 100 in the state of Ohio.[1] Many of the buildings, as in East Liverpool, are quite beautiful. East Liverpool received an especially large initial grant, because of Carnegie's affection for the community. This might help to account for the library's particularly attractive character, with a large dome on top and a rotunda beneath. In the basement there is a lovely reading room where visitors can learn much about the historical forces that shaped this part of the country.

Environmental politics concern themselves with the concrete and material. A student of environmental politics must confront what Herman

Daly and John Cobb once labeled the "wild facts."[2] While recognizing that
the materiality of a place is not entirely its destiny, given the human capacity for transformation, it would be a mistake to discount the significance
of geology and geography in shaping economy and culture. The geological features of East Liverpool, for example, were largely ignored in siting
the WTI incinerator. Placing it in the deep gorge of a river valley, over an
aquifer, runs contrary to minimal standards of common sense.

The geological traces left by glaciers provided the material substrata
for economic development in East Liverpool and the surrounding areas.
Glaciers helped to shape the contours of the area, which is hilly and rugged, with many stream beds directing water toward the Ohio River.[3] The
monstrous weight of the ice as it advanced and retreated crushed the bedrock underneath, creating large areas of glacial "fill" or "drift," a loose
gravelly soil that, in some areas of the Ohio River valley, reaches a depth
of five hundred feet.[4] This material is one of the predominant geological
features of Columbiana County, where East Liverpool is located. As one
nineteenth-century geologist noted: "The drift covers extensive areas of
Columbiana County, especially in the north and west, where the surface
is chiefly covered with it, and farther to the south and east large accumula-
tions of drift fill the valleys, and in some places, are piled against the hills,
the tops of which are not overspread by it."[5] Within this fill are layers of
coal and clay. The clay lies in veins up to thirty feet thick. The clay has a
low iron content, giving it a plasticity that is especially prized by potters.[6]

A late-nineteenth-century history of the Ohio River valley expresses
all the contradictory cultural impulses that still mark the area. In it is a
recognition of natural beauty with a clear understanding of economic potential, a dim understanding of the legitimate claims of the Native peoples
displaced by Europeans, as well as a firm belief that European settlers were
destined to occupy and develop these spaces. "When we consider," writes
Judge G. L. Cranmer, "its fertile domain—its extended area—its vast resources, and its great natural advantages, exceptional as it is in all these
respects, is it any wonder that the red man contested with such pertinaci-
ty the possession of the territory embraced within the limits of the Ohio
Valley?"[7] Cranmer was no doubt proud of the achievements of empire
building that had recently come to fruition with the announced closing of
the frontier. He approved of the national energies that were being applied
to the development of industrial America, and he was not at all reluc-

tant to use the term "empire." The Ohio River valley marked "an empire, which in soil, climate and productiveness combined, is unexcelled by that of any other upon the face of the globe." Like other white American citizens of his era, Cranmer viewed race and empire as intertwined through historical and perhaps even divine necessity. This region of the country, he wrote, "is rich in all the essentials necessary for the physical welfare and happiness of a mighty population—for the temporal welfare and intellectual and mental development of a race whose Anglo-Saxon origin and character give assurance of their superiority and excellence."[8]

While Cranmer recognized natural beauty and wrote of the "diversified scenery" and "varying beauty" that would arouse both "admiration" and "delight" in a viewer, he was most impressed by the untapped economic potential that this represented. Once "fully populated and thoroughly tilled," the "productive capacity" of the area "would supply the demands of the world." "Magnificent forests" were, in his eyes, "embryo navies" that would be large enough "to cover with their white wings the surface of every ocean and sea under the white canopy of the heavens." Underneath these forests were hidden "useful minerals" that "await[ed] only the hand of labor and industry to reveal the rich treasures of her minds, inexhaustible in the fullness of their supply."[9] Already, it seemed, human industry was at work, and "the results of the hidden chemistry of nature have been made subservient to the wants and necessities of man."[10]

What might the judge think today in surveying the area whose potential he wrote about so eloquently? Most of the forests are gone and have been tilled into farms. And the Ohio River is lined with industrial facilities for much of its path from Pittsburgh to where it joins the Mississippi several hundred miles to the southwest. While much of what he envisioned has come to pass, you have to wonder whether all the taming and tunneling that took place has really found the hidden potential that at one time represented the natural splendor of this long river valley.

The modern economic development of Columbiana County can be traced to its first white settler, Thomas Fawcett, and unfolded quickly after that. Fawcett moved west from Pennsylvania and "halted at what is now East Liverpool, about 1798 or 1800, and there purchased a tract of 1,100 acres of land, fronting on the river."[11] He built the area's first grist mill. Columbiana County as a legal entity was established in March 1803.[12] By 1830 William Scott and John Hill had built a steam sawmill on the

river.[13] But what lay underneath the ground would prove to be the basis
for economic development in East Liverpool. The first kiln was established
by James Bennett in 1840. It produced mostly yellow mugs and "yielded
a profit of two hundred and fifty dollars."[14] By 1879 there were twenty-
three potteries, with a total of sixty-seven kilns. The pottery industry was
spurred not only by the native clays, which were exceptionally suited to
making yellowware potteries, but by the profusion of natural gas, which
was "seemingly inexhaustible" and "cheaper than daylight."[15]

The pottery industry defined the economic life of East Liverpool for
most of its history, although steel mills contributed to the economy as
well, especially in the post–World War II era. Because of its association
with pottery, East Liverpool became known as the "Crockery City," and
it produced much of the pottery used in the United States. Unlike "company towns" such as Bethlehem, Pennsylvania, or Hormel, Minnesota, no
single large business entirely defined the economic and social structure
of the community. Rather, East Liverpool and the surrounding towns held
a number of small to relatively large-size concerns, most of which had
something to do with making pottery, whether for cookware or industrial
purposes. There existed, then, some diversity of ownership, but relative
narrowness in terms of commodities produced. The economy of the area
was, in other words, tied extremely closely to the enterprise of making and
selling ceramics of one kind or another.

According to William Gates's meticulously researched and documented history of East Liverpool, the greatest period of expansion for the East
Liverpool pottery business was from 1890 through 1910. Population in
the city expanded dramatically to meet the demands of rapidly growing
businesses. New potteries opened during this period, and existing ones
expanded. The most prominent and one of the oldest companies in the
city, Knowles, Taylor, and Knowles, successfully challenged English imports, having gained acclaim for Lotus Ware at the World's Columbian
Exposition in 1893. The company operated twenty-eight kilns in the city
and became the largest pottery in the United States. While the production
of housewares flourished, other businesses sprang up to produce other
porcelain products, such as electrical insulators and doorknobs. The city
was becoming crowded and dirty, an indication of its increasing prosperity.[16] While there was some labor unrest in East Liverpool, workers and
owners united in their support for tariff laws to protect local industry.

East Liverpool tended to support Republican candidates, especially the Ohioan William McKinley, because of the party's support for protection measures in the late nineteenth century.[17]

In Gates's view, the success of the East Liverpool potteries was too dependent on the protection provided by tariffs, and as a result, the pottery industry began a long, slow slide downward early in the twentieth century. As he notes: "Most local potteries began the period in prosperity, but the mid-1920s witnessed the failure of a number of the city's oldest firms. Although many of East Liverpool's small conservative potteries were already in peril, the introduction of new technologies into the industry no doubt accelerated the process. Production became centered with those firms able to employ sophisticated manufacturing and marketing methods." Not only were technical changes in production occurring, but World War I restricted access to European markets, and Asian firms, especially the Japanese, began to import inexpensive dinnerware, allowing them to compete successfully with American firms.[18]

It is worth noting that during the Depression, East Liverpool also became known for its association with one of America's most famous gangsters, Charles "Pretty Boy" Floyd. Floyd was born on February 3, 1904, in Georgia, but soon after his birth, his father moved the family to Oklahoma. Even in the years preceding the dust bowl, scratching out a living as an Oklahoma dirt farmer was not an easy enterprise, so the father turned to bootlegging to help supplement the family income. Charles took to crime at an early age, robbing a post office at the age of eighteen with a gun that he had acquired. While acquitted for that crime, he soon went to St. Louis, where he robbed a Kroger store for a reported $16,000, a crime for which he eventually spent three years in the Jefferson City Penitentiary.[19]

Floyd moved to Columbiana County after being released from prison and worked as a hired gun for the area's bootleggers. It wasn't until he left Ohio and went back to Oklahoma, however, that he began to achieve real notoriety. Working as an enforcer in Kansas City for the infamous Tom Pendergast, founder of the Pendergast machine, Floyd soon took to robbing banks. He is thought to have robbed thirty banks and killed at least ten men in the early 1930s. Many Oklahomans, desperate for a livelihood and a champion during the dust bowl and Depression, turned Floyd into a folk hero. He became known as the Sagebrush Robin Hood, a man who stole from rich bankers and used the money to buy food for the poor. He would, so the story goes, tear up mortgages during his many bank robberies.[20] He is, according to Geringer, "recalled not with a shudder but with almost a fond salute."[21] He "stole just enough from the banks to keep himself and his gang members fed, their automobiles gassed and his fellow Okies out of the poor house."[22] Floyd's reputation as a defender of the downtrodden was solidified by the Woody Guthrie song "Pretty Boy Floyd," in which Guthrie told listeners, "Some rob you with a six gun, some with a fountain pen."[23]

Whether this romanticized version of Floyd's life is accurate is a matter of some speculation. Floyd did maintain that he was not a part of the crime that made him the most wanted man in America. On June 17, 1933, a number of men attempted to free Frank "Gentleman" Nash from where he was being held in Union Station, Kansas City. An FBI agent and five other law enforcement officials were killed in the shoot-out. It was Floyd's supposed participation that led to his being elevated to "public enemy number one" after the death of John Dillinger.[24] FBI reports on the matter never expressed any doubt.[25]

Floyd fled Oklahoma and returned to East Liverpool in an attempt to avoid capture by the FBI. On October 19, 1934, he and Adam Richetti robbed the Tiltonsville Ohio Peoples Bank. Richetti was caught soon thereafter, but Floyd managed to escape. A few days later he turned up at the farm of Ellen Conkle, posing as a hunter, and asked for a ride to the nearest bus station. Conkle asked her brother Stewart Dyke to drive him into town. Floyd was spotted by local police as he was getting into Dyke's car. While some said that Floyd was shot under a tree in cold blood as he was being interrogated about the Union Station massacre, the official story is that he died in a shoot-out while running from the police in a wooded area near the Conkle farm.[26]

Floyd's body was brought into East Liverpool, propped up in the backseat between two police officers, where it was turned over to the Sturgis Funeral Home. When word got out that Floyd was dead and that his body was in the funeral home, ten thousand people are reported to have passed by to see it on display in a period of only three hours. The railing was torn off, the shubbery trampled, and the front lawn ruined. Floyd's body was put on a train and sent to Akins Cemetery in Sallisaw, Oklahoma, where he was buried. Twenty thousand people attended his funeral.

Although the pottery industry made something of a comeback after the Depression, especially with the success of the Homer Laughlin company's Fiesta ware, it was becoming clear that it would not "return to its former glory." According to Gates, "By 1950 East Liverpool was in desperate straits. The city's industrial base had been virtually eliminated and it had failed to attract new industries to replace it. With its tax base eroded it had to struggle even to maintain its already beleaguered municipal services."[27] Some potteries had closed during the Depression and never reopened. Others had moved to other cities or suburbs in the surrounding area. While the steel industry's regional importance expanded, becoming the dominant employer in the tri-state area by the 1960s, the city itself found few industries to replace the potteries that had once predominated (330–31).

Pervading Gates's analysis is a deep sense of frustration that community leaders were either unwilling or unable to diversify the city's economy, in spite of opportunities that presented themselves. When Goodyear put forward a proposal to build a rubber-manufacturing center in the area that would have employed one thousand people, local business leaders balked, apparently owing to fears that the plant might compete for local labor resources and drive up the costs of doing business. Malcolm Thompson, president of the Hall China company, refused to sell Goodyear the land that he owned where the facility would have been located (330). Gates attributes the unwillingness of community leaders to diversify to their essential conservatism, their general sense of self-satisfaction, and their incapacity to see and act with an understanding of the nature of the historical forces that were constraining them.

In the 1950s, ever-larger numbers of imports of pottery came into the U.S. market from Japan. In spite of this, President Eisenhower lowered tariffs on imported pottery, making imports an even more attractive bargain. This was a significant factor in the decline of employment in East Liverpool potteries. Employment dropped by 50 percent from 6,191 in 1953 to 3,075 by 1963 (257). By 1970 only 1,026 pottery workers lived inside the city of East Liverpool proper. The number of steelworkers now outnumbered them (258). But by the mid-1980s, the steel industry had also fallen on difficult times. The Jones and Laughlin Steel company, which had closed down, reopened after concessions from the United Steelworkers Union. While operations continued, it had become "a shell of its former self" (362).

Gates's assessment of the East Liverpool economy in the mid-1980s is a bleak one. "Today," he writes, "East Liverpool's employment picture is a shambles. The loss of its industrial base and the loss of jobs for residents in other district plants has given rise to declining population, unemployment, and poverty. Urban decline has become a factor of everyday life in the 'Crockery City'" (363).

In fact, the industrial and economic decline of East Liverpool was recognized by local leaders, perhaps because it was so difficult to ignore. Not unlike other cities in the Northeast and Midwest that suffered the loss of their economic infrastructure, East Liverpool slowly deteriorated over time. As an article in the local newspaper, the *Review*, put it: "The impact of each setback was not traumatic in itself. But the cumulative result has been nearly catastrophic, considering the decline in employment, population, commercial business, industrial bases, tax revenue, government services and other factors in the past 25 years." The newspaper editor perceived, it seems correctly, that the economic decline in East Liverpool had been an especially harsh one: "The economic and social distress . . . [in East Liverpool] . . . is comparatively worse than most cities of which we are aware."[28]

Perhaps because of his sense that East Liverpool's business and political leaders had left a long train of missed opportunities, Gates, writing at the time when the WTI incinerator was just being proposed, tends to support it. He echoes the positions then being advanced by mayor John Payne and the WTI owners. He considers the economic benefits of the plant to be "clear," yielding $150,000 in real estate taxes, as well as providing jobs. Moreover, Gates writes, based on the preliminary proposal, WTI would generate inexpensive steam energy from its plant and would attract other industries to the site, thus providing additional employment. Borrowing from a tack apparently taken by Payne during an interview, Gates further asserts that "being the first community in the United States with a facility of this type should develop a sense of pride among residents."[29]

While not disrespectful of them, Gates is dismissive of WTI opponents, including Alonzo Spencer and Rebecca Tobin, who were at the time the leaders of the newly formed "Save Our County" organization. Gates quotes an editorial in the *East Liverpool Review* sympathetically, which stated: "Foes of the facility are focusing attention on the problems they perceive the plant may bring to the community. These are sincere concerns, but procedures have been established by democratic process by which waste disposal facilities may be built and operated" (400). His conclusion is ambiguous: "The opposition to WTI demonstrates, if nothing else, that if properly motivated, area residents can organize effectively to achieve the goal of revitalizing East Liverpool" (404).

Structural Forces

The decision to site a hazardous waste incinerator in East Liverpool was made by individual business managers and community leaders. As I argue later, these decisions were made in the interests of business leaders who saw specific advantages in locating a hazardous waste facility in this area at this time. Such decisions are not, however, made within a vacuum. They are made within a context of larger structural forces that act at particular historical moments. In the case of WTI, it is possible to locate three important structural features that coalesced in the late 1970s: deindustrialization, the perception of a hazardous waste crisis, and oils shocks and the energy crisis.

Deindustrialization

The economic plight faced by East Liverpool in the 1970s was hardly unique to that community. The process of deindustrialization was unfolding not only in East Liverpool but throughout industrial America. The tri-state area of eastern Ohio, northern West Virginia, and western Pennsylvania was one of the most afflicted regions of the country. In fact, the first wave of deindustrialization landed with particular force on the city of Youngstown, Ohio, not more than an hour's drive from East Liverpool. "In September 1977," according to Terry Buss and F. Stevens Redburn, "the directors of the Lykes Corporation, owners since 1969 of the Youngstown Sheet and Tube Company, announced the closing of its huge Campbell Works facility and began laying off over 4,000 workers. Thus began a sequence of mill closings that permanently eliminated over 10,000 jobs in one metropolitan area in less than three years."[30] Youngstown was not alone. Pittsburgh, forty miles east of East Liverpool, was also hit hard by plant closings. In the early 1980s, the Pittsburgh area lost 60,000 jobs in metal production and 50,000 more in manufacturing as a whole.[31] By 1984, Pittsburgh had lost 44 percent of its manufacturing jobs.

From 1969 to 1978, the American steel industry lost 17 percent of its workforce. Its share of world steel production fell from 50 percent in the period just after World War II to a mere 15 percent by 1979.[32] The reasons for the decline of steel are complex. Steel manufacturers were unwilling to make the large capital investments in old mill towns that would have reestablished competitive viability. The highly organized steelworkers were among the highest-paid blue-collar workers in the United States, putting American steel pricing at a competitive disadvantage. The cost of raw materials increased. Lower-priced steel from Asia and other markets was becoming more easily accessible in world markets. Demand for steel was slackening as cheaper substitutes such as plastic, glass, and aluminum were finding their way into markets once dominated by steel.[33]

Yet deindustrialization occurred throughout the American manufacturing sector. From the beginning of 1979 to the end of 1980, 50,000 automobile workers lost their jobs. Due to "reverse multiplier" effects, Bluestone and Harrison estimate that this resulted in a total job loss of 350,000 to 650,000.[34] They estimate that 38 million manufacturing jobs were lost in the 1970s. The losses were widespread, all across the nation, from Sun Belt to Frost Belt. Still, the Northeast was affected with particular intensity by this crisis. From 1969 to 1976, in every northeastern state, more jobs were eliminated by plant closings than were created by new employment opportunities.[35]

The argument is often made that deindustrialization was simply a response to irresistible market forces. Decisions were made, however, in corporate boardrooms that considered profit in the most narrow and perhaps inflated terms. Youngstown Tube and Steel was a profitable company when purchased by the Lykes Corporation, a large conglomerate based in Louisiana. Lykes secured a loan to buy the plant on the stipulation that it used YTS's considerable cash flow to repay it. Instead Lykes amortized the debt and expanded its nonsteel operations. Lykes pursued a policy of planned disinvestment in YTS, so that an average investment of seventy-two dollars per year up to 1969 fell to near zero by 1975.[36]

These closures devastated the communities where they occurred. While workers in the manufacturing sector recognized that temporary layoffs were an inevitable aspect of employment in industries closely tied to business cycles, deindustrialization was a different kind of phenomenon, since these job losses would be permanent. A new term, "structural unemployment," crept into academic policy discourse.[37] The decline of self-esteem and empowerment associated with this kind of permanent job loss leads to health problems, increased rates of suicide, higher prison admission rates, greater numbers of mental hospital commitments, and more alcoholism, anxiety, and aggression.[38]

Industrial decline became a theme in popular cultural productions. Michael Moore's career as a filmmaker began when he produced *Roger and Me*, a low-budget film that depicted the economic collapse of Flint, Michigan, and the corporate insensitivity that brought it about. Bruce Springsteen and Billy Joel both had musical hits in which they depicted decline in industrial communities. Bruce Springsteen played the song "Johnny 99" in Homestead, Pennsylvania, as a direct response to Ronald Reagan's attempts to co-opt the singer into his supply-side ideology. The song's lyrics depict a character driven to robbery and murder by the loss of his job.[39] Joel released a song and video about the economic decline of Allentown, Pennsylvania.

Marie Jahoda's foreword to Gregory Pappas's seminal ethnography of Barberton, Ohio, after the disappearance of the rubber industry captures the impact of mass unemployment well. "Being forcefully excluded from active participation in the economic life of their workmates and deprived of the solidarity and comradeship that emerge in most workplaces even when working conditions leave much to be desired, the unemployed feel abandoned and time hangs heavy on their hands. Only the very strong can avoid demoralization."[40] As Pappas himself notes, "Unemployment brings to the fore the insecurity of modern society and exposes the tenuousness of our links with our community."[41] Moreover, deindustrialization has political consequences. It reduces democratic participation by undermining the institutions, such as schools, community organizations, and unions, that nourish it, as well as the sense of faith and empowerment necessary to sustain it. As Katherine Newman notes, "The unsettling, disorganizing impact of deindustrialization as it is manifested in the continuing problems of poverty and downward mobility creates major barriers to meaningful participation in the political arena."[42]

Various responses to deindustrialization evolved in the communities affected.[43] In some places, workers organized to challenge the power that was being exerted over their lives by the forces of postmodern capital. In Pittsburgh a group of labor activists, with support from some Protestant ministers, publicly challenged the managerial elite who were making decisions to disinvest in the area's steel industry. The Reverend D. Douglas Roth was pulled from a local church and arrested after he resisted calls from his church's hierarchy to step down and stop his political activities.[44] In other instances, workers, in conjunction with city political leaders, made attempts to buy and operate the abandoned plants, but with limited success (partly because steel industry executives were not interested in supporting new competitors). Congress passed limited notification laws. The federal government extended unemployment benefits. In the end, no long-term solutions were found.[45] New industries popped up in places like Pittsburgh, but without the union manufacturing jobs that had preceded them.

The WTI incinerator proposal was originally touted as an economic development project. It would help to replace the jobs lost by the closing of the pottery works. As in other economically challenged communities, local citizens organized; but ironically, rather than organizing to keep an industry alive and in a community to help sustain its economic life, the people who organized against WTI were trying to keep a new industry out. They refused to accept the notion that the replacement for difficult and dangerous industrial work would be to manage the depleted materials of industrial production. The move from an economy organized around the fabrication of material to one based on the annihilation of waste seemed a significant and unacceptable transition to make for many reasons.

The Hazardous Waste Crisis

A "hazardous waste crisis" became the subject of increased attention in the late 1970s and early 1980s. As J. R. McNeil notes: "Before 1980 such wastes generally attracted only passing notice: they were part of the cost of doing business. In the United States in 1936, chemical companies dumped 80 to 85% of their toxic wastes, untreated, into adjacent pits, ponds, and rivers."[46] Hazardous waste was, in a sense, "discovered" in the 1970s, at first sparked by press attention to Love Canal and then Times Beach.

Love Canal had been the brainchild of William T. Love. He imagined that by digging a channel between the upper and lower parts of the Niagara River, power could be generated that would provide energy for the model community that he envisioned.[47] The canal was never completed but instead became a convenient dumping ground. In the 1920s, the city of Niagara Falls began using the canal as a waste disposal site, and the U.S. military dumped chemical warfare materials there. In the 1940s, Hooker Chemical became owner of the site and began dumping its wastes, which turned out to be roughly 21,000 tons of chemicals, many highly toxic, over a period of two decades. At first, this material was contained in metal and fiber drums, but over time the drums deteriorated and then leaked. Eventually Hooker covered the area with clay in an attempt to contain the chemicals. The city grew during this period, and the canal sat close to an area with expanding residential populations. Whether the company was eager to transfer ownership or whether it was pressured by the Niagara City School Board to do so is a matter of some dispute.[48] Whatever the case, Hooker sold the land above and immediately surrounding the canal for one dollar and exemption from future legal liabilities. Over time, and partly as a result of the city's decision to install a sewer system, disturbing the stored chemicals, they began to migrate into residential areas. How far they migrated and with what effect is contested, but by 1977 it was clear that the parts of the community closest to the canal had been subjected to serious chemical contamination. The neighborhood was eventually declared a "disaster area." New York State bought seven hundred residential properties and relocated their occupants.[49] Many of the houses nearest the contamination were bulldozed and buried.

Love Canal received significant media attention for two years. The attention that it generated is largely responsible for Congress's relatively quick passage of the Comprehensive Environmental Response, Compensation, and Liability Act (CERCLA) in December 1980.[50]

Times Beach, Missouri, became the second American town to be evacuated because of chemical contamination. In February 1982, Ann Burford, Ronald Reagan's first EPA administrator (eventually forced to resign), traveled to the community to announce that the federal government would provide $36.7 million for a complete buyout of the town. The problems at Times Beach resulted from the activities of a waste hauler named Russell Bliss. After Bliss sprayed oil in the stables of Judy Piatt in 1971 to keep the dust down, numerous birds nesting in the roof died, and she and her daughters became ill. After an investigation, completed in 1982, it was discovered that the oil contained dioxin, the product of waste from a local chemical plant. The plant's managers had paid Bliss to dispose of it. Bliss, it turned out, had sprayed not only Ms. Piatt's stable with the contaminated oil but also the unpaved streets of Times Beach, as well as racetracks, parking lots, and farms throughout Missouri. When the Meramec River flooded the town in December 1982, public health officials warned residents not to return to their homes. Dioxin levels one hundred times those considered harmful to human beings had been found throughout the community. The EPA suggested a buyout, which was eventually accepted by most of the town's residents.[51] The Times Beach incident is memorable not only for its impact on the people who lived there, and its contribution to national awareness of chemical contamination, but for the notion that dioxin is the "most toxic substance" created by humans.

Times Beach was not the last community to be evacuated. In 1983 a reported 2,800 people around the United States had been moved from their homes and businesses, at a reported cost of forty million dollars, all of it paid for by funds generated by CERCLA.[52]

Americans were fast becoming aware that hazardous waste was a problem in more than two or three "hot spots." Love Canal may have been the poster child of irresponsible disposal, but the problem was pervasive, and not confined simply to the industrial Northeast. A 1978 story in *Chemical Week,* an industry magazine, quoted EPA findings that 336 million metric tons of industrial waste were produced each year, with 29 million to 45.8 million metric tons being potentially hazardous. Of this, only a reported 9.6 percent was said to have been disposed of "adequately," which included burial in "secure landfills" (2.3 percent) and "incineration" (5.6 percent). Less than 2 percent was being recovered for other uses. Most of the rest was put into large unlined lagoons or unsecured landfills, dumped into sewers, spread on roads, or incinerated without permitting. The article reported that waste was growing at an annual rate of 3.4 percent.[53] As one industry journal noted, "The fact that the U.S. needs to build more hazardous-waste facilities is often lost in the toxic haze that surrounds Superfund, the $1.5 billion fund that is supposed to pay for the cleanup of more than 400 abandoned dumpsites that might one day blossom into another Love Canal or a Times Beach."[54]

The massive quantities of hazardous waste that were being uncovered at Love Canal and other places were largely the result of changes in the processes of production that occurred in the post–World War II era. The war effort and the burgeoning consumer economy that followed it depended heavily on substances generated from chlorinated hydrocarbons. Plastics, pesticides, and pharmaceuticals were being produced by connecting chlorine and carbon (derived from petroleum) into long chains of highly stable molecules. The residual materials that resulted from the production of these chemicals were often toxic and environmentally persistent (as were the chemicals themselves). As demands for commodities dependent on these processes exploded in the postwar boom, ever-larger amounts of waste were generated as by-products.[55] The hazardous waste crisis was a perhaps not entirely conscious cultural recognition that these industrial processes had external costs that had not until then been appreciated by policy makers and the public.

Responses to the Crisis

One ready response to the perceived waste crisis was denial. Managers in the chemical industry viewed hazardous waste as a public relations problem that was being created by heightened public concerns regarding chemical contamination. In his 1983 outgoing address as chairman of the Chemical Manufacturers Association, William G. Simeral, a vice president of Dupont, encouraged the industry to change the "misconception" that the chemical industry was "poisoning America."[56] Industry officials were suggesting that the chemical industry needed to drop what had been a "low-profile" approach to their companies and develop "community relations." Managers were worried that their industry was perceived as one that "wears a black hat and rides a black horse."[57] The industry had ready defenders, such as Elizabeth Whalen, who declared in *Toxic Terror* that "for the last decade, Americans have been in the grip of a virulent strain of 'chemical phobia.'" Whelan asserted that Love Canal was simply the result of media-generated hysteria.[58]

Congress developed two major regulatory responses to the perceived crisis: the Comprehensive Environmental Response, Compensation, and Liability Act (CERCLA or Superfund) and the Resource Conservation and Recovery Act (RCRA). CERCLA was enacted by Congress on December 11, 1980. It included an inventory provision, which required persons who had disposed of hazardous substances to report on their past activities. This resulted in a list of over 35,000 sites. CERCLA also developed rules to define liability for cleanup and created a fund (the Superfund) to provide public financial assistance for cleanup efforts.

While CERCLA represented an attempt to get a handle on the waste that had already been generated and dumped, it did nothing directly to reduce the amount of hazardous waste being produced. In fact, by the late 1970s, it seemed that more, rather than less, hazardous waste generation would be the rule for the foreseeable future. Significant changes in industrial processes to reduce toxics were apparently not a priority for the managers of petrochemical industries. Moreover, aspects of pollution control measures of the late 1960s and early 1970s had the effect of "displacing" air and water pollution. Devices that captured pollutants, such as precipitators and settling ponds, concentrated hazardous wastes that had formerly been dispersed through smokestacks and outflow pipes. These had to be disposed of somewhere. And as old waste sites became "Superfund sites" and were cleaned up, the collected materials would have to be sequestered in landfills, burned in incinerators, or (least likely) reconstituted into some form of usable product. This created business opportunities for waste management companies. While chemical producers may have resisted the imposition of new regulatory structures, the waste disposal industry may have welcomed them.

The major federal law that regulates the disposal of hazardous waste is RCRA. The measure was enacted by Congress in 1976 as a major revision of the 1965 Solid Waste Disposal Act (SWDA). SWDA gave primary responsibility for the disposal of waste to state governments. The primary role of the federal government, operating through the Department of Health, Education, and Welfare, was to encourage volume reduction at municipal landfills (by compacting materials and recycling), and to discourage open burning to prevent air pollution. SWDA made no distinction between municipal, industrial, and hazardous wastes.[59]

RCRA distinguished between industrial and municipal waste problems. Its interventions into municipal waste matters were limited, encouraging states to establish "sanitary landfills" and to close "open dumps" (45). RCRA's approach to industrial waste was more stringent than previous regulatory regimes of hazardous and industrial waste disposal. A tracking system was instituted. Generators would be required to identify hazardous waste according to EPA criteria and to ensure that those wastes reached a RCRA permitted facility for their disposal, tracking them via an EPA-mandated record-keeping system. This became known as "cradle-to-grave" management. Thus hazardous waste generators and haulers are covered by RCRA, just as are facilities for waste treatment, storage, and disposal (TSDs) (45). All TSDs, whether landfills, deep-well disposal facilities, surface impoundment sites, or incinerators, are, in theory at least, required to obtain permits. The permitting process can be lengthy, but facilities can be awarded "interim status" permits while they await a full permit (46). There are also significant RCRA valid exceptions, such as cement plants that burn hazardous waste as a fuel in their operations.

RCRA was passed in 1976, during the presidency of Gerald Ford, but a significant period of time elapsed between its passage and its implementation. The initial implementation rules, proposed in 1978, were deemed unworkable, so a new set was offered in 1979. These new regulations were not promulgated until April 1980, and their effective implementation date was established as November 1980. November 1980 was also the month that Ronald Reagan was elected president of the United States. Reagan was hardly supportive of the new regulatory structure. He appointed Rita Lavelle, whose antipathy to environmental regulation was as deep as the president's, as the EPA official with primary responsibility to enforce both RCRA and CERLA. According to Jeffrey Miller and Craig Johnston, her "chief qualification appeared to be her acquaintance with Edwin Meese, Reagan's Attorney General, old friend and confidant" (46). The choice for EPA director was Anne Gorsuch, also considered to be largely unqualified for the position, and hostile to environmental regulation in general (48).

With Gorsuch as director, enforcement actions at the EPA dropped by 75 percent, with the only CERCLA actions filed being those that had been initiated during the Carter administration. Aspects of RCRA were continuously postponed. Democrats in Congress were incensed and held a half dozen hearings looking into the administration of the EPA under Gorsuch. The hearings not only investigated enforcement but also probed the whole set of relationships that seemed to have been established between Lavelle, Gorsuch, and the industries that they were presumed to be regulating. Eventually Lavelle was convicted of perjury and obstruction of a congressional investigation, and Gorsuch resigned after she was threatened with prosecution after refusing to produce documents for a congressional investigation (49). As Miller and Johnston note, "These events left congressional confidence in EPA's ability to implement RCRA at absolute zero" (49).

The deterioration of Congress's confidence in the EPA resulted in the passage of the Hazardous and Solid Waste Amendments (HSWA) in 1984. The amendments were organized partly according to the belief that the EPA would promulgate requisite regulations only if strongly encouraged or even coerced into doing so. Thus Congress put a "hammer" provision into the amendments, which mandated that unless the EPA promulgated a regulation required by RCRA or HSWA on time, then a complete ban on the substance involved would be imposed. Moreover, congressional regulations became more specific with regard to technological options for disposal, including a ban on land disposal of substances that could not be kept from migrating, and specific requirements on how landfills and impoundments would have to be constructed and monitored. Congress also began the process of bringing small waste generators (1,000 kilograms a month or less) under the RCRA umbrella, and developed a program to control leaks from underground storage tanks (50–51).

Rationalizing the process of hazardous waste disposal via RCRA benefited large waste management firms. The Times Beach case had focused attention on small-scale illicit haulers that engaged in irresponsible dumping practices. These fly-by-nighters, who would simply dump wastes into holes in the ground or into rivers and streams, or burn them in an irresponsible manner, were considered to be an important part of the hazardous waste crisis, and they were causing public relations problems for both the chemical and waste management industries. They were also cutting into the waste industry's profits. A report by Foster D. Snell noted that managers in the waste industry "reported competition from low-priced operations which simply collect and deposit hazardous wastes in dumps, sanitary landfills, and other locations." Moreover, some producers of waste considered its proper disposal a "fringe" that could be eliminated by sloughing it off to illicit dumpers.[60] RCRA was supposed to confront the problem of the "race to the bottom" to states with the lowest-cost disposal and the least inclination to require strict regulation. At the end of the 1970s, Rhode Island had become the mecca for hazardous waste disposal, where landfills would accept waste for five cents a gallon.[61] RCRA made clear that industrial waste disposal would have to be taken seriously as a cost of doing business. Cradle-to-grave tracking and an extensive permitting process would presumably reduce, if not eliminate, the shoddy practices of small firms while giving an advantage to companies large enough to have the necessary assets and expertise to deal effectively with RCRA requirements.

RCRA was thus supported by the waste management industry partly as a response to public concern over growing problems of hazardous waste contamination, but it was also seen as a means by which the industry could consolidate. Smaller operators would be eliminated through a rationalized regulatory structure. But as Steve Siegel, the vice president of the waste disposal company SCA, noted, RCRA would be "only as effective as the money it gives to enforcement."[62] More important from the standpoint of citizens in affected communities was that the administrative agency responsible for enforcing RCRA, the EPA, would often be highly sympathetic to the interests of the large firms that have consolidated their hold over the disposal of hazardous waste. The EPA's approach to WTI provides evidence of this.

Given the increases in hazardous waste that were being predicted and encouraged by Superfund, and given the possibilities for consolidation in the industry provided by RCRA, the hazardous waste industry became a potential growth sector. Demands for "proper" burial and licensed incineration, sanctioned by federal and state regulatory authorities, fostered conditions for developing highly profitable industries. Some estimates were that a cleanup of the targeted 4,170 priority sites would cost as much as $100 billion.[63] These predicted profits were well recognized by the waste management industry. The president of Republic Services Group, a large waste management firm, noted, "The more waste going into your landfills, the more profit."[64] The 1980s marked a period of strong growth for the waste management industry in general. Incineration was a significant part of the picture, and in fact, the amount of hazardous waste incinerated increased from 1985 to 1988.[65]

Important for understanding the vagaries of WTI, however, is the recognition that the hazardous waste "crisis" did not create the economic boom predicted. Growth has not been as strong in the last ten years. Much of the increase in revenues for the waste industry in recent years has come from wastewater treatment and solid waste management. Revenues for the hazardous waste disposal industry actually declined from 1990 to 1999 from $6.3 to $5.5 billion.[66] This can partly be accounted for by the fact that total chemical releases have continued to decline over time, from 20.47 million pounds in 1988 to 19.6 million pounds in 1998.[67] By the mid-1990s there was an overcapacity of hazardous waste incineration. In 1993 hazardous waste incinerators were running at only half capacity. And in May 1993, a freeze was put on the construction of more hazardous waste incinerators, and several facilities were canceled owing to lack of demand.[68] The same could be said of hazardous waste landfill capacity. The legal scholar Michael Gerrard wrote in a 1994 article that "most legal commentators and some politicians have decried a critical national shortage of hazardous waste disposal capacity to attempt to impose facilities on unwilling communities. The waste management industry, the trade press that covers the industry, and the financial analysts that study it, however, paint a very different story."[69] On-site remediation, treatment, and waste minimization had all contributed to the trend. Waste Management, the nation's largest hazardous waste disposal firm, was put on Standard and Poor's "Credit Watch" list in 1993.[70]

Concentration of the industry, however, has increased steadily over time. In 2001 the top five firms in the industry—Waste Management Inc., Allied Waste Industries Inc., Republic Services Inc., Onyx NA, and Safety Kleen Corp.—had combined revenues of $20.96 billion, whereas the next five had combined revenues of only $1.74 billion. The bottom five had combined revenues of less than $50 million.[71] Recent figures reflect a continuation of long-running trends.[72]

Consolidation in the industry was facilitated by RCRA, but it was also encouraged by other developments as well, including economies of scale. Solid waste is now shipped across several states in container railcars from urban areas such as New York City to rural places such as West Virginia. RCRA encouraged this development by requiring an upgrading of landfills (40–41). Solid waste disposal was, at one time, a primarily public sector problem, but with privatization of municipal services, waste disposal has been privatized as well. Large private companies, unlike municipal governments, have commerce-clause-protected prerogatives to ship wastes virtually anywhere (41). Large companies also have the legal means to protect themselves from citizen lawsuits and other attempts to encumber them with legal liability (42).

The Energy Crisis

A third prism through which the East Liverpool incinerator needs to be viewed is the energy crisis of the 1970s.[73] The crisis was provoked by the Yom Kippur War, and a backlash by Middle Eastern oil-producing nations against the United States and Western European states that had supported Israel financially and militarily. OPEC (the Organization of Petroleum Producing States) imposed an embargo on much of the industrialized world in October 1973. The effects were most immediately felt by millions of automobile drivers. The United States experienced price hikes for gasoline of 400 percent, and even with that there were shortages that resulted in long gas lines.[74] While the effects on electrical power generation were less immediately acute, they were real, especially given what were at the time relatively recent moves to substitute oil for coal in power generation. Moreover, it was also becoming clear that nuclear power would make a much more limited contribution to power generation than had once been anticipated, given public opposition and rising costs. OPEC ended the embargo in March 1974, but its impact continued to be felt in a heightened sense of interest in alternative energy sources and conservation measures. In 1979, OPEC reduced production, again initiating a sense of crisis and vulnerability regarding dependence on foreign energy.

Within this context, waste incineration was proposed as a potential source of energy that could help to offset shortages from oil. Trash burning was hailed as a "renewable energy source," a "cost-effective" method to dispose of trash that had formerly been a "source of irritation" and a "nuisance to be disposed of." W. R. Grace's Cryovac, which could incinerate used scrap film, was touted as a means to reap benefits from fuel savings and reduction of disposal costs.[75]

In 1984 the now infamous Cerrell Report was released. The study, done for the California Waste Management Board, became legendary for its apparent candidness. The report gained notoriety by suggesting that because of political difficulties associated with siting incinerators in affluent neighborhoods, the state of California would best be advised to place them in poor and minority ones.[76] Less remembered is that the report touted the environmental potential of waste-to-energy facilities as an alternative to municipal landfilling and hazardous waste dumping. "The environmental advantages of this process are enormous: an alternative energy source in waste products reduces the amount of land that need be spoiled for land-filling purposes, and metal and other byproducts filtered from the wastes can be recycled. Most importantly, however, the development of an alternative energy source will help lessen the costs and dangers associated with dependence on oil and coal resources."[77] In 1991 an engineering journal described the waste issue as "more 'people problems' than technical ones" and asserted that "many plant wastes can be used beneficially as alternative or supplemental fuels," with "organic material from manufacturing processes" having "particular value."[78] Engineers were also recommending dried sewage sludge as a possible fuel. A massive sewage sludge burner was built in Los Angeles at the Hyperion Treatment Plant.[79]

Because of the combustible compounds that are part of the mix, hazardous waste incinerators were viewed as a particularly valuable source of energy generation. As an article in *Chemical Engineering* put it: "The impetus to recover energy from these incinerators is the escalating cost of producing equivalent energy from fossil fuels and uncertainty over future prices. The potential gross value of the recoverable energy from each incinerator could reach as high as $2 million to $4 million per year, depending on the thermal capacity of the incineration system and the energy form and levels that can be effectively used."[80] The WTI facility was, in fact, first presented as a "waste-to-energy" plant that would help to solve the nation's energy problems. Alonzo Spencer told me he had originally supported the WTI plant, partly because of the benefits that were promised in its capacity for energy generation.

Citizen Responses

While the 1980s saw the beginnings of consolidation of waste management, and a rationalization of the process of disposal through a new regulatory structure, paving the way for successful capital formation, democratic responses would arise in reaction to this new system. As waste disposal became more rationalized, it also became more visible, and this visibility helped create the conditions for successful community opposition to disposal facilities, whether licensed and regulated or not. What the chemical and waste management industries viewed as a means to lend legitimacy to their enterprises was not necessarily interpreted as such by the communities that would host these licensed facilities. A new environmental grassroots movement was being born, organizing around issues of toxics burial and incineration. Industry officials were not pleased with this challenge to what they perceived as legitimate and legally sanctioned business practices. The manager of one waste management disposal system was quoted in *Industry Week* in 1983: "The siting process in general is not a rational one. How can it be when we're confronted by angry workers and housewives? It's being decided by people with no training."[81]

Industry officials were frustrated and at times angered that the "proper" disposal of these substances was being met with the same degree of hostility as their irresponsible disposal by fly-by-night operators. But citizen groups were translating the headlines regarding the dangers of chemical waste into a movement that was outside the boundaries of well-known environmental lobbying groups such as the Sierra Club, the Wilderness Society, and the Natural Resources Defense Council. These new groups were much more difficult for industry to deal with, because they did not necessarily play by the established rules of logrolling that had historically defined environmental lobbying. *Business Week* labeled these groups the "new environmentalists." They were not only critical of industry; they also often targeted the EPA as the regulatory authority that was legitimating the entry into their communities of various unwanted facilities. Mark Griffiths, a lobbyist for the National Manufacturers Association, stated with dismay that "the same aura of crisis over air pollution we saw 10 years ago has been transferred to hazardous substances."[82] A *Business Week*/Harris poll found that while 74 percent of Americans in 1983 were against relaxing air pollution control standards, a whopping 86 percent were against relaxing hazardous waste disposal standards.[83] (The same article referenced the WTI facility, noting that while unemployment in East Liverpool was 14 percent, there was tremendous opposition against the facility, at a time when industry officials and some community leaders were still promising 300 jobs and $1.5 million in tax revenues.)[84]

RCRA, in fact, legitimated grassroots opposition with its citizen lawsuit provision. Because of congressional distrust of the EPA during RCRA's early implementation, Congress, in later amendments, imposed an enforcement check on its actions. Citizens were given the authority to enforce RCRA regulations to stop "imminent and substantial endangerments" as well as violations of the statute. While other environmental statutes also allowed citizen lawsuits, and while other statutes also allowed EPA to bring actions to stop "imminent and substantial endangerments," only RCRA allowed citizens to bring lawsuits to alleviate "imminent and substantial endangerments."[85] That is, only RCRA gave citizens the legal right to attempt to shut down an operating facility if it could be shown to be a danger to a local community.

Using legal and other means, anti-incineration activists turned out to be quite successful, much to the chagrin of industry, in limiting the number of hazardous waste incinerators that could be built. Nearly 250 incinerator projects were canceled in the 1980s, citizen opposition being a primary factor in most cases.[86]

CHAPTER 2.

Be Careful What You Ask For: The Genesis of WTI

Society bristles with enigmas which look hard to solve.
It is a perfect maze of intrigue.
—*Honoré de Balzac,* Letters of Two Brides

I n a discussion with a colleague about my findings regarding the WTI incinerator, he mentioned seeing an art exhibition at Cornell's Johnson Museum in which an artist, whose name he could not remember, had artistically mapped various corruption scandals, including those involving BCCI, Jackson Stephens, and the Rose Law Firm. My interest piqued, I contacted the museum to find out the name of the artist.

Mark Lombardi, born in Syracuse, New York, was, at the age of forty, on the verge of being fully embraced by the New York art world. Lombardi had started with what is termed "neo geo abstract" painting. He seemed inclined to pursue this relatively arcane form of the avant-garde until 1994. While speaking on the phone and doodling on a napkin, Lombardi had an insight that would change his artistic vision and shape it for the next six years. He embarked on an enterprise in which he would attempt to visually map the networks that undergird global corporate and political power. The titles of some of his works give a sense of where he was headed: *World Finance Corporation and Associates, c. 1970–1984, Pat Robertson, Beurt SerVaas and the UPI Takeover Battle, c. 1985–91, 2000, Bill Clinton, Lippo Group and China Ocean Shipping Co. aka COSCO, Little Rock–Jakarta–Hong Kong c. 1990s (5th version), 1999,* and *Banca*

Nazionale del Lavoro, Reagan, Bush, Thatcher, and the Arming of Iraq, c. 1979–90 (3rd version), 1996.

In my initial encounter with Lombardi's work, the piece that drew my attention was *George W. Bush, Harken Energy, and Jackson Stephens c. 1979–90, 5th version, 1999.* I knew Stephens to be the Arkansas investor who provided the funds for the initial partnership that became WTI. I knew that Stephens had ties with Jimmy Carter, Sam Walton, the Rose Law Firm, and Bill Clinton, but the ties to George W. Bush were new to me. Given Stephens's connections within the energy industry, this perhaps should not have been surprising.

Lombardi used only publicly available documents for his data sources, mostly newspapers such as the *New York Times,* the *Wall Street Journal,* and the *Financial Times.* He purportedly inscribed ten thousand index cards with the pieces of information, using them to track and organize connections between global economic and political elites. This is artwork perhaps only imagined in the wildest dreams of C. Wright Mills, William Domhoff, or Karl Marx. At the center of each work lies a corruption scandal. Not only was Lombardi documenting the presence of complex and powerful global networks, but he seemed to be suggesting that these are, in important respects, criminal enterprises.

Lombardi's paintings have been described as being "limned in a double light of international fame and cryptic realpolitik."[1] He "possesses the instincts of a private eye and the acumen of a systems analyst." Lombardi is engaged in "filtering the dizzying spectrum of contemporary power relations through his idiosyncratic vision."[2] The effect, even when looking at the images in a collected book, is unsettling. "In the strangely contemplative and yet galvanizing presence of these images, the graphic equilibrium with which he invests his subjects is transformative."[3] Lombardi is attempting to generate a comprehensive and comprehensible guide to the vast elite networks that circumscribe global economic and political power.

After doing a bit of research, I sent an e-mail to Terri Swearingen about Lombardi's work. I thought she might find it interesting, given that Jackson Stephens was one of the original WTI partners. Terri was one of my key contacts in East Liverpool. She was one of the main local organizers against WTI. I'd met with her several times, and she had provided me with mountains of information about the plant. In my e-mail, I included the electronic address of one of the articles that I had found. She wrote back to tell me that she'd already been told about Lombardi. "Two other friends," she said, "recently sent me this information. Remember I told you about Charlie Cray and Brian Lipsett (along with Alan Block) spending so much time here at my house with 'butcher block' paper lining my walls, with a chronology and all kinds of notes? Wish I still had it! I'm going to call Brian to see if he saved it. You know, it contained so many of the names I see in Lombardi's work! I can't believe how familiar all these names are to me! Isn't that amazing—that I was hearing these names back in the early 90s?"[4]

The people working against the WTI incinerator, it seemed, had entered into some of the same territory as Mark Lombardi. They were drawing similar maps. They were trying to decipher the connections and locate the centers of power that were manipulating state and national regulatory agencies to protect the incinerator from the opposition that had lined up against it. While their concerns may have been more practical, they too had developed an appreciation for, and obsession with, the aesthetics of power. In the dozens of chronologies that Terri had put together, many of which she had given me, she seemed to be following some of the same rules that Lombardi followed: "(1) Get all the facts that exist. (2) Create a time-line or some spatial relationship to order them. (3) Create a uniform representational system. (4) Test the schematic plan. (5) Create a composition. (6) If another fact is uncovered, create an updated version."[5]

The desire to get to the center of the labyrinth, to understand the workings and corruptions of power, is central to noir. The New York art curator Richard Klein recognized Lombardi's work as a kind of noir text. "Of course," Klein said, "the work relates to Conceptual [art] precedents, but it also really reminds me of crime writers like Robert Ludlum or John le Carré—complex plots with innumerable characters that are hard to keep track of." Klein also recognized the importance of accountability that lies at the heart of Lombardi's work and is essential to the noir ending. "If heaven and hell exist," Klein noted, "Lombardi's drawings are like PowerPoint representations that St. Peter might create to determine accountability."

Lombardi's actual life could be the plotline of a neo-noir film. His colleagues all seem to agree that he was on the verge of major success by the opening of the year 2000. His exhibit at the "Greater New York" show had catapulted him into the higher reaches of the New York art world. His colleague and friend Fred Tomaselli stated that "he was having a great time of it—a dream come true."[6] Then, on March 22, 2000, "less than a month after the triumphal opening at P.S. 1, Mark Lombardi hung himself in his apartment" (10). Even with his success, Lombardi may have been a troubled figure, how troubled is not entirely clear. The obsessiveness of his drawings probably reflected deep anxieties, perhaps paranoia. According to the gallery owner Deven Golden, Lombardi's apartment in New York, where he did his work, "was three hundred square feet, and I think he had one window. It was permeated with the smell of cigarette smoke. There were drawings piled under the bed." Then a water pipe broke and severely damaged his masterful *BCCI,* which he apparently spent days and nights reconstructing. According to Lombardi's girlfriend, Hilary Ann Maslon, he looked bad and was acting strangely, "very manic, very erratic" (20). Still, as gallerist Christian Viveros-Fauné notes, "A flood doesn't add up to hanging yourself from the rafters" (21).

There was no evidence of foul play. The police dismissed any suggestion of murder. No one, they determined, had broken into the apartment. The detective who investigated Lombardi's death referred to him as a "classic case . . . above average intelligence, on the verge of success, and he had never spoken about or threatened suicide" (22). Yet Lombardi had spoken of a new kind of project, in which he would display his networks in lit boxes, using graphs to display three-dimensional patterns of wealth and power. But "those drawings are gone. They weren't in the apartment. It's a mystery."

The line between fact and fiction, life and art, cannot be conclusively drawn. My idea for interpreting some of the history of the WTI incinerator as noir came from citizen activists that I interviewed. Alonzo Spencer told me that he sometimes felt as though he were inhabiting a film. He suggested John Grisham as a possible reference point. Why the plant was kept operating was an indecipherable puzzle to him. WTI is not a huge operation. It employs only about one hundred people. It does not apparently generate large profits. At one point, the facility appeared to be on the verge of bankruptcy, only to be saved through an intervention by the U.S. EPA, which authorized WTI to burn waste from Superfund sites.

Alonzo suggested that Jonathan Turley, a law professor at George Washington University, had perhaps gotten closest to unraveling the mystery. Turley had taken on an investigation of WTI as director of the

GW Environmental Crimes Project. His findings are damning. He concluded not only that "WTI officers, employers and attorneys may be held criminally liable for knowingly violating RCRA requirements," but that EPA officials themselves "may be held criminally liable for fraud," given the various points at which they colluded with WTI managers to avoid proper regulatory oversight.[7] Turley submitted his findings, along with supporting documents, to the FBI. He also included a cover letter in which he stated the following:

> The Project has had discussions with the White House and various federal officials on WTI. Because of the possible involvement of Ms. Hillary Clinton and other administration officials, the criminal aspects of this case are not being discussed at this time with any member of the Administration. Nevertheless, the Project has reason to believe that Mr. Stephens and the White House staff are aware of the potentially criminal nature of this case.[8]

Terri, Alonzo, and Turley met with FBI staff in Washington. The agency was reluctant to pursue a further investigation. After a time, Turley moved on to other issues. But who could blame local citizen activists if they saw themselves as characters in a noir film or novel?

Waste to Energy

To understand the political complexities involved in the WTI incinerator, it is important to start at the beginning. Why East Liverpool was chosen as a site for what became known as "the world's largest hazardous waste incinerator" is not clear. Each step along the way, from the acquisition and use of the land on which the facility stands, to its permitting, test burn, and eventual operation, was fraught with procedural and legal irregularities. Still, the incinerator project seemed to move inexorably from conception to completion, often with the assistance of public officials in very high places, many of whom seemed willing to sacrifice not only principle but institutional legitimacy to bring the plant to operation.

The first step to siting the incinerator was the creation of the Columbiana County Port Authority. The CCPA was created by the Columbiana County Commission on March 14, 1977, with the express purpose of working with the state of Ohio to develop port facilities on the Ohio

River. On September 9, 1977, the Ohio Department of Transportation and the CCPA agreed to undertake a study to assess the feasibility of such a port. In November the consulting firm of Ernst and Ernst was contracted for the job. Ernst and Ernst released an unfavorable prognosis in April 1978. Their report questioned the value of such a port and stated that such a facility "built with tax money was not needed or justified in Columbiana County."[9] An independent audit was necessary to secure money from the state legislature for the project. The Ernst and Ernst finding was not helpful in this regard, raising significant questions about the value of the project to the local economy. In response, the East Liverpool Chamber of Commerce, under the directorship of Ray Lorello, undertook its own "Port Potential Survey" and found that a port could be economically viable and a successful addition to the area economy. With this survey in hand, the county could approach the legislature. Lorello was eventually named as a consultant by the CCPA and became a member of the Port Site Selection Committee.

In November 1979, the Ohio legislature appropriated $3 million to the Department of Transportation "to be used to acquire property and make such improvements as are necessary to enhance the use of Ohio's rivers."[10] The mandate seems fairly clear: the money would be used to build some kind of port facility. It also suggests that any acquired property would be conveyed to the state. On January 28, 1980, the Ohio Department of Transportation and the CCPA reached an agreement that paved the way for acquisition of land through eminent domain. That agreement, which would bring the Port Authority into compliance with state law, required that it develop a site plan that would (1) establish goals, (2) provide maps and descriptions of future projects, (3) indicate possible acquisitions, and (4) establish a process for public involvement. A site plan and various maps for a "River Transfer Facility" were developed by the Dravo Corporation.[11] The public was notified of this plan, and hearings were held on July 17, 1980. On August 25, the plan was adopted. That original plan has never been modified.

During the initial public hearing, the Port Authority's chair, Russell Albright, mentioned some of its goals, which included establishing an industrial park and leasing unused space to WTI and to a grain elevator company. Albright described the proposed WTI operation as an "industrial waste facility," which would receive waste from barges on the Ohio

River.[12] No mention was made of hazardous wastes or of incineration. On September 16, the Army Corps of Engineers prohibited the use of the facility's proposed dock for industrial waste transfer. The CCPA shifted its strategy, stating that funds generated by the "industrial waste" operation would be used to develop the port and attract other customers.[13] In the end, no detailed plan, as required by state law, was ever submitted for a WTI facility. No bids were ever solicited for the building of a facility as was required by state law. No port has actually ever been built on the property in question. The Columbiana County Port Authority to this day remains a port authority that controls no port.

It seems clear that public officials involved with WTI knew relatively early on that a hazardous waste incinerator would be built at the site, although the information was not made public. Don Brown, a business associate of Jackson Stephens, a primary investor in WTI, "met several times with members of the CCPA, including Russell Albright and Carl Pelini," in late 1979 or early 1980. The first "formal" contact between the parties was made in a letter dated May 27, 1980. In it, Brown wrote that WTI was interested in buying or leasing twenty acres of land for an "industrial waste incineration facility." Yet no mention was made of such a facility in the plan submitted for public comment. The Ohio attorney general eventually determined this to be "legal," because the Ohio Code does not require identification of specific businesses in the submission of such development plans, although the code does require description of "construction and improvements" that would occur.[14]

In any event, there is little doubt that the CCPA knew that an "industrial waste facility" was a reasonable possibility at the site, and the East Liverpool public was not informed of this before the public hearing held on July 17, 1980. At the hearing, Albright mentioned that the CCPA had been working with WTI to bring a "$60 million industrial waste disposal facility within the confines of the proposed site project."[15] He also mentioned that the facility would burn wastes to create electrical power, and that this in turn would attract other industrial concerns to the area.[16] Because public objections to such a plan need to be made five days before the hearing under Ohio law, in this case the public was given no opportunity to file any formal objections. Moreover, the CCPA never held additional public hearings required for modifications of the plan. So at the time of the initial proposal for building what would eventually be proposed as the "world's largest hazardous waste incinerator," no public comment was allowed.[17]

On May 15, 1981, Waste Technologies Inc. signed an option to lease 22.5 acres of land from the CCPA to build a hazardous waste facility, although the land was still privately owned by a company named River Services. In August the land was condemned by the Ohio Department of Transportation through eminent domain, and the CCPA became the actual owner. Noteworthy is that the legal entity that signed the lease was not the same one that had formed the original partnership and submitted the permit application to both the Ohio EPA and the U.S. EPA. That firm, Waste Technologies Industries, was now a subsidiary of Waste Technologies Inc., which was in turn a subsidiary of Stephens Inc.

WTI was originally a partnership, consisting of four separate companies, each a subsidiary of a larger parent company. Keeping track of the various partners, subsidiaries, and owners of WTI would become a nearly impossible undertaking over time, as the company did apparently everything in its power to disguise actual ownership. Even keeping the initial partnership straight is no easy matter. (See Figure A1 in the Appendix.) Each partner, a part owner in the facility, was set up as a subsidiary of a parent firm, thus shielding the parent from direct ownership of the facility. Koppers Environmental Corporation was a subsidiary of Koppers Company Inc., a manufacturing and construction firm. Mustang Fuel Corporation was an energy company and a subsidiary of Energy Technology Company. Waste Technologies Inc. was a subsidiary of Stephens Inc., a large investment-banking firm controlled by Jackson Stephens. Finally, Von Roll America was a subsidiary of the Swiss engineering firm Von Roll AG. Von Roll had built a number of waste incineration facilities, although the company had not operated any, until it eventually took over operation of the WTI facility.

Of these partners, Stephens Inc. was the most important. The company was founded and presided over by Jackson Stephens, and its headquarters was located in Little Rock, Arkansas. Jackson Stephens was the son of A. J. Stephens, a businessman and state legislator, who was a lifelong Democrat and raised his two sons, Witt and Jackson, in the small town of Prattsville. Witt, an eighth-grade dropout and sixteen years older than Jackson, made a fortune on municipal bonds and natural gas. Jackson attended the Naval Academy, where he became the roommate of Jimmy Carter.[18]

While the Stephens fortune was not initially large by national standards, it was large enough in the small and impoverished state of Arkansas
to make the family an important force in state politics. Younger brother
Jackson took over the family business in 1957 and diversified its holdings
outside of natural gas. The company was a major investor in Wal-Mart
and made a huge windfall when the discount retailer went public. Jackson
Stephens became "the man who owns Arkansas."[19] Stephens Inc. would become the largest investment-banking firm outside of Wall Street. Jackson
Stephens also gained notoriety by bringing the Bank of Commerce and
Credit International into the United States, over the clearly stated objections of the nation's highest bank regulator, by encouraging BCCI to buy
the National Bank of Georgia. At the time, Burt Lance, Jimmy Carter's
first budget director, who had been forced to resign because of his history
of financial improprieties, held a large amount of stock in the NBG.[20]

Stephens also cultivated a business and financial relationship with
Mochtar Riady, a wealthy Indonesian businessman who controlled the
Lippo Group. Riady became friendly with Stephens in the mid-seventies
and sent his son to Little Rock in 1977, where James became ensconced in
the social, political, and economic life of the state's elite. At the time, Bill
Clinton was the state attorney general and became friendly with James.
James Riady and Lippo were eventually charged with illegally funneling
more than $1 million of foreign campaign donations to the Democratic
Party during the 1996 campaign. Riady was a close associate of John
Huang, an assistant director at the Commerce Department (appointed
by Clinton), and organizer of the Buddhist temple fund-raiser that caused
so many problems for Al Gore.[21]

In his various business dealings, Stephens often drew on the expertise
of Joseph Giror, a securities law expert and chairman of the Rose Law
Firm. One has to be careful when treading the murky world of the Little
Rock elite of the 1970s and 1980s. For a time, the firm became "the favorite
target of every conservative conspiracy theorist in America."[22] I do not
want to lead the reader into the mire of Whitewater, Ken Starr, and secret
land strips (where Latin American drug exports supposedly landed). Still,
it is undeniable that there were political and economic interconnections
between top Arkansas lawyers, business investors, and Clinton administration officials that were particularly incestuous even by the historical
standards of small-state politics in the United States.

Giror made Hillary Clinton the first female associate in the Rose Law Firm when she moved to Little Rock in 1977 with her husband, who had won the state Democratic primary for attorney general. She was introduced to Giror by Vincent Foster.[23] Rose Law is the oldest firm in the state, a partnership that was founded in 1820, and the firm that acted as lead council for the Little Rock School Board as it fought desegregation in 1957. Giror sold four Arkansas banks that he controlled to Worthen Banking Corporation, a holding company that had been set up by Jackson Stephens and Mochtar Riady. The holding company was made possible by changes in the banking laws that had been initiated by Bill Clinton during his second term as governor. Clinton also initiated changes in the state's usury laws to allow such entities to charge higher interest rates.[24] Giror eventually left the Rose Law Firm under a cloud created by his association with FirstSouth bank, a failed S&L. When he left, he took much of Jackson Stephen's business with him, although there continued to be links between Giror, Stephens, and the remaining Rose partners. The Rose Law Firm was then taken over by three of its members: Hillary Clinton, Vince Foster, and Webster Hubbell.

From 1982 to 1992, the year that Bill Clinton became president, Stephens Inc. was the major underwriter and seller for the Arkansas Development Finance Authority, a state bonding agency, which was directly under the supervision and control of the governor's office. Stephens Inc. reportedly benefited tremendously from this association (18). The relationship between Rose, Stephens Inc., and Governor Clinton remained a tight one. Rose often did the legal work for a company that had a financial interest in 61 percent of all the bonds that were issued in the state (18). Witt Stephens reportedly often referred to Bill Clinton as "that boy" (18). Jackson Stephens, although more inclined to support Republican candidates than his father or older brother, contributed heavily to Clinton's gubernatorial campaigns and to the Clinton presidential bid in 1992. When the Clinton campaign was flagging in 1992, the Worthen Bank, controlled by Stephens, provided a loan to keep it afloat.[25] Another player in this game was Clinton's childhood friend "Mac" McLarty, Clinton's first chief of staff, who was CEO of Arkla Inc., the largest natural gas utility in Arkansas. Arkla was owned by Stephens Inc.[26] The close relationship between Stephens, Clinton, and various "friends of Bill" served Stephens

Inc. well and may help to explain the protections that WTI received from the Clinton administration in 1992 as the incinerator moved toward operation against tremendous public and political opposition.

Jackson Stephens was also a business associate of Donald Brown. Brown had grown up in East Liverpool. It may have been Brown who suggested to Jackson Stephens that a hazardous waste incinerator in East Liverpool was potentially a good investment. This stemmed perhaps from a misguided sense of civic obligation along with a desire to benefit financially from the enterprise. Brown called East Liverpool mayor John Payne in January 1980, suggesting that a "waste-to-energy facility" be located in East Liverpool. Brown and Payne had been high school classmates at East Liverpool High School, and then college roommates at Kent State University.

When Russell Albright, at the July 1980 public hearing, made the incinerator proposal public, he put an environmental spin on it. WTI would be a "waste-to-energy" plant. The original permit application, put forward to the Ohio Hazardous Waste Facilities Board on September 4, 1981, stated that WTI would be such.[27] (The permit, it turns out, was never signed by the property owner, as was required by the U.S. Resource and Conservation and Recovery Act.)[28] In fact, a brochure entitled "Waste-to-Energy" was published by WTI in September 1981, the company's first stab at public relations. According to the brochure, "The energy created at the WTI facility, from previously 'useless' materials, is equivalent to 175,000 barrels of crude oil and can mean less dependence on foreign energy."[29] The brochure was part of what was described in the permit as a "rigorous grass roots public relations program." WTI's managers held a stated determination to inform the public on the grounds that it would be "capable of supporting industrial projects when the communication is honest and candid and when community concerns are effectively addressed."[30] Yet the term "hazardous waste" shows up nowhere in WTI's brochure, or, in fact, in the permit itself. Rather, the more innocuous "industrial waste" is preferred. When the permit was made available to the public, aspects of it deemed to be "trade secrets" were excluded. Importantly, this included the contents of the waste material that would enter the plant for processing. To this day, the contents of what is burned at the WTI facility are unknown to the public. Ohio, unlike some other states, does not require public disclosure of materials burned at hazardous waste incineration facilities.

Early in the project's planning, Democratic mayor John H. Payne became a crucial defender. In January 1982, Payne, along with representative Douglas Applegate, met with WTI officials, including Donald Brown, in an attempt to secure a $4.3 million UDAG (Urban Development Action Grant) for developing the port facility. Brown suggested that the grant was an important part of the project, commenting on "the importance of the UDAG grant to us. . . . We sure hope there's a port sitting underneath us."[31] Payne also decided to run for a second term with the explicit intention of seeing the facility move forward.[32] Payne had been approached in January 1980 and flew to WTI's headquarters in Little Rock.[33] The UDAG application was eventually dropped in May 1982 at the initiation of HUD officials, who suggested that it be resubmitted after the permit application was approved.[34] The city never reapplied for it.

In March 1982, Arch Petit, a consultant, expressed optimism that a permit for the plant would be granted by the end of the year. At this time, the plant was still being presented as a waste-to-energy facility, but with the addition of second line that would detoxify steeling pickling acid, turning it into calcium carbonate. Company officials were suggesting that the facility would pay $1.25 million in property taxes, with a plant valued at $25 million for tax purposes, increasing total property value in the city by one-third. During this period, Petit suggested that opposition to the facility was minimal and came from "across the river and down the river."[35] This was apparently in reference to local groups that had sprung up in nearby Lisbon and Wellsville, Ohio, and Chester, West Virginia. Petit also claimed that "no organized environmental group is opposed to such a project as ours."[36] Yet in the East End of East Liverpool, where the plant was to be located, a group called the East Liverpool Parents for the Protection of Our Children had already formed.[37] Opposition, in fact, grew quickly. By June 1982 a local newspaper reported that "the name Waste Technologies Industries has become synonymous with controversy."[38] Supporters, on the other hand, continued to tout its contributions to energy production. Plant manager Robert E. Good was upbeat, stating that steam and electricity generated by the plant would attract other industries to the community.[39] That the facility would be a magnet or "seed" for other business operations that would want to make use of its services was a commonly cited justification.[40]

On July 25, WTI filed with the Ohio EPA for a state hazardous waste permit. Eventually, facility opponents would discover that the state permit lacked the landowner's signature as required by Ohio law.[41]

In December 1982, the U.S. EPA, specifically EPA official Bill Muno, began to show real support for the project. One question that was raised early on had to do with increased particulates that would be generated by the plant's operation. Muno suggested that even though the East End and in fact Columbiana County as a whole were out of compliance *without* the plant, it was "just over the line for being a non-attainment site." According to a study by the Batelle Institute, the plant would emit only 78.8 tons of particulates a year, "small enough to be exempt from the [U.S. EPA] requirements." That new plants could not be located in nonattainment areas was, Muno said, a "common misperception."[42] Thus, even though Columbiana County was out of compliance with federal clean-air standards on ozone and sulphur dioxide, the plant could be built, because it was not considered a "major" pollution source, that is, one that emitted one hundred tons of specified pollutants annually.[43]

Questions were also being raised about the siting of the plant. Specifically, it was to be built on a floodplain. WTI first suggested that it would fill in the site to the level of a hundred-year flood, and then acceded to filling to the level of a five-hundred-year flood. In a letter dated December 29, 1982, the Ohio Department of Natural Resources (ODNR) wrote to the U.S. EPA Region 5 to express its concerns regarding this issue. In the letter, the department stated that "because the proposed HWMF [hazardous waste management facility] will be receiving, storing, and treating hazardous and toxic waste, it is inappropriate to locate it in a flood hazard area so near a public water supply provided by the Ohio River." The letter noted that since no hazardous wastes were going to be loaded onto the site from the river, there was no reason for the site to be located on the river. The ODNR cited a federal executive order on floodplain management that state agencies be required to look at other sites than floodplains when considering facilities development,[44] which stated, "Regardless of site preparation, flood hazard areas are inappropriate for a hazardous waste management facility."[45] In what seems to be a violation of federal regulations, then, the facility was built on the floodplain without consideration of any other sites. (The EPA has denied a permit in at least one other instance in which a hazardous waste facility was to be located in a floodplain.)[46]

In early January 1983, the East Liverpool City Council went on record against the plant, but the vote was complicated by council member James Scafide's statement afterward that he hadn't actually made up his mind.[47] Later that same month, the Columbiana County Commission voted 2–1 against the plant.[48] On February 15, Councilman Scafide, apparently now with his mind more firmly made up, submitted a resolution to the council to direct the mayor to cease his support for the plant, specifically before the Ohio Hazardous Waste Facility Approval Board. The motion passed 4–3.[49] In March 1983, Anne Gorsuch resigned as EPA chief under a cloud of suspicion regarding the administration of the Superfund program. Ronald Reagan, who had continued to defend her, stated that her resignation was an "occasion for great sorrow," and it testified to her "unselfishness," her "personal courage," and her "loyalty to the nation."[50] Gorsuch had been brought down by Rita Lavelle, who helped to facilitate toxic waste disposal permits for business officials with whom she had cozy relationships. She had lunch with executives of firms that she was investigating. This information had been given to congressional investigators by EPA whistle-blower Hugh Kaufman.[51] Kaufman would eventually become an important supporter of the WTI opposition.

In March 1983, West Virginia asked to be included in the review process of the plant. Senators Robert Byrd and Jennings Randolph expressed concerns about possible problems with the plant's operations, as did West Virginia congressman Alan Mollohan. Ohio senators Howard Metzenbaum and John Glenn also expressed reservations. The only congressman with some jurisdiction who said that he would "not get involved" was Ohio's Douglas Applegate, whose district included Columbiana County. Don Brown accused West Virginia's stand as being "politically motivated." "I really think it's really turning into an issue of who controls the Ohio River and drinking water."[52] As a result of delays to the permit and continuing resistance, Charles Waterman, an attorney representing WTI, threatened to "terminate" the project.[53]

The state body that would grant a permit in this case was the five-member Ohio Hazardous Waste Facility Board (OHWFB). The process involved a public hearing, followed by an adjudication hearing. The adjudication hearings before the board took place at the end of March. They were presided over by an attorney named Richard Brudzinski. During the hearings, Payne's associations with Brown were made known. Ron Alexander, an attorney for the opposition group called the Community Protection Association, produced a letter, written a month before the Ohio EPA's approval of the project, from Steve White of the Ohio EPA to Charles Waterman, the attorney representing WTI. In it, White appeared to say that he was restricting the review process for WTI's benefit. "My staff," he noted, "is attempting to restrict its requirement for additional information to a minimum." During cross-examination, White denied that he was cutting corners. They were requiring "enough" information on the application, but not "additional" information."[54] Also during the hearing process, John Rupert, an environmental scientist for the Ohio Department of Natural Resources, expressed reservations about the siting of the facility. Specifically, as did a number of others, he questioned whether siting the facility in a floodplain was wise and also noted that the facility would be located over a "high-yield" aquifer, the purity of which made it a potential source of drinking water. The ODNR, however, had no jurisdiction over the actual siting of the facility and could only put its concerns on the record.[55]

After six months of review, followed by the hearings, Brudzinksi recommended that the board not grant the permit on June 14, 1983. He determined the WTI permit to be incomplete and ruled that more information would have to be made available before a permit could be granted. Specifically, Brudzinksi expressed concerns about emergency procedures, how the waste would be handled, how the groundwater would be protected, and how much waste would be put into the city's municipal wastewater facility. Opponents of the plant expressed "elation." But project manager Robert Goode stated that he did not see a problem with supplying the additional information, and that WTI planned to do so.[56] By the end of June, however, he was expressing frustration with the process. Goode stated that he understood that they needed to expand on parts of the permit, but that the information that the siting board was requesting would take a considerable investment. Did they want to make that investment without having a permit? "Where," Goode asked, "do we stop? Do we spend a million dollars? Do we spend two million dollars?" The investors were getting "nervous."[65]

In the meantime, Donald P. Brown, vice president of WTI, was, according to his account, "laid off" from WTI . Based on ownership changes documented in the Ohio attorney general's report (see Figure A4 in the Appendix), it seems that Brown was maneuvered out of the company by having been given stock in a subsidiary that was dissolved, leaving him the owner of a firm without any assets. He soon left to take a position at an environmental services company in Akron. He was the second person to have left a high position in the company. The first was Arch Petit, who had been the first president of WTI. Petit had left for another position in Koppers Inc.[58]

On June 24, 1983, at 1:30 p.m., Vladus Adamkus, the Region 5 EPA adminstrator, entered the picture for the first time. At that moment, he signed the Resource Conservation and Recovery Act (RCRA) permit, giving the U.S. EPA's seal of approval for the project. Adamkus's support was not reluctant. As it was later made known, he signed the permit in spite of the absence of a landowner's signature as is required by federal law. In retrospect, we now know that two agencies, one state and one federal, were willing to overlook the lack of a landowner's signature on the permit. Adamkus was reported to be "extremely pleased" to have the project in the region "because it will afford area industry another means of disposing of hazardous materials in a safe and regulated manner."[59]

The importance of the lack of a landowner's signature on the original permits is difficult to overstate. The requirement is not a mere formality but is supposed to indicate an acceptance of joint responsibility or legal liability for any problems stemming from a plant's operations. Eventually, EPA regional administrators would deny knowledge of the importance of the signature, but in fact, the reasons for having the landowner's signature on the RCRA permit are made clear in the preamble, which states: "Some facility owners have historically been absentees, knowing and perhaps caring little about the operation of the facility on their property. The Agency believes that Congress intended that this should change and that they [property owners] should know and understand that they are assuming joint responsibility for compliance with these regulations when they lease their land to a hazardous waste facility. Therefore, to ensure their knowledge, the Agency will require owners to co-sign the permit application and any final permit for the facility."[60]

The U.S. EPA Inspector General stated in its July 15, 1992, Special Report that "the intent of having the landowner sign the permit application is to ensure that the landowner realizes that it assumed joint responsibility for the hazardous waste facility under RCRA when it leased the land to the operator." The lack of a signature from the CCPA was not a mere oversight. The board *refused* to sign, because it did not want to accept legal liabilities associated with the facility, liabilities that would ultimately have to be assumed by the taxpayers of Columbiana County.

At the end of July 1983, the first of what would become one of many reorganizations of the four original WTI partners was announced. Koppers Co. of Pittsburgh sold Environmental Elements to a group of EE's managers, in a move to divest itself of some of its less-profitable operations. Robert Goode suggested that this would have no impact on the WTI plant itself.[61] At this time, Congressman Applegate, who had expressed ambivalence about the facility early on, was becoming increasingly frustrated with the unwillingness of the EPA to answer queries that he raised about the permitting of the facility. In a letter to William Ruckelshaus, Applegate stated that he had asked for copies of the draft permit for his office's review before the EPA's signing, which he did not receive in a timely manner. He also expressed concerns over the incompleteness of the permit application, and he had questions about the entire permitting process. "In sum," he stated, "Mr. Ruckelshaus, *I would be much more comfortable with the situation if it were not for a decided feeling that EPA wants this facility as much as WTI does* and that this permit is too important to the agency to deny no matter what the consequences to East Liverpool."[62]

On August 11, the Ohio Hazardous Waste Facility Approval Board heard a second round of oral arguments on the case. At the meeting, attorney Charles Waterman read a letter from Mayor Payne supporting the permit for the plant. At that point, however, Payne's endorsement probably held little weight. He had been overwhelmingly defeated in the Democratic primary.

In the time leading up to the granting of the permit, there had been tremendous local opposition to the plant's siting in the area. The Hancock County Commissioners, from Hancock County, West Virginia, went on record against it in 1981, as did the Madison Township Trustees, from

West Point, Ohio, and the Trustees of Yellow Creek, Ohio. In Columbiana County itself, the physicians at the city hospital went on record opposing the plant on December 8, 1992, as did the Columbiana County Board of Health on December 10, 1982. The Columbiana County Medical Society voted against the incinerator in January 1983. The East Liverpool Unit of the Ohio Nurses' Association voted 98–0 against the incinerator, also in January 1983. In February 1983, a petition opposing the plant, with fifteen thousand signatures, was delivered both to Governor Celeste and to various officials in Washington. In 1983 the city councils of Toronto, Ohio, Steubenville, Ohio, and Weirton, West Virginia, all went on record as being opposed to the facility.

On April 27, 1984, the Ohio Hazardous Waste Facilities Board chose to overrule the hearing examiner's findings that the permit application was incomplete and issued a permit to operate the WTI facility. In August 1984, the Ohio state legislature revised its hazardous waste incinerator siting criteria to prohibit the siting of hazardous waste management facilities within two thousand feet of any home, school, hospital, or prison, or within a floodplain.[63] The WTI facility was grandfathered under the old rules.

Legal Challenges to the Permit

Once a permit is granted for the operation of any hazardous waste facility, it is extremely difficult to have it revoked. This is especially true if the facility has the support of the U.S. EPA, which the WTI facility clearly had. This is not to say that there are not avenues, both legal and extralegal, for challenging permits. Opponents of the East Liverpool plant challenged the permit vigorously for two decades. But once the OHWFB acted, for the plant's movement toward operation to be halted, a legal grant would have to be *revoked*. Revoking legal grants that are supported by powerful interests usually requires the intervention of fortuity or catastrophe. In East Liverpool's case, neither intervened to the degree necessary to undermine the inertial force that the permit represented.

The first of many legal challenges to the plant's permitting was brought by the state of West Virginia, the Columbiana County Board of Health, and the Community Protection Association, a local activist group. The lawsuit directly challenged the Ohio Hazardous Waste Facilities Board's decision to grant the permit. The lawsuit claimed a variety of procedural and substantive errors in granting the permit. Central were charges that possible alternative sites had not been explored and that the board's finding of "minimal environmental impact" was faulty. The first charge in particular seemed to be an obvious violation of the permitting process. Under RCRA regulations, alternative sites for siting hazardous waste facilities must be explored, but in the case of East Liverpool, no other site was given even minimal consideration. The plaintiffs also charged that the board did not comply with Ohio EPA standards, and that West Virginia should have been granted "party" status in the adjudication hearing.[64]

The Ohio Supreme Court was unsympathetic to the plaintiff's challenges against the permit. The court determined that limiting public testimony to five minutes during the public comment phase of the permit process was legitimate. Also, the court found that the examiner had no insurmountable conflict of interest, even though he had previously been employed by the hazardous waste industry. The Hazardous Waste Facilities Board, moreover, had the authority to approve an incomplete permit with the understanding that more information would be forthcoming. Although the site was located, as noted, close to a school and residential area, this was determined, in itself, not to be in violation of any standards. And though no alternative sites were examined, which was contrary to state siting standards, the court found that locating the best possible site for such a facility would be "an impossibility and would frustrate the objectives of the legislature in providing environmentally safe facilities for hazardous waste. (It could always be argued that there was another possible site that was not compared.)" (26). According to the supreme court, exploration of alternative sites was not statutorily mandated "in every case" by RCRA, and board findings regarding "minimum risk of contamination" were lawful and "supported by the requisite degree of evidence" (84–86). The court also found expert testimony, offered by company witnesses, to be credible in claiming that "the risk of injury to the people of East Liverpool is so low it is negligible for all practical purposes." At the same time, the court found little credibility in testimony suggesting that property values might be depressed by the plant's construction and operation (26). The court also accepted the board's finding that little risk existed of possible explosions at the plant, noting the care that the company said would be used in handling of the materials (28). The appellate court, in other words, gave broad discretion to the state's Hazardous Waste Facilities Board, suggesting that any legal challenges would have to reach a very high bar before they would be taken seriously by any court. In December 1986, the Ohio Supreme Court upheld the appellate court's validation of the Facilities Board's decision to grant the permit.

Judge Ralph S. Locher wrote a passionate dissent, however, in which he excoriated the majority for failing "to address the real environmental concerns at issue." While the majority, he suggested, approved "WTI's perfunctory compliance with the 'form' of Ohio's hazardous waste laws, the majority ignores the 'substance' of environmental protection" (88). Whereas the majority opinion was grounded in questions regarding formalistic compliance with narrow legal rules and deference to the administrative authority of the Hazardous Waste Board, Locher hoped that the court would deal with the actual ecological and health issues raised by the siting of the plant. Locher was incensed that no attempt had been made to abide by RCRA's requirement that alternative sites be examined. And he contended that a permit should not be granted "as a matter of law" in cases where a facility would located "on the bank of a major waterway," where it would "operate above a community's potential major source of drinking water," when it would be within the borders of a municipality, and when the "*exact* nature and volume of wastes is unknown."

While admiring the technological accomplishment represented by the proposed facility, Locher expressed doubts as to whether operators could guarantee safety. The majority, following the board, had concluded that the technology used in the incinerator was so advanced that it mitigated the need to propose alternative sites. Locher doubted the conclusion, finding that "the board seems blinded by the technological sophistication of the plant when time and again human error has managed to overcome 'fail-safe' technology from Bhopal to Chernobyl to the Rhine. However, proper planning requires fallback measures to ensure that even a 'minor accident by plant management standards does not turn the southern portion of this state into a wasteland'" (89).

Locher was also concerned with the plant's siting near the Ohio River, the "ecological balance" of which "could be destroyed by an accident of even *de minimis* proportions"; near an aquifer that supplies drinking water to Columbiana County; and near residential areas with "schools, taverns, churches and the business district of East Liverpool" (88–89).

Locher's skepticism would turn out to be prescient. He was also the only judge on the Ohio Supreme Court to note that "the pleas of the citizenry of East Liverpool and surrounding areas have been virtually ignored."

Judge Locher's opinion was an anomaly. He was concerned with the broad picture of what a hazardous waste incinerator would mean for the environmental integrity and public health of the area. The court's majority, following the usual path in such cases, was concerned only with the narrow consideration of technical legal matters. And when a possible conflict existed between the interpretation of legal rules and the authority of a state administrative agency, the court chose in each case to defer to the state.

The period from 1986 to 1990 was a relatively quiet one in the political history of the facility, as the plant was under construction, and legal challenges seemed to be exhausted. As the facility moved toward completion, however, in the early 1990s, opposition began to pick up steam again. At the same time, there seemed to be a debate occurring within the EPA itself. One nagging question difficult for the U.S. EPA to overlook was the additional burden of particulate matter that would be produced by the facility.

Congressman Applegate had noted in his July 1983 letter to William Ruckelshaus that WTI's own estimate was for a release of ninety-five tons of particulates a year. This was within a mere 5 percent of triggering the need for a discharge permit under the Clear Air Act, which could not be obtained, because East Liverpool was already at twice the acceptable standard for particulates, and hence a "nonattainment" area. In a March 25, 1987, memo from U.S. EPA Air and Radiation Branch chief Steve Rothblatt to deputy regional counsel Dave Ullrich, Rothblatt noted that "when this permit was issued, the 110(a)(2)(I) construction ban was in effect for particulate matter in an area including the site of the proposed facility." Rothblatt stated unequivocally that "construction of this source is prohibited."[65] This finding within the U.S. EPA itself, as with other questionable aspects of the permit, was not enough to undermine its validity in the eyes of state and federal regulators.

Alonzo Spencer

I met Alonzo Spencer on one of my first trips to East Liverpool. I'd been introduced by Terri Swearingen. We drove by Alonzo's house in the East

End. There was large poster stating "WTI Equals Death" on his front door. I knew that Alonzo was one of the earliest opponents of the facility, so I wanted to ask him about those early years. I was interested in how he got involved in the opposition and what his take was on the political maneuverings that were behind the permit's acceptance by the OHWFB.

Alonzo told me that he was at first a supporter of the proposed incinerator project when he learned of it in 1978. He recognized the economic difficulties that the city was facing. He viewed the proposal as an opportunity to bring new jobs into the community. Moreover, he liked the idea of a "waste-to-energy" facility being brought into the community. Local residents were also being told that the facility would increase the tax base. Supporters of the plant, including Mayor Payne, brought a film of similar incineration facilities that were operating in Europe. They showed clean-looking plants—efficient and attractive—surrounded by water.

Alonzo began to have doubts after seeing a pediatrician discussing hazardous waste incineration on a Saturday afternoon television program. According to the doctor, emissions generated by hazardous waste facilities could be potentially harmful to children. Alonzo and a group of citizens began to meet and discuss the potential risks of the incinerator. Most people at the meetings were women. A group of area barge owners also opposed the facility. The county was proposing to build a port facility as part of the operation, and the barge owners saw this as potential competition from a state-funded agency. The group that Alonzo was meeting with evolved into Save Our County, a still-functioning opposition group. Becky Tobin was elected president. She was married to a local judge. Alonzo became vice president. Save Our County began to make connections with other antitoxics activists across the state and eventually the country. When Lois Gibbs spoke in Wheeling, Alonzo and others went to see her. At the time, she was in the process of forming the group that would eventually become Citizens' Clearinghouse for Hazardous Waste. She became a source of additional support, information, and advice.

Alonzo Spencer's commitments to environmental activism can be traced back through a life of political engagement that early on was associated with civil rights struggles in southeastern Ohio. East Liverpool, when Alonzo was growing up there, was a segregated city. The YMCA was not open to African Americans. The municipal swimming pool was open to black residents only one day a year. Alonzo was on an undefeated high school football team. When they went to Columbus for the state championships, black players were put up in private residences. The white players stayed at the Diceler-Wallace, one of Columbus's fanciest luxury hotels. Black players and their families were under the impression that hotel operators would not accommodate black customers. Later, however, when Alonzo was being recruited by Ohio State for track, he was put up in the Diceler-Wallace. It turned out that the hotel wasn't segregated, but the East Liverpool football coach had decided, on his own, that the black and white students shouldn't be allowed to stay together in the same hotel. This was in 1946.

In the 1960s, the NAACP organized demonstrations in East Liverpool to desegregate local businesses. Alonzo and others sat in at a local lunch counter with the expectation that they would be arrested by the one African American local beat cop. No one objected, however. The Ohio Public Accommodations Law, passed in response to the 1964 Civil Rights Act, was perhaps more easily accepted in southeastern Ohio than, say, in Mississippi. The schools had not been segregated, although there were no black teachers until Alonzo's wife was hired in 1965.

East Liverpool potteries, the main employers in the community for nearly a century, did not hire black workers. In the 1960s, Roy Wilkins came to speak. He was invited by local labor unions. Many of the owners and managers of the local potteries were present. In his talk, Wilkins suggested that it was time for the potteries to start hiring African Americans. His words seemed to have an effect, because black workers were hired after that. Unfortunately, at that point, the potteries themselves were in serious decline.

Alonzo had been active in civic life throughout this period. He had been president of the East Liverpool NAACP chapter and the Youngstown chapter of the ACLU. Yet he told me that he hadn't really thought much about environmental politics before the incinerator became a local issue. The environmental movement during the 1970s was still primarily the domain of white activists, mostly concerned about wilderness preservation. Alonzo was part of a growing grassroots movement that would not only challenge the siting of toxic waste facilities but transform the environmental movement itself.

When Alonzo Spencer first became involved with anti-WTI activity, he was told to stay away from the issue, because it was something for the "white community" to decide. He was told to stay in his place. He was threatened with having his house burned down. At one point, he and his friend and fellow activist Virgil Reynolds went to the Chamber of Commerce to ask for the names of a group of local residents that had gone to Europe to visit an incinerator there. Alonzo and Virgil were threatened by the secretary. She called the police.

From Alonzo's perspective, the benefits that were supposed to flow to the community from the incinerator's operation were not forthcoming as promised. For one thing, no serious proposal was ever put forward for a "waste-to-energy" plant. Thus no businesses were attracted to the area because of cheaply generated local energy. In fact, opponents believe that the presence of a large hazardous waste incinerator in the community discourages new businesses from locating there.

The supposed financial benefits have been elusive as well. Originally, proponents argued that the facility would use millions of gallons of municipal water in its operations. The city would attain a significant financial windfall by selling this water to WTI. But opponents investigated the European design that was being proposed, and determined that the addition of a spray dryer, which uses a lime slurry to absorb waste, would eliminate the need for large amounts of water. They were correct about that. WTI presumably pays some taxes, but the amount has never been a matter of public record. The facility pays a "tipping fee" for every unit of hazardous waste delivered, but considers this a "gift" to the city. There is a written agreement between the city and the operators. Alonzo said that he took the agreement to an attorney to see if it was essentially a binding contract. In the lawyer's opinion, it was. He took this information to the city solicitor, but his office didn't seem interested. In 2004 the facility cut the amount paid per unit by 50 percent. This left the city's finances in a state of considerable stress. On one of my trips to East Liverpool, I noticed that signs had sprung up around town encouraging residents to vote yes on a new school tax assessment. Its necessity was the result of the decrease in city income from WTI tipping fees.

To this day, Alonzo receives one phone call every day. Each time the person calls and hangs up. Alonzo asked phone company officials to trace the call, but they weren't able to do it, because of a security system being used by the caller. To break through it would require the expenditure of a fair amount of money. It hasn't seemed worth it. So every day his phone rings, and when he picks it up, no one answers: another minor mystery in the noir text of WTI, but perhaps a telling one.[66]

CHAPTER 3

The Center of the Onion:
Property and Ownership

Find out someone that hath the Use and Value of Money
amongst his Neighbours, you shall see the same Man
will begin presently to enlarge his Possessions.
—*John Locke*, Second Treatise on Civil Government

As the WTI facility progressed toward operation, one of the most vexing questions that surrounded it involved ownership. Over time, determining ownership of the facility became an increasingly difficult, if not impossible, undertaking. At the same time, the question of who owned the plant was important to its opponents, because ownership meant accountability. If health or environmental problems materialized or an accident occurred, the determination of ownership would be essential for determining legal liability. Knowing ownership was also important for technical reasons related to RCRA. RCRA required that once a permit was granted, for it to remain valid, ownership could not change hands.

Transformations of property's meanings, and hence the meanings of ownership, have been dramatic in the postindustrial era. For one thing, the significance of "dematerialized" property has increased, as patents and copyrights are now a primary subject of legal and political disputes regarding the meanings and entitlements of ownership. At the same time, partly as a result of property's dematerialization, the reach of private property, the privatization of what was once public or "nature," has expanded. Human body parts, genetic information, animal and human cell lines, "life" itself—all are now subject to control via patent law. More and more of what was once a global commons is privately controlled; ownership has become concentrated in the hands of a relatively small number of highly privileged individuals and institutional actors while becoming globally dispersed and increasingly less controlled or controllable by once powerful regulatory states. Not coincidentally, as the global commons has become more privatized, what ownership means in concrete terms has become ever more difficult to determine.

One reason for noir's persistence is that it provides such a rich source of narratives and metaphors for understanding the elusiveness of power flows in our age of globalization. Among the best examples of noir's capacity for generating anxiety about the shifting contours of political and economic power is Roman Polanski's *Chinatown*.[1] The film tracks the trail of private detective Jake Gittes through the world of California water politics on the 1930s. The political centerpiece of the plot is an attempt by powerful interests in Los Angeles to fake a drought to encourage farmers in the San Fernando Valley to sell their land cheaply, land that will presumably provide the material basis for eventually unimpeded suburban sprawl. The powerful men involved with the scheme have few if any moral scruples, and central theme of Polanksi's film is the association of political and economic power with adultery, incest, kidnapping, and murder. *Chinatown* was loosely based on the real politics behind Southern California's transformation from desert to oasis. William Mulholland, head of the Los Angeles Department of Water and Power in the first decades of the twentieth century, may not have been as morally bankrupt as the film's chief villain, Noah Cross, but Mulholland has been described as the man who "brought the Owens River to Los Angeles through a combination of determination and deceit."[2] Much is left murky in the film, including the ultimate identities and motivations of the powerful.

Legal Ownership

In historical terms, ownership was a floor concept in the development of liberal capitalist societies. It is generally associated with possession. As Lord Mansfield said, "Possession is very strong; rather more than nine points of the law."[3] Ownership grants a kind of power, a power over property, power over what one possesses. One can shape, sell, reconfigure, or even destroy something that one owns. But power over property involves more than simply power over some inert substance. Ultimately the power

of ownership or possession involves asserting power over other human beings. With ownership comes the right to exclude others from one's property. Also, an owner can rent a property and thus require payment for its
use from others. Since property can also include ideas and creative works,
others who seek to draw on those ideas can also be required to pay a price
for their use. The more property an owner has, of course, the more power
that the owner can assert, and, generally speaking, this would imply more
power over more people. Property and power are inextricably linked in a
liberal society in which property rights are sacrosanct.

Hypothetically, ownership implies obligations as well as rights and entitlements. In legal terms, these are often couched as "liabilities." If harms
flow from the entities that someone owns, then those harmed can assert
legal claims against an owner. Owners obviously want to avoid such liabilities, and they can do this in a number of ways. An owner might exercise care to minimize harms that might occur on her or his property. An
owner could buy insurance to shift the liability to a third party. Owners
are always, of course, entitled to deny claims of harms charged against
them. Also, owners can attempt to hide ownership so that potential claim-
ants have difficulty locating those responsible for liabilities that may be
incurred.

Assessing liabilities might be relatively straightforward in the case of,
say, a homeowner. If the mail carrier slips on icy steps, the homeowner
might be held liable for injuries incurred. While the level of responsibility might be in dispute, the ownership of the property probably wouldn't
be. But in advanced capitalist economies, the meaning of ownership can
move from the obscure to the bewildering. The complexities stem from
transformations that began in the nineteenth century, resulting from the
evolution of the modern business corporation. The limited liability corporation was invented, as the name suggests, to limit the legal liabilities of
corporate owners, whether a small number of partners or a large number
of shareholders. As corporations have become larger and more complex
over time, not only did ownership become more dispersed, but opportunities for obscuring it have proliferated as well. These proliferations could,
in turn, provide cover against legal liabilities.

Limited liability developed in the late nineteenth century, in response
to the increasingly expansive character of the Industrial Revolution. Business had acquired a voracious appetite for capital, and in order to obtain

it, businesses sought a mechanism to reduce risk to investors. With limited liability, owners might lose initial investments, but they would not
be responsible for debts incurred or other liabilities beyond that initial
amount. State legislatures viewed limited liability as a means to attract
business investment into their state economies. As E. Merrick Dodd has
noted, "An important phase of the early development of American manufacturing enterprise was the yielding on the part of one legislature after
another to the demands of American manufacturers for limited liability."[4]
Limited liability corporations paved the way for what is now a fairly radical separation of owners from managers of large corporations. Not only
would shareholders be sheltered from the debts incurred by bankrupt
firms, but it would not be possible to sue them for other liabilities that the
business had incurred, except under very narrow circumstances.

Shareholder protection under limited liability has not, however, ever
been absolute. Common-law rules evolved that made it possible, as the
phrase went, to "pierce the corporate veil" and find shareholder liability
for a corporation's conduct. The circumstances under which this would
be possible, however, were narrowly drawn.[5] The generally accepted rule
that circumscribed the circumstances under which a corporate veil could
be pierced can be found in the early-twentieth-century case *United States
v. Milwaukee Refrigerator Transit Co.* The case involved a brewing company that had organized a refrigerator company that it then required to
ship its products to various parts of the United States "with the intent of
exacting from the railroad companies a large proportion of the freight
moneys for interstate and foreign shipments controlled by it,"[6] in violation of the Elkins Act of 1903, which prevented rebates (essentially kickbacks) on shipping costs.[7] Given nineteenth-century case law establishing
the "personhood" of corporations, the court established a presumption
that a corporation was a "legal entity as a general rule, and until sufficient
reason to the contrary appears." However, under some circumstances, the
corporate "veil" could be lifted and the business entity would be viewed
as "an association of persons." This would be possible "when the notion of
the legal entity is used to defeat public convenience, justify wrong, protect
fraud, or defend crime."[8]

The standard is obviously vague. Richard Farmer has stated a widely
shared view that the corporate-veil doctrine "cannot be cohesively articulated."[9] Piercing the corporate veil is difficult, not only because of the in-

determinacy of the standard, but also because of the historical unwillingness of courts to pierce it except under very limited circumstances. As
Farmer notes, "Limited liabilities for the shareholder in its subsidiary is
the rule and piercing the corporate veil to reach the assets of the parent
corporation is the exception to this rule."[10]

Complicating matters even further is the capacity of limited liability
corporations to set up one or more subsidiaries. These can provide additional insulation between the parent corporation and those seeking damage judgments. Under the common-law doctrine, a set of factual inquiries
is initiated to determine the degree of control that the parent company has
over the subsidiary. For example: Does the parent corporation own all or
most of the subsidiary's stock? Is there significant overlap between corporate officers of the parent and subsidiary? Are employees of the subsidiary paid from the same accounts as the parent? Is the subsidiary grossly
undercapitalized? Does the parent use the subsidiary's property? Has the
subsidiary fulfilled the formal legal requirements to be such?

Because there are multiple and complicated factors at stake in piercing
corporate veils, the doctrine is inconsistently applied in various jurisdic-
tions. In Ohio the parent must use its control over the subsidiary to commit fraud for the veil to be pierced.[11] In Texas the bar is very high. "Proof
of an identity of shareholders or of corporate directors and officers, or of
domination by the parent of its subsidiary's affairs, will not justify treatment of the two as one business unit. Nor does the parent's ownership
of 100 percent of the subsidiary's stock alone defeat their separate existence."[12] In Pennsylvania, on the other hand, the bar is relatively low, so
that "whenever one in control of a corporation uses that control, or uses
the corporate assets, to further his or her own personal interests, the fiction of the separate corporate identity may properly be disregarded."[13] In
Connecticut, corporate officers can be held personally liable for torts,[14] including environmental harms.[15] Courts cannot agree on which standards
should apply in a given case: the standards of the state where the parent
company is located, or the standards of the state in which the aggrieved
party is a resident.[16]

"Piercing the corporate veil," then, involves complicated legal considerations that can involve partners and subsidiaries, stretching across several states, as well as international boundaries. Piercing a corporate veil
can, in other words, mean piercing several of them, and each case can

present its own difficulties. Such legal protections obviously increase the legal power and protections of corporate managers and owners, which is precisely what they were designed to do.

Corporate managers felt threatened by the social and environmental movements of the 1960s. Partly as a result of political pressure brought by these movements, new regulatory schemes were enacted into law. Also, businesses perceived themselves as being increasingly vulnerable to tort claims against practices in which they engaged that may have caused health problems or environmental damage. Corporate legal departments developed strategies to fend off possible lawsuits. One such strategy was to proliferate subsidiaries to make it more difficult for potential plaintiffs to get at the assets of the parent company. This strategy seemed particularly useful given the difficulties that litigants faced, under common-law doctrines, in piercing corporate veils. Partly in response to these industry tactics, RCRA specifically required the presence of a landowner's signature on permit applications. The thinking was that even if facilities changed hands, disappeared into quagmires of subsidiaries, or went bankrupt, landowners, by signing the permit, had accepted joint legal responsibility for any liabilities that may have been incurred. In fact, the landowner's signature has been deemed important enough by the EPA itself that the agency has denied a permit when a signature was not present.[17]

In the case of the WTI incinerator, the managers faced a dilemma. On the one hand, the owners, like owners of similar facilities, wanted to shield themselves from potential lawsuits. The proliferation of subsidiaries (see Figures 1–6 in the Appendix) seems to provide good evidence of that. On the other hand, plant operators needed to maintain a continuity of ownership to sustain the validity of the permit. Precisely because of past problems with shifting ownership of facilities, RCRA required that an ownership change trigger a permit reapplication. Permit reapplications are to be avoided under any circumstances, given the costs and time involved, especially if, as in the WTI case, there is significant political opposition. Permit reapplication would be even more problematic in the WTI case, because of the real possibility that the permit would have to be written under revised Ohio hazardous waste regulations, regulations that had been rewritten in direct response to WTI's siting. The revised regulations prohibited incinerators from being built on floodplains and near homes and schools. WTI would have great difficulty, it would seem, surviving a review under these rules. Moreover, if a new owner was brought on board, it might have to face scrutiny under Ohio's "bad boy" law, which required an investigation into a permit owner's past criminal record. WTI's owners thus had to perform a difficult balancing act. This resulted in a bizarre set of attempts to proliferate subsidiaries and disguise owners while also attempting to maintain continuity to protect the integrity of the permit. This became even more complicated as things moved forward and some of the initial investors began to withdraw from the arrangement, perhaps because it was becoming a financial drain and a public relations fiasco.

Terri Swearingen and others who had organized against the incinerator in the mid-1990s made a determined effort to discover who the actual owners of WTI were and whether an ownership change had occurred that might trigger a major permit modification process. Terri consulted with Alan Block, an expert in corporate environmental crime, from Penn State University. Block advised her on how to track down corporate ownership by searching incorporation documents, SEC filings, and filing Freedom of Information Act requests with state and federal agencies. The results turned into a poster-sized chart that detailed forty-four corporate names associated with ownership of the facility. Much of the information turned up in the 1993 Ohio attorney general's report, the result of an investigation that was triggered by Ohio law, which required that the owners of hazardous waste facilities be reviewed to determine the continued "reliability," "expertise," and "competence" of the permit holder. In this case, the attorney general's investigation took three years to complete.[18] Its findings relied heavily on legwork and analysis undertaken by anti-WTI activists.

The attorney general's report is a 150-page document that attempts to trace the legal history of the WTI incinerator from the initial proposal and lease agreements through its permitting and eventual trial burn. Confined to a series of technical legal matters, the report is both an indictment of the practices of WTI and a set of narrow legal findings about the statutory appropriateness of its conduct. The most important legal finding of the document was that WTI's ownership had changed since the authorizing of its initial permit. In the words of the attorney general's report: "WTI has evolved into a different business entity than the one that was permitted by the Hazardous Waste Facility Board in 1984. WTI has never applied for any permit revision or modification as a result of those changes in the business (although it did, at the request of Ohio EPA, apply for a permit change meant to reflect the fact that one of the current partners, Von Roll (Ohio) Inc. is also acting as the operator of the site). Consideration of the facility's reliability, competence and expertise should include consideration of WTI's failure to apply for the permit changes as the facility's ownership changed" (2).

Ownership changes at WTI were not, and still are not, easy to disentangle. (See Figures A1–A5 in the Appendix.) In 1986, Waste Technologies, Incorporated, transferred its ownership interests in the incinerator (WTI) "to a company owned by the same company that held about 99 percent of Waste Technologies, Incorporated." The new company was named "Waste Technologies Incorporated" (without a comma). In other words, one of the original partners sold its interest to a company that was essentially itself, but with a new name, identical to the old except for the absence of a comma (2–3). According to the attorney general, this alone constituted a change of ownership that required a permit modification. But that was not all.

In 1986 another WTI partner, Von Roll America Inc., created a subsidiary and transferred its partnership interest to the new company, Von Roll (Ohio) Inc. This was also a change according to the Ohio attorney general. Von Roll America was in turn a subsidiary of a Swiss company, Von Roll AG (alternatively, Von Roll Ltd.) (48). Von Roll America's managers did send a letter to the Ohio EPA stating that they did *not* believe the sale of the WTI ownership share to Von Roll (Ohio) Inc. constituted a change of ownership requiring permit modification, indicating an awareness of the possibility that the change was significant. The Ohio EPA, seemingly ever compliant, responded that it had "no objection to your characterization of the transaction and the withdrawal of the two investors" (3).

Each of the previously owned partners also had its own story of complicated ownership transfers and arrangements to tell. Koppers Environmental Corporation, for example, was a subsidiary of Koppers Company Inc. when the WTI partnership was formed. According to the attorney general's report, "at some point," ownership of Koppers Environmental was transferred to Environmental Elements Corporation, another subsidiary of Koppers Company Inc. This entity then changed its name to Environmental Elements Ohio (Inc.). Environmental Elements then apparently created a subsidiary, New Enelco Corporation, which would buy all the stock of Environmental Elements Corporation from the parent company, Koppers Company Inc. Legg Mason Inc. also bought some stock in Environmental Elements Corporation. Environmental Elements Corporation then formed a holding company, Environmental Elements (Delaware) Inc., and transferred the stock of Environmental Elements Ohio (Inc.) to it. Thus the Ohio attorney general's office, in its report, could state, without apparent irony, that on May 14, 1990, when the required disclosure forms were submitted to the state for proper review, "Environmental Elements Ohio (Inc.) was owned by Environmental Elements (Delaware) Inc., which was owned by Environmental Elements Corporation, which was owned by New Enelco Corporation, which was publicly traded and owned by individuals and by Legg Mason, Inc." Then, after the disclosure forms were filed, New Enelco Corporation merged with Environmental Elements Corporation, retaining the name Environmental Elements Corporation. This company still owned Environmental Elements (Delaware) Inc., which still owned Environmental Elements Ohio (Inc.)

In 1990, Von Roll America Inc. purchased all of the stock of all remaining partners (Energy Company Technology Company and Waste Technologies Incorporated [no comma]) that it had not previously owned, making Von Roll the sole owner of the WTI facility.

Terri indicated to me that opponents believed that Chemical Waste Management had at one time owned the facility. The details of Chem Waste's involvement are spelled out in a series of memos and incorporation documents that Terri and other opponents collected via Freedom of Information Act searches. A detailed analysis of the documents was written up by Block, with the help of the opponents who had helped to gather and review the materials. According to Block, Chem Waste had for years desired to purchase the original partnership, but the company wanted to avoid a permit modification that would trigger a review of its corporate activities under Ohio's "bad boy" statute, a law that required review of the legal history of firms applying for hazardous waste disposal permits. Federal and state officials were divided on whether Chem Waste's acquisition would initiate such a review, but Ohio EPA director Richard Shank took the position that it did. The attorney general's report concluded that the sale had never been finalized. Block, on the other hand, believes that Chem Waste may have bought WTI but exercised an option to withdraw from the sale to avoid the scrutiny that could have resulted from a permit modification review.[19]

All told, the attorney general's 1992 report documented nine changes of ownership since the permit had been granted. Four of these were substantial enough that they warranted status of "new persons" under the laws regulating hazardous waste incineration. Under state law, each of the changes should have resulted in the filing of new or amended permits. In no case had such amendments been filed.[20] The report essentially concluded that the original permit was no longer valid. WTI officials were also apparently worried. In one of her document searches, Terri discovered a letter from Blake Marshall, president of Von Roll, to Dan Quayle, at the time vice president of the United States and chairman of the Council on Competitiveness. In it, Marshall asked for support from the vice president, because he recognized that WTI was "quite possibly operating without a valid permit."

Yet while the Ohio attorney general's findings were potentially very significant, the attorney general's office did not have the power to require a permit reapplication. That power rested with the Ohio EPA. At first, Ohio EPA officials seemed to agree with the attorney general's office. They noted that Von Roll no longer controlled the permit and "was essentially operating its Waste Technologies Industries incinerator in East Liverpool without a valid state permit."[21] Yet the agency decided to allow the plant to remain open while a review of its state permit was being conducted, a decision highly favorable to the plant. After conducting its own investigation, the state EPA found that while the changes of ownership had possibly resulted in legal violations, they were not substantial enough to warrant revoking the permit or stopping operations at the incinerator while the review went forward.[22] The Ohio EPA ordered the company to redo its permit to reflect the changes that had occurred,[23] and then turned the matter over to the Ohio Hazardous Waste Facilities Board. WTI submitted a permit modification request to have Von Roll Inc. named as the owner of the facility. The OHWFB took more than two years to make its determination. In the meantime, Agnes Martin, who lived in Jackson County, Ohio, about 150 miles from the plant, filed a complaint with the Ohio EPA, contending that legal violations related to ownership changes were significant enough to revoke the permit. Both the Ohio EPA and the Environmental Review Board dismissed her petition.[24] The Ohio Court of Appeals ruled that she did not have standing, given that she could not show direct harm from the facility's operation. The court also held that Martin had essentially reiterated the charges leveled in the attorney general's report, charges that had already been investigated by the Ohio EPA. Her complaints were dismissed.[25] In December 1992, WTI began limited burning of hazardous waste.[26]

Corporate Cultures

In its review of the permit modification request, the OHWFB had to determine whether the new owner was "credible, reliable, competent, and trustworthy."[27] During the time that the HWFB was undertaking its review, a number of matters related to Von Roll came to light that cast some doubt on, if not the firm's "reliability" and "competence," at least its "credibility" and "trustworthiness." In February 1996, executives of Von Roll's parent company, Von Roll AG Switzerland, were convicted on criminal charges stemming from the company's supplying parts for an Iraqi "supergun" project. Three months later, evidence emerged of connections between two Von Roll subsidiaries and an organized crime boss in New Jersey.

Iraq's "supergun" was the brainchild of the Canadian-born engineer Gerald Bull, an editor of *Jane's Armour and Artillery*, who was once called "perhaps the greatest gun designer of the century."[28] Bull had originally conceived of the supergun as a mechanism for launching satellites into space. Brilliant and mercurial, he had difficulty selling his concept to either U.S. or Canadian civilian or military authorities. His obsession with the supergun, and the need for capital to finance the project, drove him into the subterranean world of international arms sales and eventually, in 1989, into the orbit of Saddam Hussein. With Hussein, Bull finally found the enthusiastic partner that he had long sought. Needless to say, Hussein was not interested in using the gun to launch satellites, although this was apparently the cover story Bull told employees working on the project.

Bull contracted to design and build two huge artillery pieces for the Iraqis, "Baby Babylon," and "Big Babylon." The smaller gun would have a bore of 350 millimeters and a barrel 100 feet long, the larger one a 600-millimeter bore and a 200-foot barrel. According to Bull biographer James

Adams, "There is no doubt that if these two artillery pieces had been built and worked as Bull hoped, then Iraq would have had an artillery system that would have been several times more powerful than anything else in any army in the world."[29] Israeli territory would have been within the range of the larger gun. Before work could be completed on either project, however, Bull was assassinated in his Brussels apartment.

At the time of Bull's dealings with Hussein, Iraq was under an international arms embargo. Switzerland's forty-year-old neutrality law also prevented such sales. In September 1994, three Von Roll AG executives, including a former chairman of the company, were charged by Swiss authorities with violating Swiss law by selling cylinders to Iraq that could be used for constructing one of the superguns. Von Roll stood by its employees and released a statement read that in part: "That the machine parts could be used for a weapon had already been ruled out because of their size. Our employees could not have foreseen the possibility of these parts having a military use."[30] During the trial, Von Roll maintained that the gun's purpose was to launch satellites, an implausible story that Gerald Bull had himself maintained in an attempt to avoid legal difficulties.[31] In February 1996, however, a Swiss court ruled that the cylinders were indeed war materials, and all the charged Von Roll employees were convicted of violating export rules, given a one-month jail term, fined, and assessed court costs.[32] Von Roll continued to maintain the innocence of its executives. In East Liverpoool, WTI official Raymond Wayne stated that the company was "outraged" by the convictions.[33] But James Adams, in his biography of Bull, is dismissive of the attempts by the various companies involved to escape responsibility for their conduct. Bull's company SRC's association with the project was well known, and "the only work they had done was designing weapons." Eventually Swiss authorities raided Von Roll's Berne facility, where they discovered the recoil mechanism for Big Babylon.[34]

A second set of events casting doubt on the integrity of Von Roll's management came to light soon after the supergun convictions. The 1993 Ohio attorney general's report on WTI had minimized charges that Von Roll had links to organized crime. In 1996, however, the exact nature of those connections became clearer. The central character in the case was Thomas Petrizzo. Petrizzo was reputed to be a capo for the Colombo crime family, who, according to the *New York Times,* "rode in convoys of Colombo gangsters in 1991 and 1992 hunting for rivals in a family war."[35] He was eventually tried, but not convicted, for murder in connection with these activities. Petrizzo was also owner of a legitimate business, a steel-fabricating firm—A. J. Ross Logistics—which had fashioned steel reinforcement bars for many New York skyscrapers. In 1988, New Jersey Steel, a subsidiary of Von Roll AG, paid $2 million for a one-third interest in A. J. Ross Logistics.[36] One year later, Von Roll Transportation, another Von Roll subsidiary, successfully bid on a $142 million contract with the New York and New Jersey Port Authority to build a monorail at the Newark Airport. Petrizzo's firm bid on a portion of the project, unsuccessfully. Petrizzo was nonetheless included in the final contract as a "consultant" and paid $1.2 million for his services. In 1993, New Jersey Steel again paid Petrizzo a consulting fee, this time $120,00 in connection with the modernization of a facility that the company owned in Sayreville, New Jersey.[37]

In May 1996, Petrizzo admitted to prosecutors that when his firm had been denied the bid on part of the monorail project, he had approached Von Roll's management with threats that there would be labor problems unless he was given some part of the contract. The $1.2 million, it turned out, was essentially an extortion payment. Petrizzo eventually pleaded guilty to mail fraud. This was in addition to a previous guilty plea for embezzling a half million dollars from a Teamster pension fund and defrauding the Bank of New York for $6 million.[38] When questioned about Petrizzo in 1995, Von Roll's attorney Walter H. Beebe had said that Petrizzo was brought in at the recommendation of the Port Authority, a claim that, at the time, was denied by an official at the authority.[39] Neither Von Roll nor any of its employees was ever criminally charged. Yet the long-running associations with Petrizzo, along with Von Roll's willingness to accede to his blackmail, were, as might be expected, alarming to citizens in East Liverpool. Terri Swearingen stated that the revelations "show how far Von Roll will go to make a profit. They have no regard for laws or people."[40]

The evidence of improper business relationships was troubling enough that New York City School Construction Authority inspector general Toby Thatcher sent Von Roll affiliate New Jersey Steel a letter asking for a meeting, raising the question of whether NJS would be allowed to continue bidding on school district construction projects.[41] Yet neither the scandals nor the ownership changes seemed to make much of an impact on the members of the Ohio Hazardous Waste Review Board. The board simply acceded to WTI's request for a permit modification.

Another Legal Challenge

Although the protests continued to draw media attention both within the state and nationally, plant owners were undeterred. By the end of 1992, the plant had been completed, and the operators were moving forward with the EPA-mandated trial burn. On January 13, 1993, Greenpeace filed a lawsuit against the incinerator in the federal district court for northern Ohio to attempt to stop this. *Greenpeace v. WTI* was filed under a provision of the Resource Conservation and Recovery Act allowing for challenges to the operation of activities that create "an imminent and substantial endangerment to health and the environment." Specifically, Greenpeace claimed that "because incineration at the WTI facility will result in emission of dioxin and dioxin-like compounds, WTI will cause an imminent and substantial endangerment to health and the environment in violation of the Resource Conservation and Recovery Act."[42] (There were actually eight counts in the complaint, including one that challenged the validity of the permit on technical grounds, one that charged a violation of Ohio nuisance laws, one that challenged the siting of the facility, and one that charged a violation of the National Environmental Policy Act.) Greenpeace brought the lawsuit under the citizen suit provision of the RCRA, and the plaintiffs hoped to enjoin the plant's operation. They hoped to prevent not only the eight-day trial burn but also a yearlong "post trial burn" that would be permitted if the trial burn itself was successful. Because of procedures established under RCRA, the permit at this point could only be challenged under the fairly strict standard that the facility created an "imminent health or environmental risk." Proving this is not, and was not in this case, an easy matter.

The case presented a tangle of complicated jurisdictional matters. The Ohio Environmental Protection Agency was involved with overseeing the permit, as was the U.S. EPA, but each oversaw operations at different time periods. RCRA allows challenges against some kinds of administrative actions and not others. The discretion of the EPA to grant permits, for example, could not be challenged in district court but would have to

be taken to the court of appeals. The district court dismissed all state-
law claims as well, ruling that it had no jurisdiction over them.[43] Since
the facility had a state permit, the state's finding could not be challenged
in federal court. Having cleared away a variety of claims regarding challenges to the legitimacy of the permit, district court judge Aldrich was
left with RCRA itself, which provided injunctive relief if it could demonstrate to the court that WTI "has contributed or . . . is contributing to the
past or present handling, storage, treatment, transportation, or disposal
of any solid or hazardous waste which may present an imminent and
substantial endangerment to health or the environment."[44] Only one substance of those that would eventually be emitted from the facility posed,
in Judge Aldrich's analysis, the potential for the endangerment alluded to
by RCRA. That substance was dioxin. At the time, the EPA did not have
promulgated guidelines for dioxin emissions, and this fact both helped
and hurt opponents of the incinerator. On the one hand, they couldn't
claim that any standards might be violated by the plant's operation. On
the other hand, since there were no specific levels, they could claim, via
expert testimony, that the dioxin emitted by the plant would provide a
"substantial endangerment." (In 1999, EPA established the Maximum
Achievable Control Technology Standards [MACT]. Under these guidelines, 99.99 percent of destruction and removal of dioxin-listed wastes
must be achieved.)[45]

Dioxin's toxicity has long been the subject of intense debate. As a primary ingredient in the defoliant Agent Orange, dioxin was heavily scrutinized as a possible source for health problems in Vietnam veterans. Yet
while it has been associated with cancer in the public imagination and
by many epidemiologists, its potential toxicity has been questioned by
various environmental skeptics, including Elizabeth Whalen, in her 1985
book *Toxic Terror: The Truth about the Cancer Scare,* and more recently
by Michael Fumento in *Science under Siege.* During the trial, Greenpeace
lawyers attempted to introduce internal EPA documents in which agency
experts had cast doubt on the methodology used to evaluate the safety
of hazardous waste incinerators. A confidential memo suggested that the
risk of exposure to dioxin in the food chain in the East Liverpool area
was one thousand times greater than from inhalation. In its evaluation
of risks, the memo suggested, the EPA had essentially been looking in
the wrong place. Judge Aldrich at first refused to allow the memo into

the record, because it had not been obtained through proper channels. (Opponents had found it in a wastebasket in Carol Browner's office, after she had walked out during a meeting with them.) Aldrich changed her mind once opponents made the memo public during the trial.[46]

Yet though the EPA had no established standards for dioxin release, it had conducted the first phase of a two-phase risk assessment study, concluding that over a seventy-year period, one million "maximally exposed individuals" would yield "1.3 additional cancers." For Judge Aldrich, this level of risk was great enough to meet RCRA's standard. She approved the eight-day trial burn but enjoined the one-year post-trial-burn period of operation until the EPA had conducted a complete study of its possible health and environmental effects—until, in her words, "the U.S. EPA determines what the risk is and what risk is acceptable."[47]

Aldrich's decision raised the hopes of incinerator opponents. But they were soon dashed by a Fourth Circuit Court of Appeals ruling overturning Judge Aldrich. The court considered the lawsuit to be nothing more than "a collateral attack on the permitting decisions of the federal EPA," an attack that the "RCRA judicial review provision plainly forbids."[48] The appeals court considered the lawsuit an attempt to circumvent the direct review process that required that they appeal any EPA permitting decision in federal appeals court (the deadline for which had been missed). The violations were, according to the circuit court, simply "technical violations," and none gave rise to the "imminent and substantial endangerment" requirements of the RCRA. "Technical violations" to the permitting process included the circumvention of the requirement that "no hazardous waste facilities be located within 2,000 feet of a residence or school" and that "the facility be designed to avoid a washout from a one-hundred-year flood" (imposed by Ohio statute). According to the court's majority, such concerns were "simply expressions of displeasure with the alleged inadequacies of EPA review." Such concerns should have been raised "with the appropriate agencies" (160). The court found that the plaintiffs were essentially attempting to "eviscerate" the permitting process (162). They reversed all aspects of the district court's decision that prevented operation of the plant.

In what seems to have been an attempt to intimidate opponents, and in response to the appeals court's finding, WTI sued Greenpeace for attorney's fees. RCRA allows for fee shifting when lawsuits are frivolous or imposed for an "improper purpose." Perhaps because of the dismissive tone of the appeals court's ruling, and of course to intimidate future plaintiffs, WTI brought the action forward. They asked for $375,000 in damages. Neither the district nor appeals courts found any merit to the claim, however. As the appeals court stated in the case of *Palumbo v. Waste Technologies Industries,* "plaintiff's suit could be viewed as a good faith, though unavailing, attempt to test the parameters of 42 U.S.C. sec. 6972(a)," and thus not subject to Rule 11 sanctions (37 F.3d 1494, 1994).

Back to the Future

On my second trip to East Liverpool, I made plans to meet with Terri Swearingen again as well as with Alonzo Spencer. Terri had informed me that things were "heating up" over the incinerator again, since WTI was now up for a Title V air pollution control permit, which, if granted, would give an additional imprimatur of legitimacy to the operation. Significant questions persisted, however, as to whether the plant deserved to get this permit. For one thing, allegations of operational problems at the plant had been confirmed in a successful whistle-blower lawsuit brought by Donna Trueblood. Trueblood had contacted the Ohio EPA about irregularities that were occurring at the plant, including the mislabeling of hazardous materials, without alerting her supervisors, and as a result, she was first harassed and then fired. An administrative court had ruled that her firing was illegitimate and ordered her reinstatement. When she arrived at the plant for her posting, though, she was refused entry.

There were other problems as well. In response to the draft permit for the plant, a self-trained local citizen activist, Teresa Mills, went through the highly technical application document and found dozens of shortcomings. The draft permit had been issued on November 29, 2002, but no notice had been given until January, meaning that WTI had had the document for two months before giving citizens access to it. Moreover, the Ohio EPA had given only fifteen days' notice for a public hearing, rather than the thirty required under Title V. Notice of the draft permit was not published in the *Weekly Review,* the local newspaper (although it had been in the newspapers of some surrounding communities). Most importantly, the Ohio EPA "failed to identify all applicable requirements in the Title V permit while going into great detail describing requirements that do not apply to the WTI."[49] Mills was frustrated that the staff at the Ohio EPA had seemingly cut and pasted general permit requirements into the draft permit, rather than giving site-specific requirements for the particular facility. According to Terri, complaining to the U.S. EPA about shoddy practices was fruitless, because they would contend that administering the rules was up to the state EPA.

Questions persisted about WTI ownership. During my earlier visit to East Liverpool, indications had surfaced that WTI had been sold by Von Roll to Heritage Environmental Services. Finding out exactly what had occurred was, as usual, no simple task. Alonzo's pursuit of this matter led to the usual frustrations. This time, however, things seemed bizarre even by WTI standards. The issues were laid out in an exchange of letters between attorney Charles Waterman at the Columbus, Ohio, law firm Bricker and Eckler, who had handled the case for WTI since the beginning; officials at the Ohio EPA; and Alonzo Spencer.

On November 10, 2000, Waterman sent a letter to Gary Victorine, deputy administrator for the U.S. EPA Region 5, stating that Von Roll U.S.A. Holding Inc., at that point owner of 100 percent of the shares of Von Roll America Inc., was "contemplating a sale to Heritage [Environmental Services LLC] of not less than a 51% equity interest in Von Roll America, Inc., the owner of the reference facility." Having noted this, however, Waterman asserted that "as a result of this transaction the identity of the owner and operator of the permitted facility will *not* change, i.e., Von Roll America, Inc., will still be the owner and operator of the facility." Waterman suggested, in other words, that while Heritage Environmental Services LLC would own "not less" than 51 percent of the equity in WTI, it would not be the owner or operator of the facility. Waterman was concerned about how a possible change in ownership might affect the permit. He stated: "Please advise whether this proposed stock transaction will require a modification of the reference U.S. EPA permit under 40 CFR §270.40 or any other provision of RCRA and its implementing regulations. Your consideration of our request is appreciated."[50]

Terence Branigan, associate regional counsel for Region 5, replied in a letter dated August 28, 2001. In it, he essentially repeated Mr. Waterman's assertion, stating that "your letter indicates that the identity of the owner and operator of the permitted facility will not change as a result of this transaction and that Von Roll America, Inc. will still be the owner and operator of the facility." He then states, "Based upon the information submitted, the U.S. EPA does not believe that it would be necessary to modify the permit referenced above to add Heritage Environmental Services, Inc., to the permit solely as a result of the proposed stock transaction." Without clarifying precisely why this might be the case, he continues, "We may, however, review this issue should U.S. EPA receive information that Heritage Environmental Services is participating in the management or operation of the facility." Branigan separates ownership from operation in a way questionable in comparison to standard EPA practices in such cases. His inclusion of the phrase "your letter indicates" seems to indicate a refusal to commit to a definite determination of ownership.

In a letter dated September 20, 2001, Alonzo Spencer challenged Branigan's response to Waterman:

> Mr. Charles H. Waterman altered a U.S. EPA document with no prior authorization changing the expiration date on that document and you did nothing about it. Mr. Charles H. Waterman knowingly provided false information to the Ohio EPA Director Donald Schregardus, and the director acted on that false information allowing Von Roll America to continue illegally operating and you did nothing about it.
>
> Based upon Mr. Waterman's past actions, we believe Mr. Waterman should be in jail.
>
> Now we are informed that you have determined that the change of ownership in Von Roll America's permit is not a modification of that permit. You are basing that conclusion solely on information submitted to you by Mr. Charles Waterman. . . .
>
> In the twenty plus years that I have been involved in this moral struggle, this may be the most troubling decision you have rendered involving this facility.[51]

The past actions that Alonzo is referring to involved Waterman's providing the name of Von Roll (Ohio) as one of the "original partners" of WTI, in a 1990 letter to the Ohio EPA, information that was false and apparently designed to disguise an ownership change. Waterman's statement was exposed after Terri Swearingen learned from her search of incorporation documents that Von Roll (Ohio) was incorporated in 1986, whereas the original partnership was formed in 1980. Alonzo's allegations about Waterman's conduct were public and undoubtedly known at the Ohio EPA.

Branigan responded in another letter:

A permit modification is generally required under RCRA *when a corpo-ration that owns a permitted facility like WTI sells (or otherwise transfers ownership of) the facility to someone else.* A permit modification is also generally required when a corporation transfers control over the opera-tions of a permitted facility to someone else. However, *when someone merely sells the stock of a corporation that owns or controls the permitted facility, the sale of the stock does not—by itself—necessitate a permit modi-fication.* If the purchaser of the stock thereafter attempts to exercise con-trol over the permitted facility or its operations, U.S. EPA would review whether these attempts require a permit modification to name the stock purchaser as an owner or operator of the permitted facility.[52]

Branigan suggests that "merely" selling 51 percent of the company's stock does not, in and of itself, transfer ownership. To the casual observer, this seems counterintuitive, but under standards of determining corporate ownership, his claim may be difficult to dispute (although not necessarily valid). One possible interpretation is that the transfer of ownership of Von Roll America Inc. did not mean that the ownership of WTI had changed hands, even though VRA owned 100 percent of WTI's stock. Under this theory, Heritage Environmental Services LLC acquired ownership in a company whose sole asset was ownership of a company whose sole asset was a hazardous waste incinerator, but Heritage Environmental did not own the incinerator itself.[53]

It turned out, however, that Heritage Environmental Services LLC may indeed have been involved with the operations of WTI, making the rest of Branigan's rather convoluted argument moot. On January 18, 2002, Branigan sent a letter to Waterman, repeating his assertion that "the proposed stock transaction would not *by itself* necessitate" a permit modification, but the matter would be reviewed to determine if there was additional participation by Heritage Environmental Services LLC in the operations of the plant. Branigan also wanted to know whether the stock transaction had taken place, whether VRA and Heritage Environmental had separate boards of directors and employees, and whether VRA alone was operating WTI. Moreover, he had received information that Heritage was operating a transfer station near WTI and that Von Roll employees had been doing work there. He was also interested in a press release from October 2000 suggesting that Von Roll and Heritage Environmental were considering a merger.[54]

Things, as usual, turned out to be more complicated than first appear-
ances might indicate. During the Trueblood whistle-blower suit, a number of stipulations had been made about facts that both parties agreed
to. Among these was the name of the company, which, it turned out, was
not Heritage Environmental Services LLC but Heritage Environmental
Services/WTI LLC.[55] The attachment of "WTI" to the end of the Heritage
Environmental Service's name seemed to indicate the appearance not only
of yet another subsidiary but of one with responsibility toward, if not operational control over, the facility. This suspicion was further reinforced
by other facts that came to light in the Trueblood case. It turned out that
while Heritage Environmental Services/WTI LLC was one party to the
case, Heritage Environmental Services was another. HES now apparently owned and operated a transfer station next to the incinerator, where
hazardous wastes were being temporarily stored for disposal at WTI.
Even more interesting, it seemed as though employees, including Donna
Trueblood, from the WTI plant were working at both the transfer facility
and the incinerator. In other words, not only was there an entity HES/
WTI, but HES itself may have intertwined with the operations of WTI.

    Alonzo Spencer was understandably incensed when he learned via the
lawsuit that the representatives of WTI had given the wrong name for the
majority owner of Von Roll America. He sent a letter to the East Liverpool,
Ohio, EPA Field Office in which he asserted: "Charles H. Waterman, Attorney for Von Roll America, Inc., Heritage Environmental Service LLC
has again submitted information to the Ohio EPA that he knew or should
have known to be false. As in the previous incident, the Ohio EPA accepted
and acted on that false information. Those individuals at the EPA knew or
should have known Waterman's information was false."[56] The Ohio EPA,
however, was remarkably deferential to Waterman's versions of facts.

    At the February 25 public hearing on the Title V permit, Ohio EPA rep-
resentatives stated that HES/WTI was now a majority shareholder in the
facility. This prompted Alonzo Spencer to send a letter to Patricia Natali,
the Ohio EPA inspector of the WTI site, asking that the Ohio EPA petition the Ohio attorney general "to investigate and determine if Rudolph
Raengerle, Fred Sigg, Heidi Dugan, Cindy McCall, Raymond Wayne and
Michael Parks" (managers of the WTI facility) had "knowingly provided
untrue, inaccurate, false and incomplete information to the Ohio EPA or
the U.S. EPA."[57]

When I spoke to Alonzo on the phone before my trip to East Liverpool, he told me that he thought he had finally caught WTI and the Ohio EPA in the ownership trap. Here was written evidence not only that Waterman had given false information about the name of the company that had bought Von Roll America Inc., but that HES itself was in control of a facility that had operational control over aspects of WTI's operations. Still, Alonzo was not hopeful that the Ohio EPA would bring sanctions against the plant or open the pandora's box of permit modification. Nor would this even affect the application for a Title V permit. "They can be very clever," he assured me. Alonzo seemed to see this as a kind of game, a game with very significant consequences for his community, but a game nevertheless. Powerful forces in private industry and state and federal government wanted the incinerator to operate. In the end, it seemed not to matter whether fair or even legal procedures were followed, only that rules be interpreted so as to keep the hazardous waste incinerator operational. When I spoke to Terri about all this, she told me former congressman Doug Applegate's comment continued to haunt her, when he stated in a 1983 letter to the U.S. EPA that he couldn't help feeling that "the EPA wants this facility to be operating as much as the industry does." That, she felt, was the one consistent theme in the incinerator's history.

Inside WTI

Diagrams in incineration manuals provide technical information and many important clues about how a facility functions, but they are hardly a substitute for the gritty realities of an actual operating system. I had been told that WTI offers tours, so I contacted Raymond Wayne, the public relations person at the facility, and set up an appointment. In my e-mail to Raymond, I told him that I taught environmental politics at Ithaca College. Obviously resourceful, he looked up my college Web site and found my vita. He noticed that I'd written a couple of papers on WTI. He asked me to send him a copy of them for the "WTI library." I admired his savvy and sent him a couple of things that I'd written.

I arrived for my interview on February 27, 2004. I parked the car, feeling somewhat conspicuous in my 1987 Volvo station wagon, replete with stickers from the local area music scene. I approached a guard who pointed me toward the reception area. I entered, introduced myself to the receptionist, and waited a few minutes for Raymond to come down from his office. He was cordial, dressed in a Carhartt jacket. He handed me a hard hat and some goggles. We had a bit of a connection, in that he had attended college in Erie, Pennyslvania, not far from where I'd grown up in Jamestown, New York.

We started the tour with a look at the labs. Under the Resource Conservation and Recovery Act, hazardous waste must be tracked "from cradle to grave." Raymond explained how the lab technicians worked to analyze the material. He said that a customer would send a sample of materials for disposal, and the lab technicians would look at it to determine what it was and whether they could accept it. Once a determination was made, the customer would be able to send that waste to the facility, at which point it would then be checked again. As described by Raymond, this was a meticulous process, and no doubt, the technicians worked hard to properly label waste materials and keep them separated. It was important to keep incompatible wastes from mixing. If they improperly mixed, explosions were a potential outcome. Raymond told me that they had never had a problem with this in the past. The technicians were conscientious and well trained.

Raymond expressed pride in the facility and in Von Roll as a company. He told me that Von Roll set the highest standards for hazardous waste incineration. They were engaged in test burns to meet the most recent Title V air quality standards. The company was on the cutting edge of incineration technology, in his view, and was able to use its technical know-how to keep a competitive advantage within the industry. According to Raymond, the company was pushing for even higher regulatory standards, because it knew that WTI would be able to meet them. He seemed to be completely committed to the facility.

As Raymond explained it, waste entered the facility in two forms: liquid and solid. Liquid waste came in containers as well as tanker trucks. The containers could be of virtually any size, but from what I observed, most seemed to be large metal drums. Eventually Raymond showed me the "front wall" of the incinerator, where these drums were carried by conveyor belt into the kiln, to be burned, drum and all, at a temperature of approximately 2,000 degrees. Wastes were also pumped into the kiln via pipes from storage tanks, after they had been emptied there by incoming trucks. Solid waste was also burned in the incinerator. This was composed of material that was considered hazardous under RCRA guidelines, because it had some kind of chemical contamination. It was dropped into a pit and was eventually moved by crane onto a platform and pushed into the incinerator. Dirt was also burned in the incinerator, entering via a chute.

We left the window from which the technicians could be observed, and walked outside toward the facility's storage areas. We stood near the center of the company's property, from which we could observe all aspects of the operation. On one side was the incinerator itself. On another side were the storage tanks where waste was stored. Large tanks were also visible, where water was stored. Raymond told me that all the rainwater that fell onto the property was collected and used in the incineration process. Any water that left the property for the Ohio River was treated and met all water quality standards. The property itself, including places where loaded trucks had their waste siphoned out, was terraced on downward levels, so that if there was some kind of a leak, it would flow toward the center of the property, where it could be contained. Moreover, all the buildings were kept at lower pressure from the outside, so that any gases that might escape would be contained. This air was then funneled into the incinerator. From this perspective, the safety features did indeed seem impressive.

He next took me into a building in which the containers of liquid waste were stored. Here row upon row of fifty-gallon drums sat on large shelves, their contents labeled, where they awaited their final disposal. In another room, the initial steps in the conveyor process could be viewed. Raymond told me that the conveyor system was based on the ones used by the automobile industry. This was indeed an advanced form of Taylorism. Few workers were visible, just those who were using forklifts to move the waste into the system. From there, everything was done via computer, run by operators working on the second floor near the incinerator's kiln. Raymond again stressed the necessity of keeping wastes separate as they entered into the system. There were five conveyors that moved material toward the front wall of the kiln. Keeping things sorted properly was one of the most important jobs that the operators were engaged in.

Out on the open grounds of the facility, Raymond pointed out a natural area, immediately outside the facility's fence. Employees had planted native species of grass in an area that looked like two or three acres. Bird feeders had been set up along the facility's perimeter and were attracting species endangered in the Ohio River valley. Below was the Ohio River. The facility was built on fill, to a level above the five-hundred-year flood-plain. Raymond pointed that several years ago, when the Ohio flooded, Pittsburgh was underwater, but the river's waters remained comfortably below the level of the plant.

Finally, Raymond and I entered the operations room on the second floor. Here I met the operations manager, Jim Brinker, as well as several others who were engaged in the process of keeping the facility functioning properly as tons of waste were moved into it. The control panel was on one side of the room. When Raymond and I entered, one of the operators was eating his lunch. The place had a casual but serious atmosphere. Several video display screens showed different aspects of the operations. One screen displayed the inside of the kiln itself. There wasn't much to see, mostly a reddish haze, but Jim told me that if it got too dark, smoke was forming, an indication that there might be a problem with the burn process. Other displays showed entry points into the kiln and the areas around them.

There were also several large computer monitors, each displaying brightly lit images. The colors were stunning. The monitors reminded me of a NASA control room, brightly lit and cheerful, and capable of displaying large amounts of data in various forms, both visual and numeric. The operator sat at a terminal that showed a set of variously colored lines. The monitor displayed data on kiln temperature, the amount of oxygen feeding into the kiln, and so forth. Regulatory guidelines specified burn rates and temperatures, because these were some of the variables that determined what would eventually be released from the stack. If temperatures became too high or too low, or if the oxygen mix wasn't proper, then the system would automatically shut down. Not only would this indicate a violation of regulatory guidelines, but, Jim pointed out to me, fluctuations in temperature beyond approved levels could damage the equipment. Everyone had an interest in seeing that the system operated smoothly. The operating room had the feel of what I imagined an airplane flight control deck to be. Rather than planes, though, waste streams were being managed on an ongoing basis, coming from different sources and arriving in different forms.

It turned out that Raymond had given some of the writing that I'd sent him to the folks in the control room, and they had read it. But if they were hostile or suspicious of me, they were good at hiding it. Everyone was cordial, although it was clear that I was an outsider, visiting a very tight-knit team. Jim told me that he had worked at the facility from the beginning of its operations, first as an operator, eventually working his way up to operations manager. He'd seen the plant move from the drawings phase, through construction, into the start-up and various test burns. I much appreciated his generosity and patience in explaining the different aspects of the incinerator's operations. It was obvious that he loved what he was doing. It was not hard to imagine why. The processes by which the plant was kept functioning at peak performance were complex and challenging. Not only did the material have to be moved into the incinerator and burned within very specific parameters, but the discharged gases had to be cooled and cleaned in the ongoing attempt to reduce the amount of toxins that would be released into the atmosphere and the surrounding community. Jim, no doubt, understood the facility's engineering aspects better than anyone else. He'd been working with the kiln for ten years. He told me that he'd been to Japan as a consultant on an incinerator there as well. In terms of the operations aspects of hazardous waste incineration, he is undoubtedly one of the world's leading experts.

At one point, as I was listening to him talk intently about how the system worked, he noticed the other workers listening to him. He was clearly respected by the other workers, who commented good-naturedly on his intense interest in, and knowledge of, the processes that he was explaining. I asked him if he believed in the environmental safety of the facility, knowing pretty much in advance what the answer would be. The others in the room expressed their faith in the system as well. Jim said that he'd been at WTI long enough to have remembered the candlelight vigils and Martin Sheen's presence at anti-WTI demonstrations. I asked him what he thought about the opponents. He said they were just "saving face." After all, WTI was considered within the environmental-services world to be a top-notch facility, and it had survived tremendous regulatory hurdles and several court challenges. He looked at me and said, "The people that are *really* opposed to us won't come in here." I took that as a compliment of sorts.

All the crew members expressed pride in their medical and fire training. They felt that they were better qualified as emergency workers than were some who worked outside the plant for the city, something that they implied caused resentments among them. One of the crewmen took me to the solid waste pit, showing me how he used a crane to move the waste that was dumped in from trucks to a bin, from which the material was pushed into the incinerator. He told me that this was his favorite job. He said that there was something of an art to it, not to add too much, and to grab amounts that were manageable. This was the one part of the operation that was not clean and antiseptic from any observer's standpoint. I found the smell coming out of the pit to be nauseating, a feeling that stuck with me for about an hour after I left the plant. The smell was a combination of garbage and chemicals. This was a job that I could not imagine having. I wouldn't have been able to stand it for an entire day, much less the many years that the worker had put into it.

I walked out of the room with Raymond. We crossed by the incinerator's front wall, where I stopped to watch some of the fifty-gallon drums of hazardous waste being fed into the incinerator's kiln. We walked down the steps and outside the building, where you could look up and see the kiln as it slowly rotated, keeping the material inside moving around for an optimum burn. Two trucks were underneath a chute from which the burned residues were discharged for eventual transport to a disposal site in Indiana. As we walked back to the reception area, I turned around to get a wide look at the incinerator. Raymond showed me some of the bricks that were used to line the walls of the kiln. They were very heavy and about a foot thick. The spray dryer was nearby, an addition that was fought by the plant's opponents. Next to it was a container, like a small silo, which stored lime to be used in the dryer. About a month previously, an accident had occurred here involving a truck driver and the lime slurry. What happened is not entirely clear, but the driver was found by WTI employees lying inside his truck's tank. He eventually died from burns resulting from contact with the lime. At least some of the safety measures that Raymond had spoken of so highly seemed to have gaps.

We walked toward the river. Raymond told me that I had some of the facts wrong in my paper. For one thing, I had written that Greenpeace had hoisted a banner on the WTI stack, but in truth, the activist had gotten caught in the enclosed ladder on the way up. "You can't always depend on newspapers," he explained. As we talked back to the office, Raymond asked me what I thought of the facility. I told him that I thought it was an engineering marvel, a technical marvel. I was being neither disingenuous nor, I believe, incorrect. An operation such as this one, from an engineering perspective, is truly impressive. Whether it is enough of an achievement to answer the critics who suggest that no matter how well such a facility might be run, it can never be safe enough to be placed so close to populated areas, is another question.

I left WTI and drove across the river to Terri's house. While the distance between the facility and Terri's dining room was relatively short in terms of actual distance, when I arrived, I had traversed a huge cultural space. Terri had copied a large raft of documents for me. She gave me some of the latest updates on what was happening at the facility, including rumors of serious financial problems. There was also a rumor that a number of high-level employees had been discharged, including longtime plant manager Fred Sigg. Rumors were always circulating around WTI, however. Terri took them with a grain of salt.

I have to say that I felt much more at home talking about these issues with Terri. Whatever the technical merits of the incinerator, my heart was with the cultural opposition, the forces of democratic dissent, rather than with the engineers with whom I had spent the past two hours. Terri and Jim were clearly worlds apart, and if I had to choose sides, there's little doubt about which side I'd be on. I had wanted to spend some time with Terri asking about the various political actions that they had taken during the heady days of the early 1990s. She hooked up her computer and went through the pictures that she presented for talks at college campuses and for activist groups. There were pictures of "Hands across the River," when several thousand people had met on the West Virginia–Ohio bridge. There were pictures from the weenie campaign. There were numerous pictures of large crowds of people outside of the WTI fence, in some cases climbing over it. I really got the sense of how large a political issue this was at one time, drawing environmental and community activists from all over the United States.

CHAPTER 4.

Don't Give Up the Fight: Rhetorics of Resistance

> Capitalism inevitably and by virtue of the very
> logic of its civilization creates, educates and
> subsidizes a vested interest in social unrest.
> —*Joseph Schumpeter,* Capitalism, Socialism, and Democracy

Environmental justice activism evolved during the 1980s, representing a more diverse set of faces within the environmental movement.
Environmentalism, and its predecessor "conservation," had been primarily associated with the preservation of wilderness until the appearance of
Rachel Carson's *Silent Spring* in 1962.[1] Carson helped to spur a revolution
in thinking about the relationship between the "human" and the "natural." A naturalist who had before the success of her first book, *The Sea
around Us,* worked for the U.S. Fish and Wildlife Service, Carson viewed
human and natural systems as interdependent.[2] She was the first popular
author to expose the pervasiveness of environmental threats, particularly
in the form of chemical contamination, to human health. In spite of her
contributions, however, even throughout the 1960s, environmentalism
tended to be associated with the white middle class, interested in protecting the last shreds of disappearing "nature," especially in the western
United States. The environmental movement was not initially embraced
by African Americans or white working people, who often, with some
justification, associated it with the concerns of the privileged. For these
reasons, those involved with environmental justice issues have sometimes
been reluctant to label themselves as environmentalists.[3]

Environmental justice movements have made two immense contributions to environmental politics. First, advocates of environmental justice
expanded the meaning of "environment" beyond "conservation" of "nature" or "pristine wilderness." Cities were often ignored by environmental activists, if not viewed with outright hostility.[4] In the words of one
environmental justice advocate, "The environment, for us, is where we
live, where we work, and where we play."[5] Second, environmental justice
movements challenged, and then fundamentally altered, the class, race,
and gender structure of environmental activist politics. The underlying
premise of environmental justice was and is that environmental harms
are unevenly and unfairly distributed nationally in the United States and
globally.[6] Environmental justice was personified by grassroots efforts to
challenge the dispersal of toxics into poor, black, and brown communities. Love Canal was the location of one of the first actions that could be
considered a part of the environmental justice movement. Lois Gibbs
eventually became a national leader. In 1982, citizens of Warren County,
North Carolina, led by African American women, used tactics of civil disobedience, essentially lying down in front of trucks, to prevent their community for becoming home to the state's toxic waste landfill. More than
five hundred people were arrested.[7]

Perhaps the most important founding document in the movement's
history was a report issued by the United Church of Christ's Commission
on Racial Justice. The report found that 40 percent of hazardous waste
disposal capacity in the United States is located in communities that are
predominantly African American and Latino. In fact, the best predictor
of whether a person resided near a hazardous site of some kind turned out
to be race, which was even more important than poverty.[8] Other studies followed. Robert Bullard's seminal work *Dumping in Dixie* found a
statistically significant correlation between the proportion of people of
color in a given community and the presence of toxics.[9] Environmental
justice activists borrowed from the pages of the civil rights movement to
create nonviolent resistance and public spectacles that would expose environmental threats posed by petroleum and chlorine-based industrial
operations. Anti-incineration campaigns of the 1980s and 1990s should
be seen as a part of this larger set of political movements. The movement's
emphasis on lived experience and everyday life also had important gender
implications. Women have often been leaders in the environmental jus-

tice movement. Anti-WTI activism fit the model of this evolving form of political activism. The leadership was diverse in terms of race, gender, and class.

In 1984, the "Cerrell Report" was published. The study was commissioned by the California Waste Management Board, seeking guidance on how to site "waste-to-energy" facilities in the state. The authors began with the premise, often expressed since, that incineration facilities are a much safer alternative to previously favored disposal methods, primarily landfilling, often in unregulated and unmaintained dumps.[10] The study gave detailed consideration to public resistance to proposed facilities. In fact, the authors divided "subgroups" into those "least resistant" and those "most resistant" to having facilities in their neighborhoods.[11] The report concluded that residents of the Northeast and the West were most likely to resist facilities, and that residents of rural areas were less likely to resist than residents of urban ones. Yet already industrialized areas would be more likely to accept a site than nonindustrial ones.[12]

Perhaps the most inflammatory finding of the report, however, fell under the heading "Personality Profile." Here the report is as astonishing in its candor as it is appalling in its recommendations: "Certain types of people are likely to participate in politics, either by virtue of their issue awareness or their financial resources, or both. Members of middle or higher-socioeconomic strata (a composite index of level of education, occupational prestige and income) are more likely to organize into effective groups to express their political interests and views. All socioeconomic groupings tend to resent the nearby siting of major facilities, but the middle and upper-socioeconomic strata possess better resources to effectuate their opposition. Middle and higher-socioeconomic strata neigborhoods should not fall at least within the one-mile and five-mile radii of the proposed site."[13]

As with any political movement that confronts power in a direct fashion, the antitoxics and anti-incinerator movement has had its share of critics. Not unexpectedly, the authorities that were being challenged did not accede to demands that they cease engaging in the production and distribution of toxic wastes. Antitoxics activists were branded with the "NIMBY" (not in my backyard) label. The implication was that they were often simply obstructionists, or worse, representatives of an ignorant mass whose members were unable or unwilling to grasp the scientific "facts" involved with waste disposal, particularly in terms of the concept of "risk." Implicit in criticisms of NIMBYism is that activists are selfish, refusing to share the costs of waste created by an affluent industrial society. As Gregory McAvoy notes: "The Nimby syndrome gained prominence in the 1970s as researchers and the popular press were concerned that citizens could oppose routinely and most often successfully facilities like those for hazardous waste disposal. In its early and popular usage, the Nimby syndrome characterized citizens as: (a) overly emotional, uninformed, and unscientific in their opposition to these facilities; (b) motivated by narrow, selfish interests; and (c) obstructing policies that would provide for the collective good."[14]

NIMBY's meanings expanded in ways that made its use even more problematic. NIMBY became associated with the position that no undesirable entity be located in one's neighborhood, not just incinerators and nuclear dumps, but low-income housing developments, facilities for deinstitutionalized mental patients,[15] "antenna farms,"[16] and recycling facilities.[17] While the merits of resistance might be more clearly justifiable in some cases than others, all NIMBY proponents were often grouped together as generally selfish people who were so obsessed with their own individual rights and private property values, that they were unwilling to absorb their share of the social costs that must, in an advanced capitalist economy, be borne by someone.[18]

Proponents of hazardous waste incineration, and of other industrial facilities, have characterized NIMBY activists not only as ignorant and selfish but also as doing public harm by stalling the progress of industrial development and the economic benefits that accrue from it.[19] Roberta Barbalace goes so far as to assert that community resistance to hazardous waste facilities *fosters* environmental harm, because it "prevents the construction of new environmentally sound sites, and forces HW facilities to be built upon pre-existing, already contaminated sites that are frequently located in depleted neighborhoods."[20] In other words, NIMBYism is a form of environmental racism. Much was written by public policy analysts and law professors on how to use negotiation techniques or incentive systems as mechanisms for gaining community approval for undesirable industrial facilities.[21] A philosophical debate emerged regarding what a "just" distribution of waste might look like and how it could be achieved.[22]

Barry G. Rabe's *Beyond Nimby*, published in 1994, in the wake of ten years of antitoxics organizing, is a good example of an academic policy analysis approach to hazardous waste disposal. On the one hand, Rabe is highly critical of the waste disposal industry and the regulatory authorities that were attempting to facilitate hazardous waste siting in the 1980s. Neither of the two most widely used approaches to siting—market-based incentives and regulatory mandates—had resulted in quelling community opposition. Market-based solutions were hardly ever, if ever, accepted by citizens of local communities as adequate compensation for the social and environmental harms that flow from accepting a toxic waste disposal site. Regulatory mandates involving even the most "state-of-the art" facilities were viewed by local citizens as attempts on the part of government bureaucracies to shove an unwanted facility down the throats of an unwilling public.

Rabe is also, however, quite critical of antitoxics activists, whose uncompromising intransigence he sees as representing an unrealistic response to a social and environmental problem that must at some point be addressed. We need, after all, to put the stuff someplace. NIMBYism provides no solution to the hazardous waste disposal problem. As Rabe puts it, "Although some salutary effects of the Nimby phenomenon should be acknowledged, the virtual inability to open new hazardous waste treatment and disposal facilities in either Canada and the United States raises a host of serious public health, environmental, equity, and intergovernmental concerns."[23]

In contrast to the conflictual model inspired by most hazardous waste siting, Rabe suggests a cooperative model. In Canada, the province of Alberta's approach was, according to Rabe, exemplary in this regard.[24] The province proposed the construction of a large waste disposal and management facility that included both incineration and landfilling, while organizing a province-wide policy of hazardous waste reduction and recycling. The siting was to rely entirely on "volunteerism." Public dialogue was to be encouraged in any community considering the site, and no community would be forced to accept it. As a result, not only was the site accepted willingly in the town of Swan Hills, but Swan Hills was chosen over other willing communities in the province.[25] Alberta had overcome the traditional NIMBY syndrome, generating a "win-win" situation.

While some communities in the United States have been more successful in dealing with the waste disposal problem than others, no American state has developed a comprehensive policy along the lines of Alberta. The Alberta case remains an intriguing one, but it did not provide a model for hazardous waste disposal in the United States. So while Rabe's study provides an excellent, meticulously documented account of a "success story," it had a limited impact on policy-making processes. More significant, perhaps, is the question of whether the Alberta model is actually a good thing from an environmental perspective. Rabe himself raises the question of whether Swan Hills has made the disposal of hazardous waste in the province "too easy," but he arrives at no firm conclusion. Alberta, he notes, developed a comprehensive waste management strategy, fostering minimization while providing for disposal.[26] But the underlying assumption of the Alberta model is that the creation and disposal of hazardous wastes on a very large scale are inevitable, and therefore facility siting should be undertaken in the spirit of cooperation and compromise rather than conflict and resistance.

The WTI proposal took a more typical path of hazardous waste siting in the United States. WTI was not part of a comprehensive hazardous waste plan. Moreover, considerable citizen opposition, which was extremely vocal early on, was mostly discounted by public officials. The process took on an air of inevitability, as first local, then state, and finally national officials did what was in their power to keep the project on track, in spite of serious and valid objections raised by prominent people and ordinary citizens in the affected community. Citizen opponents felt excluded from initial siting decisions and felt as though they were not offered meaningful choices. In fact, suspicions about the legitimacy of the entire process haunted citizen activists from the outset. These suspicions, mixed with doubts about the plant's safety and apprehensions about long-term health and environmental consequences, have helped to sustain an active anti-incineration movement for many years.

Were East Liverpool citizens thus engaged in a selfish and unthinking kind of NIMBYism? In fact, East Liverpool opponents were not simply lashing out. While supporters of cooperation and compromise on incinerator siting might disagree with Terri Swearingen or Alonzo Spencer's actions, they would not be entitled to cast either as an irrational "anti." They, like other anti-incineration opponents, held a theory of political action. This theory is often expressed as "stopping up the toilet." Proponents of this view take the position that citizens have an obligation to make siting and construction of such facilities as difficult and expensive as possible. Only an increase in costs of disposal will shift businesses and policy makers toward supporting more sustainable ways of organizing the economy. Under this theory, the problem with hazardous waste disposal is not too many NIMBYs, but too few. The fewer sites available, the more the toilet is clogged up, the greater the pressure to change the nature of industrial practices. While the struggles may be local, the political vision is global. As Luke Cole and Sheila Foster note: "The movement for environmental justice seeks much more than merely to *stop* the siting of waste facilities, and other locally undesireable land uses in low-income communities and communities of color. . . . The movement for environmental justice is also about creating clean jobs, building a sustainable economy, guaranteeing safe and affordable housing, and achieving racial and social justice."[27]

Stopping up the toilet, then, is both a set of tactics and a radical theory of political action. At the local level, it seeks to prevent the siting of specific facilities and to galvanize democratic forces against corporate interests and the regulatory agencies that so often seem to facilitate their activities. In a larger sense, its refusal to compromise offers a challenge to the entire system of industrial production. As Kevin DeLuca notes, "Mainstream environmental groups have accepted the parameters of the industrial system and just work to mitigate its most adverse effects, but environmental justice groups question the premises and challenge the practices of industrialism that produce the wastes in the first place."[28]

Radical Actions

The 1980s were the heyday of radical environmental activism. Ronald Reagan had been elected president in 1980, and he appointed Anne Gorsuch as EPA director and James Watt as secretary of the interior. Each was seen by environmentalists as being entirely too cozy with the industries that they were supposed to regulate, petrochemicals in the case of Gorsuch, mining, timber, and cattle in the case of Watt. Both would eventually leave office discredited. Before they left, they generated much controversy, and each helped to generate considerable opposition from environmental activists. Watt's actions as secretary of the interior helped to inspire the organizers of Earth First! Dave Foreman, founder of Earth First!, had a flair for guerrilla theater. In the spring of 1981, members of Earth First!, along with Edward Abbey, author of *The Monkeywrench Gang* and *Desert Solitaire,* unrolled a giant polyurethane "crack" down the face of the Glen Canyon Dam. The dam's construction in the 1960s blocked the flow of the Colorado River and despoiled the fabled Glen Canyon, a natural wonder, arguably as beautiful and archaeologically as significant as the Grand Canyon. Rik Scarce notes that the action "introduced Earth First! And Earth First! humor, a wit on level with that of Lenny Bruce—political, challenging, poignant, and hilarious to the thoughtful, irreverent or insulting to the rest. More importantly, though, the crack symbolized a break with environmentalism's past.... No more muddling through. No more compromise.... After the crack the environmental movement would never again be the same."[29]

The tactics and ethos that defined Earth First! had been prefigured by the actions of Greenpeace in the 1970s. Greenpeace had been organized in 1969 in British Columbia and gained worldwide attention when it sailed a rented boat, the *Greenpeace,* toward the Aleutian island of Amchitka in the hopes of stopping an American nuclear test there. While the activists did not even get within a thousand miles of the test site, the publicity that they generated caused enough embarrassment that the U.S. government halted nuclear tests there.[30] Greenpeace quickly grew into an international movement, challenging French nuclear testing and Soviet whaling practices. Eventually it expanded its activities to include antipollution and antitoxics campaigns. Greenpeacers "bolted shut effluent pipes leading from chemical plants and skydived off power plant smokestacks to publicize pollution." They were "*active* activists."[31]

Greenpeace activists were both self-conscious and sophisticated in their approach to media. Robert Hunter, director of Greenpeace during the early challenges to Soviet whaling practices, described the media theorist Marshall McLuhan as "our greatest prophet." Greenpeace would use direct action to launch "mind bombs," which would destabilize public consciousness and lead to cultural and political transformation. Thus, even if a particular action was unsuccessful (in saving an individual whale or preventing a single instance of nuclear testing), real success would be defined in terms of shifts in values, expectations, and policies.[32] Greenpeace and Earth First! represented a new face of environmental politics, not only in their willingness to engage in civil disobedience and direct action, but also in their capacity to deploy new rhetorical strategies, to deploy what

DeLuca has called "image politics."[33] The practice of image politics represents certain dangers. When adopting them, activists are challenging the rational and bureaucratic standards associated with "civility." Thus they can be cast as having voluntarily removed themselves from the sphere of reasoned discourse, and as such risk being marginalized. But a dismissive stance toward the rhetorical significance of "image events" "supports those in positions of authority and thus allows civility and decorum to serve as masks for the protection of privilege and the silencing of protest."[34]

Greenpeace and Earth First! were characterized differently by the press. Greenpeace activists in their tiny boats facing down huge Russian whaling ships were often cast as crazy/brave. Rather than radical greens, challenging the forces of industrial fishing, they were rugged individualists challenging the dangerous and hegemonic power of the Soviet Union. They had shifted, as one news account put it, from "sailing around the Pacific trying to stop American and French nuclear testing" to their current project of "trying to stop the Russians from the massive hunting of whales off the California coast."[35] Earth First!, on the other hand, was treated as a terrorist organization. While Earth Firsters engaged in a diverse variety of tactics, including acts of nonviolent civil disobedience, public spectacles, and tree sitting, the press tended to focus on acts of ecotage, especially tree spiking. After lumber worker George Alexander was injured when the saw he was working near fractured from hitting a metal spike, Earth First! was publicly named as the perpetrator, even after it was discovered that the spike that was responsible for injuring Alexander had been placed there by a conservative Republican landowner, who had a boundary dispute with the lumber company that had cut the tree.

Anti-WTI activism, then, evolved during a period that environmentalists were becoming increasingly disenchanted with the mainstream movement, which seemed inclined toward working out the details of the implementation of the legislative gains made in the late 1960s and early 1970s. Some radical tactics were more successful than others. Greenpeace managed to present itself as being involved in a heroic struggle. The bravery of antinuclear and whaling activists in their tiny boats was the stuff of legend. Earth Firsters, on the other hand, were often presented as hooligans or criminals. Anti-WTI activists distinguished themselves early on by the use of irony and wit as a way to challenge powerful forces. In William Gates's history of the area, *City of Hills and Kilns,* a photograph from January 1983 shows opponents dressed up in what appears to be radiation protection gear. One is holding a sign that says, "Preview the '84 Valley Girl Fashions."[36]

Challenging Power in East Liverpool

Leaders of political movements use a variety of appeals to attract and inspire adherents—appeals to faith, to morality, to justice, to interest. Leaders of the WTI campaign used all of these appeals, but they were especially effective in attracting support and sympathy by creating ironic spectacles that both communicated their messages and tweaked the noses of the powerful. Irony's power against the powerful is obvious. Irony unmasks, and power relies on masks to maintain the fictions of its imperatives. Irony creates communities of the knowing, the insiders who "get the joke," often at the expense of a target or a victim. When a powerful figure is targeted, irony, if successfully deployed, shifts the balance. The weak and the strong, at least momentarily, have changed positions. Power's vulnerabilities are exposed. When a target responds with chagrin, anger, disdain, or even flight, the success of the ironic spectacle is advanced and even magnified. In the public arena, the only successful response to ironic challenges is perhaps recognition, some indication that one knows how to play the game of ironic reversals. This is an extremely difficult maneuver for the powerful to successfully manage. George Voinovich, Ohio governor during the period of greatest conflict in the WTI case, was especially ill suited to fend off the clever attacks of WTI protestors.

The cleverness of the WTI opponents is clearly displayed in a poster that was printed in 1991. "Wanted," it states in large letters above a picture of the smiling governor, "for endangering the people of the State of Ohio." Underneath is a "description," which notes: "Eyes: Blind to the facts," "Ears: Deaf to the calls of citizens," "Height: Shrinking under pressure from polluters and those wanting to turn Ohio into the world's waste capital," "Disguise: Sometimes presents himself as a public servant," "Last Seen: Backing away from protecting the citizens of East Liverpool from the world's largest hazardous waste incinerator." "Caution," it warns in bold letters, "This man is a danger to the people of Ohio!" Included under "specific acts by Mr. Voinovich against the people of Ohio" is that he "sheepishly refused to uphold Ohio's laws and stop the world's largest hazardous waste incinerator from being sited less than 1,000 feet from an elementary school in East Liverpool." At the bottom of the page is a warning: "If you see this man do not try to comprehend alone! Contact: Tri State Environmental Council."

The size and format of the poster draw the reader in. In American culture, the wanted poster is a familiar and compelling motif, an object of fear and fascination. It triggers associations with Western outlaws and Chicago gangsters. A passerby sees the governor's picture and is intrigued. Why would Governor Voinovich be on a wanted poster? Other familiar elements remain intact: physical description, possible disguises, crimes committed, warnings about possible dangers. In each case, though, ironic shifts have occurred. The reader is drawn into the joke, perhaps appreciates it, and recognizes it as a comment on political power, potentially magnifying the appreciation.

Terri told me that the activists always tried to tie a number to their actions. When they staged a takeover of the Ohio EPA, they chose ten people. These became the "Takeover Ten." At another point, they staged a demonstration featuring grandparents. These became the "Grand Eight." They made a large banner with the motto "Whatever It Takes." At one point, they took school kids on a trip to Columbus, where they held a public contest: "Pin the Brain on the Governor."

The "weenie" campaign again evidenced the activists' capacity for effectively deploying irony against Governor Voinovich. Terri Swearingen told me that the ideas stemmed from another action. According to the state's own capacity assessment plan, Ohio did not need the WTI incinerator, so Terri, Alonzo, and some others went to Columbus to give the governor a "math lesson." While at the governor's mansion, they put up some for-sale signs there, indicating that the governor had "sold out to the waste disposal industry." While they were there, the governor left the residence. On the way out, he told the protesters, "I have nothing to say to you people." The phrase "you people" particularly irked Terri. He was treating the protesters as though they were unruly children. As the governor ran to his car, Terri said, she thought he was a "weenie." This turned into Voinovich being a "weenie on waste." The idea of doing a "roast," Terri said, came from Johnny Carson, in other words, "roasting someone," or making fun of them.[37]

In late November 1991, opponents traveled to the governor's mansion in the affluent Columbus suburb of Bexley to have a "weenie roast." Twenty-two East Liverpool area residents showed up in a yellow school bus, just as the governor was on his way out of the residence. As he hurried away, demonstrators yelled, "Run, run!" A spokesman said that the governor was not trying to avoid protesters but was simply on his way to an Ohio State football game. But as a car spirited him away, he responded to the protesters' pleas for a dialogue by saying, "'I'm not going to talk with you. I have nothing to say.'" Demonstrators called the governor a "weenie" and held up signs accusing him of child abuse.[38] The governor's spokesman later responded by castigating the protesters: "I stopped behaving that way after I got out of the second grade," he was reported to have said. "These people are more interested in publicity than in protecting the environment."[39] This was probably the least effective rhetorical response that could be marshaled in such a case. The governor was the schoolmarm, ineffectively trying to discipline clever, playful miscreants who had a morally compelling case to at least be heard.

Aware that the weenie campaign had garnered significant media coverage, opponents followed up with a pun-filled press release. In it, Terri Swearingen was quoted as saying, "We're here today because we believe this weenie needs to get off his buns and stop WTI. Frankly, Governor Voinovich is in quite a pickle, and we would relish the thought of the Governor being able to mustard the courage to ketchup with the rest of the world on the incinerator issue. Our response would be, Hot Dog."[40] Opponents also went to area grocery stores and placed stickers on packages of hotdogs with a small picture of a weiner and a caption stating, "Governor Voinovich Is a Wienie on Waste: Tell the Governor . . . Don't Burn Ohio, Stop Incineration."

Two weeks later, opponents returned to Columbus to continue to the weenie campaign. They seemed to be winning at least some of the press over with their clever ribbing of a flustered governor. This time, "They came," according to the *Plain-Dealer* reporter T. C. Brown, "from the East bearing gifts of gold, frankfurters and mirth."[41] Since Voinovich was out of town, protesters wielding foil-covered hotdogs left a series of gifts with his receptionist, including grade-school math books and flash cards "to help calculate the state's capacity to burn waste."[42] The weenie campaign continued in various guises for about a year. Every time the activists went to Columbus, which was as often as once a week in 1991, they would buy

hotdogs from stands near the state capital and bring them to the governor's secretary. People around the state would also mail cans of Vienna
franks to the governor's office on a regular basis.[43] The campaign seemed
to be having some effect. Voinovich declared a moratorium on the future
constructions of toxic waste incinerators in Ohio, for which he was ap-
plauded by a Greenpeace spokesperson. Terri Swearingen is convinced,
partly based on the governor's own admission, that the activists made a
difference. He was simply incapable of fending off their challenges. But activists wanted him to go further, insisting that he prevent the WTI facility
from moving forward.[44] This was a step that the governor was unwilling
to take.

   In the fall of 1992, after a two-year campaign, Ohio Citizen Action
completed a successful petition campaign to have Issue 5 placed on the
November ballot. Issue 5 would have required that warning labels be
placed on products containing carcinogenic chemicals, and that businesses that discharge carcinogenic chemicals into the environment send
warning letters, twice a year, to residents in potentially affected areas.
Enforcement would be funded through a tax of one cent per pound on
toxic chemical releases.[45] In early October, the governor held a news conference to express his opposition. Voinovich appeared with four of his
cabinet members to criticize the measure as redundant, a threat to jobs,
and unenforceable.[46]

   Unbeknownst to the governor, a number of anti-WTI protesters were
standing in the back of the room. Several of them began waving the hotdogs, a now-familiar signifier, indicating that the governor was a "weenie
on waste." Voinovich did not immediately notice the protesters, but once
they were pointed out to him, he immediately left the room. Asked about
the governor's quick exit, his spokesman, Mike Dawson, stated, "We aren't
going to participate in a side show with people waving hot dogs on their
heads."[47] The picture of Connie Stein, Terri Swearingen, and Mike Casey
holding up hotdogs with slightly amused looks on their faces was too much
for the state's newspapers to ignore. The picture turned up in at least eight
of them, including newspapers that didn't often carry anti-WTI actions,
such as the *Akron Beacon* and the *Toledo Blade*. Some headlines invited
readers to join in the fun: "Protestors Hot-Dog It at Voinovich's Event,"[48]
"Weiners Cause Walk Out,"[49] "Weenie Protestors Disrupt Voinovich,"[50]
"Governor Flees 'Sideshow,' at Call for Issue 5 Defeat." *USA Today* picked

up the story in its roundup of state news. "Governor Voinovich," it said, "walked out of his own news conference . . . as foes of a hazardous waste incinerator waved wieners at him. Some environmentalists say administration officials are 'weenies on waste.'"[51] Voinovich, caught off guard, and a man with little sense of humor, seemed unequipped to deal with the spectacle being generated by the protesters.

In December, opponents of the plant challenged Governor Voinovich again, this time over the issue of a health study that the state had proposed to conduct in East Liverpool after the start-up of the incinerator. Proposing the study may have been an attempt to mollify residents, suggesting that health concerns would be a priority once operations began at WTI. The proposal had precisely the opposite effect. That it would generate antagonism seems entirely predictable. The inability of state officials to foresee the study's effect was an indication of their insulation and alienation from the democratic forces that were organizing against the plant. The ex post facto nature of the measure excluded any capacity to ensure the safety of citizens. Rather, the proposal suggested experimentation, perhaps along the lines of the infamous Tuskegee syphilis study. For WTI activists, the state health study was little more than a clumsy attempt to shroud power in the guise of medical care.[52]

Community members expressed several objections. For one thing, this was the first time that such a study had been conducted in the community, suggesting that, as one press release stated, "it was being performed in order to hide the fact that proper health studies were never done prior to permitting and constructing the WTI facility."[53] In this way, the study seemed like the product of a post hoc rationalization and public relations maneuver, rather than the result of an actual concern for the children of the East Liverpool area. Moreover, that the study would proceed only after operations at the plant began made the study suspect on scientific grounds. What would be the baseline for comparison? None would be available locally. As Ted Hill, a local pediatrician (and Terri Swearingen's brother), stated in a letter to Peter Somani, the assistant director of Ohio's Department of Health: "No transportation, storage or incineration of hazardous waste should be permitted at the WTI facility in East Liverpool, Ohio until all baseline epidemiologic studies are complete."[54] The state, of course, was not willing to postpone the plant's operations until an extensive survey had been completed. Thus the state health department's concern seemed disingenuous.

There were other problems, as well. The proposed six-month testing for lead would not necessarily pick up elevated levels given lead's half-life of one month in children's blood.[55] While testing was proposed for mercury levels, it was not clear that the state had taken account of the tremendous difficulties of administering and evaluating such tests accurately.[56] Surveillance of mortality and cancer figures would not yield meaningful information for as much as thirty years, making them virtually useless as a mechanism for checking the facility.[57]

Dr. Herbert Needleman thus found the scheme to be "medically inadequate and morally derelict."[58] What had begun as a perhaps misguided attempt to show concern for the health of children in the community had become a public relations disaster and another opportunity to take Governor Voinovich to task for his support of the incinerator. Children were not being cared for but treated as, in the words of opponents, "guinea pigs or mine canaries."[59] Activists made up pledge cards: "A Mother's Pledge, GOVERNOR VOINOVICH WILL NOT DRAW BLOOD . . . MY CHILDREN ARE NOT HIS GUINEA PIGS." The pledge went on to say: "As a mother in the Ohio Valley, I will not allow Governor Voinovich to touch my children. The only thing the Governor can do to assure me of the safety of my children, is to immediately shut down the WTI toxic waste incinerator. A bogus experiment which he calls a 'health study' will do nothing to protect my family. The Governor will not draw my children's blood in an attempt to allow toxic polluters to make my back yard their dumping ground." On the bottom of the pledge card was a signature line.

Three hundred fifty pledge cards were turned in to the governor's office. These parents had essentially refused to take part in the study, undermining the validity of any findings. State health commissioner David A. Yost offered to suspend the study if the East Liverpool city council would vote that they did not want it to be funded.[60] The council was divided. On March, the WTI opponents again took their case to the Ohio state capital. At 11:00 a.m. on Monday, March 23, 1992, children and parents arrived at the governor's office. The children were carrying cages of mice and guinea pigs. Terri Swearingen was quoted in a press release as saying that "they have come to the Capitol today to show the Governor the difference between experimental lab animals and children." The children would not, in Terri's words, "be part of a grotesque scientific experiment."[61] A poster was printed with a picture of a child behind bars. "Say No," it said, "DO NOT ALLOW GOVERNOR VOINOVICH AND HIS HEALTH DEPARTMENT TO USE OUR CHILDREN AS HUMAN GUINEA PIGS. BOYCOTT THE HEALTH STUDY." Needless to say, the study was terminated.

Ulrich Beck summarizes the problem of turning society "into a laboratory." In these kinds of cases, "research becomes a kind of groping in the fog. Laboratory experiments assume that variables are controllable. To the extent the boundaries of the laboratory are opened this controllability is canceled. Experiments in the open air and on people . . . raise not only ethical questions about the logic of research. There the controllability of the laboratory situation is lost, so is the very framework that makes a precise conceptualization and determination of variables possible at all. Checking hypotheses becomes blurred, fictive, because the opening of the laboratory boundaries requires one to assume theoretically and practically controlled influences."[62] The state of Ohio had proposed a health study, the findings of which, almost by necessity, would be suspect. The potential subjects of this research recognized it intuitively and opposed it rationally. Their rhetorical response revealed the problematics of scientific investigation and the blindness of the powerful.

Rally, Trespass, and Necessity

The rhetorical brilliance of the weenie and anti-health-study campaigns lay in the successful deployment of irony to highlight the governor's intransigence on WTI as it punctured the protective cocoon of his official position. While irony and playfulness continued to mark the guerrilla theater of anti-WTI protests, the October 1991 rally and subsequent trial drew the most national attention. Rather than using irony to undermine the authoritative legitimacy of officialdom, the October rally constituted a direct challenge to the power represented by the incinerator.

The "Hands over the River" rally occurred in early 1991. Here demonstrators from Ohio and West Virginia marched across the Jennings Randolph Bridge from opposites sides, meeting in the middle. More than one thousand people participated. During the rally, Terri talked to a supporter named Vincent Irene, who had worked with the homeless in Pittsburgh. Irene said that he knew Martin Sheen, and that Sheen was in Pittsburgh working on a movie. He believed that Sheen might be interested in becoming involved with the opposition. Irene eventually told Terri that she should fax some materials to the Western William Penn Hotel in Pittsburgh, where Sheen was staying. She still had not met or talked with Sheen when Irene told her that she should plan an action that involved him. She and others put together a three-state event that would focus on physician opposition. The event would begin in Beaver, Pennsylvania, move on to Wheeling, and finally end in East Liverpool. Physicians, including Terri's brother, would be the featured speakers, and she included Martin Sheen as well. Terri wasn't sure that he would actually be there, but was extremely relieved when he arrived at the first event. He became an active member of the opposition forces.[63]

On September 24, 1991, 150 citizens demonstrated outside a local school as WTI public relations people attempted to hold an informational meeting inside. Only ten people sat inside the school. The next day, when U.S. EPA and Ohio EPA officials held a hearing on the facility, seven hundred opponents showed up, singing, chanting, and shouting. Before they went into the meeting, they held a "funeral for democracy" replete with a flag-draped coffin. Opponents had sneaked bullhorns into the meeting, and that along with crowd chants was enough to drown out official spokespeople. Officials pulled out a blackboard, wrote on it that the meeting was adjourned, and asked attendees to send written comments to the EPA regional office in Chicago.[64] The citizens were elated that they were "in control." In the words of longtime activist Joy Allison: "That's the way it should be. The EPA and the (incinerator) industry have been in control for 11 years, but the citizens were in control tonight."[65]

On October 13, 1991, 1,200 people attended a rally near the facility. After several hours of speeches, twenty-nine people jumped over an eight-foot construction fence that surrounded the facility. Along with Terri Swearingen and Alonzo Spencer was the actor Martin Sheen, who had been born in Dayton, Ohio. Sheen said that he was led to the protest by "two words: My conscience."[66] After scaling the fence, the protesters refused to leave the company's property, kneeling together and praying as they waited to be arrested for trespass by local police. Several days later, three others were charged with criminal trespass when they tried to block the facility's entrance.[67] If convicted of the misdemeanor charges, defendants could have served up to thirty days in jail and paid $250 in fines.[68]

The trial took place in February and generated a tremendous amount of publicity. Opponents made the best of the opportunity, as they turned the trial into a public hearing on the safety of the WTI facility. The way to this had been paved two weeks earlier, when a municipal court judge, Melissa Byers-Emmerling, after a preliminary hearing, agreed to allow the protesters' attorneys, C. Joseph King and Paul Boas, to invoke the "necessity" defense. This would allow them to broaden the trial far beyond the fairly simple question of whether they had broken the law of trespass, a charge in itself very difficult, if not impossible, to deny.[69]

The roots of the necessity defense can be traced back through English common law, but courts have been reluctant to allow it. In the classic case of *The Queen v. Dudley and Stephens*,[70] the facts were truly horrifying. Three men and a small boy were at sea in a lifeboat with virtually no food and water. Believing that they all would die, the men decided to make a human sacrifice. At first, they agreed to draw lots but then settled on killing the boy, reasoning, they later said, that he was the most reasonable choice, given that he had no family for which to provide. The boy was killed and eaten, and the men were eventually rescued and tried for murder. The jury, unable to reach a verdict, turned the decision back to the court. Appellate judges were leery of applying "necessity" as an excuse for otherwise criminal conduct. In their words, "It is plain what the principle leaves to him who is to profit by it to determine the necessity which will justify him in deliberately taking another's life to save his own."[71] The determination of what constituted necessity was being made by the person who would most immediately benefit from the decision. As a result, "such a principle once admitted might be made the legal cloak for unbridled passion and atrocious crime."[72] The defendants were found guilty and sentenced to death.

The facts of the East Liverpool case are, of course, much less dramatic. The necessity claimed is less immediate (long-term health and environmental problems, rather than death by starvation and thirst). The crimes committed, on the other hand, were much less serious (a minor property crime, rather than murder). Yet precedents with a closer factual parallel, those in which "political" necessity was claimed, did not seem to offer much support for the defendants, either. In *State v. Warshow*,[73] for example, defendants had demonstrated on the private property of a nuclear power plant in Vermont. When asked to leave, they refused and were arrested for trespass. The jury, in this case, was not allowed to consider the necessity defense; rather, it was held for appellate ruling. The appeals court found that neither health risks from low-level nuclear radiation nor the potential for an accident was enough to meet the "imminent and compelling harm element" of a necessity defense. "Nor," the court stated, "can the defendants' sincerity of purpose excuse the criminal nature of their acts."[74]

Undoubtedly both judges and juries take "necessity" into account in subtle ways in making judgments regarding degrees of guilt and sentences warranted. But the explicit acceptance of "necessity" as a legal defense remains rare, and it was surprising that Judge Byers-Emmerling allowed it to be raised at the trial of the East Liverpool defendants. The most immediate impact of the ruling would be to drastically expand the kind of evidence that could be introduced by the defense. They would have a public platform for making the case that WTI posed such a threat to the community and that legal violations to stop its construction and operation were a moral and legal compulsion. The judge essentially allowed the defendants to politicize the trial. They took full advantage of the opportunity.

A rally was held in support of the protesters at the Diamond, a local Liverpool restaurant, on February 11, 1992. Speakers stood atop a bus that was supplied by a local radio station as upward of five hundred people gathered to listen.[75] Opponents came from far away in support of the defendants, including Greg Moore, from Bloomington, Indiana, who was wearing a gas mask, stating that he was "fed up" with the incinerator.[76] UAW local president David Kimmel spoke at the rally, lending union support for the action. "You're going to win this fight," he told the crowd.[77] Plant manager Samuel Kasley was not impressed. "It's just actors and rabble rousers coming from out of town that have stirred things up. . . . We're the people that are actually doing something about the hazardous waste problem. We deal with the facts and with science."[78]

From the outset, the trial's extraordinariness was apparent. A swarm of print and broadcast media were present for the preliminary hearing. Police chief Chuck Coen stated that "in the 25 years that I've been here, we've had murder cases for preliminary hearings that never attracted a crowd like this."[79] Judge Byers-Emmerling castigated four members of the jury pool for posing for a picture with Martin Sheen in the hallway during a court recess. She told them that they had "violated every law I hold sacred," and said that she should have held them in contempt but ultimately chose not do so.[80] They were, however, permanently barred from serving as jurors.[81]

Defense attorney C. Joseph King laid out the arguments for "necessity" in a brief filed before the preliminary hearing. He contended that the acts of the defendants "were necessary to prevent the greater loss" that would be caused to health and environment by the plant. The arguments for this defense were laid out in memorandums filed by the defendants before the trial. There they argued not only that a variety of health risks were associated with the plant's operations but that the "'evil' that the defendants sought to avoid was *imminent*. It was imminent, not in the sense that their protest alone would then and there prevent dangerous activity at that instance. It was imminent in that the 'shakedown' or initial pretest burning was to begin February 15, 1992 and full operations thereafter. What was imminent was the absolute need *to start the process* of stopping this facility through the method described above and immediately. Anything else, the Defendants reasonably believed, would be too little and clearly too late."[82] In other words, the defendants were arguing that they were morally compelled to call attention to the incinerator's problems, and that the need to do this was "imminent" given the relatively near-term start-up date of the incinerator. To an outside observer, even one sympathetic to the ultimate aims of the plant opponents, this might seem to be a fairly obvious stretching of the meaning of the term "imminent," if the term is taken to mean "immediate," as it usually is. "The Defendants," the brief continued, "will testify that their actions were carefully calculated, not as mere symbolic protest, but rather as an act designed to begin a process through their mass presence and the information that could be generated only by such an extreme action that would culminate in such an upheaval that the incinerator would be stopped."[83] Moreover, the defense argued that they did not have to prove *actual* imminence, but merely evidence that defendants *believed* that the facility's start-up posed an imminent danger.

Judge Byers-Emmerling found the argument to be compelling enough that she was willing to give a jury discretion to draw its own conclusions.

In her ruling on the defense motion, she noted that the Ohio Code section related to trespass states that "no person, without privilege to do so, shall . . . knowingly enter or remain on the land or premises of another."[84] But one element of "privilege" allowed that it grow "out of *necessity*."[85] Given the explicitness of the statute, the judge felt compelled to allow it to be offered as a defense. Moreover, she accepted the defense argument conflating the distinction between actual and perceived imminence. "It is not necessary for the accused to be objectively correct in his/her belief merely that he/she have a good faith belief that the belief is reasonable."[86]

During the trial, local prosecuting attorney G. Thomas Rodfong did his best to keep the eight-member jury focused on the narrow trespass charge. "When all the dust is settled and all the evidence is presented, remember that WTI is not on trial here. . . . The company did not commit the crime."[87] Rodfong focused on the specific actions taken by the defendants. A videotape was shown of the protesters jumping over the fence. Police, plant officials, and other witnesses were called to verify the video's images which, Rodfong stated, "will show exactly what took place that day at WTI."[88]

Yet once the necessity defense was put into play, it became impossible for the prosecutor to keep the issues narrowly focused. The judge agreed, for example, to allow testimony that spoke to facts that the defendants *may have known* when they decided to climb over the fence. King was thus able to call several expert witnesses who attacked the facility's safety. Dr. David Ozonoff, chair of the Boston University School of Public Health, discussed cancer risks posed by the facility, noting that dozens of carcinogens were going to be released by its operation. Ozonoff's testimony was compelling. He had, he said, "passed this picture of the incinerator site (that shows the school nearby) around my department at school and just watched everyone's eyes bug out."[89] Ozonoff concluded that "locating this here makes as much sense as designing a transportation system in Death Valley that relies on ice skates."[90]

Dr. Herbert Needleman, a professor of psychiatry and pediatrics at the University of Pittsburgh's Western Psychiatric Institute, focused on the damaging effects of lead on children's mental development. WTI, once operating, would be permitted to release 4.7 tons of lead into the local atmosphere annually. Michael McCawley, an engineer and air pollution expert from West Virginia University, and the person given the responsibility for analyzing the effects of the plant on that state's environment, testified on atmospheric inversions at the site. He noted that because of the location of the incinerator on a valley floor, and because of the particular character-istics of weather in the Ohio River valley, the result would be "like putting a lid on a pot and trapping the lower-level air."[91] "Basically," he stated, "you're living in your own garbage."[92]

Hugh Kaufman, assistant to director of hazardous waste at the EPA, and the whistle-blower who had brought Anne Gorsuch down, also testi-fied at the trial. He focused on siting regulations, ownership issues, and questions regarding the legitimacy of the permit. Kaufman noted the ab-sence of a landowner's signature. If an accident occurred, he stated, it would leave the citizens of Columbiana County with responsibility for any finan-cial liabilities that would be incurred, given that the Columbiana County Port Authority still owned the land on which the facility was being built.[93] Kaufman's position at the trial was that "the whole permit process violates the EPA's own regulations."[94] He was not, however, supported by national officials in Washington.[95]

The impressive expertise and rhetorical skills of the expert witnesses encouraged favorable media coverage. A headline for the Columbiana County *Morning Journal* had pictures of three defense witnesses. Above the first, Paul Connett, was a banner stating "It's a scam"; above the second, Hugh Kaufman, "It's illegal"; and above the third, mayor James Scafide, "It's a hazard."

After the expert witnesses testified, some defendants chose to speak in their own defense. Terri Swearingen stated that she had not gone to the site with the intent to cross the fence, but when Martin Sheen went over, she harbored no compunctions against following him. Paul Connett, a chemist from St. Lawrence University, said that he felt "there needed to be some kind of shock tactic" to get the public's attention.[96] Sheen testified that "we hoped to bring a chain reaction and bring public dialogue to help prevent a disaster."[97]

As the defense testimony proceeded, the focus of the trial shifted fur-ther and further from the narrow question of trespass to the larger issue of whether protesters were justified in challenging the plant's siting and operation. Prosecutor Rodfong was well aware that this was happening, but there was little that he could do about it. "It confuses the issues for the jury to decide," he said.[98]

On Saturday, February 15, after three hours of deliberation, the jury acquitted all defendants in the case. Plant opponents were ecstatic. Martin Sheen said that the acquittal prefigured the "dawning of a new day." The community would take control over its own destiny. "This case," he said, "set a precedent. Nothing is the same."[99] An "obviously worn" Judge Byers-Emmerling was aware of the unusual nature of the verdict. She believed that the outcome would set a precedent in Ohio, because few if any previous cases had been specifically decided on the necessity defense.[100] Rodong said that the only "necessity" in the case was the necessity of Sheen getting back to New York to appear in *The Crucible*, so he jumped the fence to bring the protest to a head.[101]

City police were unhappy with Judge Byers-Emmerling's conduct in the case. A spokesperson for the local branch of the Fraternal Order of Police read a prepared statement at a city council meeting, representing the order's view that allowing the necessity defense "did effectively give these and others the right to trespass at the WTI site if they feel it is necessary." But the judge vigorously defended herself, stating that she had to allow the defense in trespass cases, that the jury's verdict did not guarantee future acquittals, and that there was now a civil injunction against the protesters again moving onto WTI property. The city council took no action either in support of or against the judge.[102]

Plant opponents were energized by the decision. In the words of defendant Lisa Marie Topley, "We're more psyched then ever. . . . People said they were never aware of the magnitude. This is exactly what we wanted."[103] Not only did the trial give *area* residents information about regulatory improprieties and the potentially damaging health impacts of WTI's operations, but the trial was broadcast on Court TV, giving a nationwide audience access to arguments against the incinerator's operation and siting. Opponents were receiving support and questions from other groups around the country who were engaged in opposing hazardous waste sites and incinerators in their own communities. WTI had indeed been put "on trial" during the trial, so that the action succeeded in generating a tremendous favorable publicity for protesters and unfavorable publicity for WTI and EPA officials. Hugh Kaufman challenged state and federal officials to indict him for "perjury" if they believed his testimony to be inaccurate.[104]

Still, the acquittals would have no direct impact on the regulatory process. Only state or national regulatory officials had the power to alter plans for moving toward operation, and they showed little if any inclination to do so. Four days after the verdict, WTI public relations officer Julia Bircher could state confidently, "There's been no change. . . . Construction is about 94 percent complete and ongoing, and we expect construction to be completed about the end of March."[105] A short *USA Today* piece quoted WTI officials as saying that the "burner will be completed on time next month despite acquittals of 29 protestors opposed to [it]."[106] Opponents had won a significant battle, but they were still a long way from winning a war.

Activists planned a March 5 rally in Columbus. According to their press release, "Citizens rolled a full-sized bed on the Statehouse steps today with a banner declaring: 'Governor Voinovich: In Bed with Toxic Polluters.'"[107] Anti-WTI activists Virgil Reynolds, Scott Sikora, and William Bradley played the roles of Governor Voinovich and WTI executives, as they smoked cigars and traded play money for "political favors."[108] The spectacle lasted for six hours. Opponents were eager to publicize the fact that Voinovich had received $14,000 from Chemical Waste Management, a firm that had business links to WTI.[109]

A June article in the *Columbus Dispatch* noted that opponents of the facility had held a press conference in Columbus and taken a pledge to continue civil disobedience against the plant. They vowed to begin civil disobedience training and initiate demonstrations to block the opening of the facility. In response to this, company spokesperson Julia Birch said, "Civil disobedience is nothing more than violence. . . . It's terrorism. It's breaking the law."[110] But an editorial in *Weirton Daily Times* offered a different assessment. Editors noted that activists had *already* engaged in civil disobedience: "If setting beds in front of state buildings, climbing fences with famous actors, handcuffing each other to state official's desks and 'firing' them is not civil disobedience, they we're afraid to ask what is." In a move that is highly unusual for a mainstream daily newspaper, the editorial endorsed the activists' tactics. "As long as they don't hurt other people, then we will continue to admire and respect their intense dedication to their cause. In fact, we think their actions border on heroic because they are willing to risk their own well being for the rest of us and our children, even though we have not yet asked them for their help." The editor concluded, "We encourage WTI opponents to continue their protests—as long as no one gets hurt. Again, we admire their fortitude."[111]

Newspaper editors are generally a fairly conservative bunch. Their profits, after all, are tied to advertising dollars that are generated by local businesses. For the WTI protesters to gain sympathetic editorials for their actions of civil disobedience is thus quite extraordinary. They had captured the signifiers in the battle over WTI. This is perhaps their most significant accomplishment.

In the Belly of the Beast

In the summer of 1992, WTI opponents decided to take their case directly to the U.S. EPA, and in doing so, raised the stakes of their protests. On July 21, fourteen people sneaked up the back stairs of the EPA building and briefly occupied the office of EPA administrator William K. Reilly. EPA officials, including Lewis Crampton, an associate administrator to Reilly, had agreed to meet with them. At 6 p.m., when the building was supposed to be closed, several stayed to protest the lack of support that they felt they were getting. EPA officials immediately began to threaten them with arrest. Alonzo Spencer and Terri Swearingen talked on the phone to reporters while inside the office. "There's two policemen standing here." Terri said, "They've closed the blinds and they're telling us now they're going to arrest us for unlawful entry."[112]

EPA officials had apparently been ready for some kind of protest, and they chose to play hardball. An "Operations Plan," a copy of which was eventually obtained by Terri Swearingen through a FOIA request, had been put together by the Federal Protective Policy to deal with any problems.[113] Under the heading "General," it noted the scheduled meeting that was to take place at the EPA office. Under the heading "Intelligence" was written, "On Friday, July 10, 1992 . . . this same group of demonstrators used fake ID's and lied to the contract guard that they were going to the Document Section. Once they enter[ed] the building, they went directly to the Adminstrator's Office and refused to leave until the administrator talk[ed] to them. The Assistant Administrator talked with them until 6:00 p.m."[114] In response to the July 10 occupation, seven officers were assigned to the task and were "deployed in strategic areas and [ordered to] report . . . all suspicious persons and incidents in their area."[115] The EPA would be prepared if protesters attempted to engage in disruptive behavior, and they were.[116]

Alonzo Spencer, Terri Swearingen, and twelve other demonstrators were turned over to the Washington, D.C., police and taken to the city jail. They were required to post a $500 bond before release, an amount that was apparently larger than had been anticipated. Because of this, they were forced to stay in jail through the night. While many of the group had been jailed previously, the D.C. jail was a step beyond what they had experienced up to that point. Terri called the experience "bizarre, certainly . . . an experience I'll never forget." First was a holding cell, where they waited to be processed, a place where "you're afraid even to sit down, you don't want to touch anything." Next was the central holding cell. "While we were there, one guy was brought in for murder. Another guy still had blood splattered on his shoes; we heard him tell police he had to stab another guy or (the other guy) would have murdered him. . . . You see a lot of things you only read about."[117] Bill Bradley, a cancer patient, while allowed his medication, was not given water he needed to take it. When asked by a fellow prisoner what he was in for the other man responded, "They can arrest you for that?" It turned out Bradley's cellmate was a murder suspect.[118] While the experience may have been horrific, it yielded another publicity bonanza. Tales of activists' mistreatment at the hands of the EPA were carried across the tri-state area.

After their night in jail, the twelve participants were arraigned the next morning. They pled guilty to "unlawful entry" in Superior Court later that afternoon. Each was assessed a fifty-dollar fine. Ever quick to turn the rhetorical tables on public officials, Terri proclaimed, "We're all guilty. Whatever we have suffered in the last 48 hours is nothing compared to the poisonous consequences to the children if WTI is ever allowed to operate."[119]

More Actions

At the end of July 1992, the rock singer Richard Marx came to town to add his voice to the chorus of celebrities who had taken a stand against WTI. Marx, at the time, was a well-known figure, with a number of hits, including "Don't Mean Nothin," and "Hold On to the Nights" and the top-ten hit "Hazard." He was reported to have sold ten million records. He'd also garnered two Grammy nominations for best male vocalist in 1988 and 1989. Marx was born in Chicago, but he had an extended family in the East Liverpool area.[120]

Marx had come to the community in the wake of demonstrations in which more than a dozen people had been arrested. Several community members had begun a hunger strike as the facility moved closer to gaining the last of the necessary approvals to begin operations. The *East Liverpool Evening Review* prominently featured a picture of Marx on the front page. He first spoke and then held a news conference at the home of Bob and Sandy Estell, a couple who had been longtime opponents of the facility.[121] Marx was also prominently featured on the front page of the *Columbiana County Morning Journal,* appearing at a press conference with hunger strikers, Beth Newman of the Greenpeace antitoxics campaign, and Terri Swearingen.[122] His appearance, in other words, garnered a fair amount of attention in the local press, although the event did not seem to extend to the larger regional newspapers in Pittsburgh or Columbus or the national media. Marx was moderately well known, but he didn't carry the cachet of Martin Sheen. Nor was his appearance connected to a spectacle.

Still, Marx's appearance was enough to raise the ire of WTI plant officials, who invited him to tour the facility to get management's side of the story. Marx agreed to take the tour but then backed out when media made an appearance in violation of what he'd understood to be an agreement to keep them away. After some negotiations, WTI agreed to give the tour without the press being present. He met with WTI officials for three hours before his press conference. For this, he received a bit of grudging approval from the WTI management. Julia Bircher, a spokesperson for WTI, was reported to be "pleased" with Marx's visit and stated, "Very few politicians or celebrities who oppose us have taken the time to visit the plant and learn both sides of the story or both sides of the issue."[123] Still, Marx remained unconvinced.

While Marx contended that the managers of the plant were not "bad people," and that they did not want to injure local residents, he had real concerns about the facility's impact on the area residents and said he was "100 percent opposed" to its operation. He stated that the incinerator would not help the local economy, and he said that the only folks who wanted it were businesses "who need it to dump their waste." You can't, he told gathered opponents and members of the media, "afford to have this type of incinerator in your back yard."[124]

The headline of the November 23, 1992, *East Liverpool Evening Review* was indeed ominous: "450 Storm WTI." The decision to go over onto the WTI property was not this time taken in the heat of the moment. Demonstrators came prepared. At 2 p.m. on Sunday, November 22, 450 people assembled in front of the WTI facility. They came with ladders and marched to the WTI fence. Some went over the fence, and others went under it. The entire East Liverpool police department along with thirty sheriff's deputies were on hand to deal with the protesters, who were rounded up and put onto a school bus. One frightened police officer, afraid of being overwhelmed by demonstrators, sprayed tear gas on the crowd as they approached the fence.[125] This event was the culmination of a day's rally that had itself capped off a week's worth of anti-WTI demonstrations. One hundred thirteen people were arrested during the week. Seventy-three protesters were arrested after going over the fence on the November 22. After being processed at City Hall, each received a cheer from the crowd that waited for them. Police stated that given the tear gas, and given the number of children at the event, in the future, protesters might very well be charged with child endangerment and their children taken to the County Department of Social Services.[126] Clearly, however, protesters were unlikely to be deterred. As the incinerator moved slowly yet inevitably toward a January start-up, protesters were, if anything, becoming more defiant.

In 1993, after it became clear that the Clinton administration would not revoke WTI's permit, WTI opponents began to shift their efforts to Washington. On Thursday, March 19, 1993, eight people were arrested in the White House. At the end of a public tour, they sat down and refused to leave. Protesters, including Terri Swearingen and Dick Wolf, began to sing "We Shall Stop the Burn" to the tune of "We Shall Overcome." Terri told me that those on the tour that were not part of the protest seemed somewhat shocked by what was occurring. Each of the protesters was arrested on misdemeanor trespass charges, sent in paddy wagons to the D.C. "Central Cell Block," where they were held until later that night. The formal charges were "Illegal Entry/Failure to Quit." Dick Wolf said in re-

sponse, "To the charge of 'Failure to Quit,' we are guilty as charged." Vice
President Gore's press secretary stated, "We know the problems there, but
our hands are tied." On that same day, the final test burns were completed
at the WTI facility.[127]

In July 1993, opponents again took their case to Washington, this time
to the Swiss Embassy. Twenty-three were arrested for blocking traffic,
fined fifty dollars, and released. The Swiss government was targeted because Von Roll was a Swiss company, owned at this point by United Bank
of Switzerland. In the words of Terri Swearingen, "We won't let our children die for Swiss banks who finance Von Roll's dangerous and illegal
activities in the U.S."[128]

A school bus with thirty children had traveled from East Liverpool to
Washington on Monday, July 14, to attempt to meet with President Clinton
to ask him to close the facility. Clinton, at the time, was visiting flood victims in the Midwest. The bus then drove to the embassy, where adult protesters proceeded to attach themselves to one another and the bus using
galvanized steel pipes. It took the police two hours to detach all of the
protesters. Opponents of an incinerator in Allentown, Pennsylvania, joined
in with their support. A spokesman for the Swiss government showed little
sympathy or support, one suggesting that the area was already polluted
by steel mills, and another that the government had no power to control a
private business corporation.[129]

On November 1, 1994, opponents held one more rally in an attempt to
bring the Clinton administration around. The Arkansas "Chicken Rally"
was held at Lafayette Park across from the White House. Attendees were
invited to "dress like a chicken," "bring a chicken," and to "use your
imagination."[130] About sixty people showed up in "bright yellow chicken
costumes or white-and-red rooster hoods," carrying rubber chickens and
picket signs. The event took place only three days after a gunman had
fired randomly at the White House, "without incident and amid tight security."[131] The *Washington Times* did carry a picture of Terri Swearingen
dressed as a chicken.[132] The event coincided with President Clinton's visits to Pittsburgh and Cleveland in support of Democratic congressional
candidates. When asked by the *East Liverpool Review* whether Clinton
would visit a city so close to his other stops, a spokesperson responded,
"His schedule is really jammed."[133]

SLAPP

"WTI Fires Back" was the headline of the *Columbiana County Morning Journal* on Friday, March 21, 1997. The company had decided to initiate a lawsuit against some of the incinerator's main opponents. Von Roll was seeking $34 million in damages against thirty-three individuals. Fred Sigg, the facility's manager, was quoted as saying, "Enough is enough."[134] Technically, the lawsuit was a countersuit to a class action filed by David Hager. Hager had filed his lawsuits on behalf of thirty-three specific individuals and all residents who lived within proximity of the WTI facility. He claimed a loss of property values, as well as health and environmental damage. WTI's lawsuit claimed libel and defamation against the company and charged that Hager's class action was "frivolous."

Terri said that the threatened lawsuit caught her by surprise. She had already been through much. She had organized dozens of events, caught the attention of the national press, and spent time in jail. But now, for the first time since she had begun her odyssey, she was frightened. Here was the possibility that her family would be bankrupted, that she would lose her home and possessions. Even if the lawsuit was unsuccessful, the time and expense involved would be enormous. How could she even pay for an attorney who would have the skill and resources to fight a large corporation with its bank of experienced lawyers? She sought help and found the law firm of Cohen, Milstein, Hausfeld, and Toll in Washington, D.C., a firm with a national reputation in handling class action lawsuits. She and Alonzo Spencer, who was also a defendant in the case, traveled to Washington to visit a member of the firm. The building was impressive with a large atrium stretching up from the lobby. The attorney whom they talked to was noncommittal. He'd get back to her. A week later, the answer came. The firm would take the case, pro bono. Terri could sleep just a little bit easier. She would at least have excellent legal counsel, and thus a fighting chance against the lawyers who were being brought in by WTI.

Fred Sigg denied that the lawsuit was a SLAPP suit, that is, a lawsuit designed primarily to intimidate and silence criticism against corporate behavior. SLAPP suits had become a favored tactic by corporations in the 1990s as a way to keep their critics at bay. The acronym stands for "strategic lawsuit against public participation." Sigg's position was that "opponents over the years have been afforded numerous opportunities to provide public input in the decision-making process involving WTI's licensing and operation."[135] The continued opposition at this point was little more, Sigg felt, than harassment.

The WTI countersuit claimed that the Hager lawsuit was designed simply to "damag[e] Defendants' business activities, reputation and integrity." It was "frivolous" because the suit "merely intended to harass and maliciously injure the Defendants' business operations, opportunities and reputation."[136] The countersuit also claimed that the defendants were "vexatious litigators" under Ohio law, "because they have habitually, persistently, and without reasonable grounds engaged in vexatious conduct."[137] They were also accused of interfering with the company's business relationships, via filing lawsuits and in general "acted with actual malice, consisting of ill will spite and hatred in order to interfere with Defendants' business relationships."[138]

The heart of the lawsuit involved, however, the defamation charges. Most of the WTI brief was, in fact, turned over to statements made by opponents of the plant criticizing its operations. Two people were named in the defamation part of the brief: Terri Swearingen and Alonzo Spencer. WTI attorneys had apparently scoured local newspapers and examined correspondence found on file in government offices. Terri Swearingen had stated, for example, at a press conference, "If [the incinerator] has to be there, you want to have the most trustworthy people in charge. But we don't have that."[139] In a letter to the Ohio attorney general's office, Terri, Alonzo, and others had asked, "If Von Roll's controlling shareholder does not care about Holocaust victims and drug addiction, why would they care about a few hundred school children in a poor Appalachian river town?"[140] In a press release, Alonzo and Terri had stated that "it appears that Von Roll management knowingly, deliberately, and actively conspired with a gangster—Tommy Petrizzo—to engage in racketeering activities."[141]

These and other charges were arguably true. Evidence from newspaper stories, memorandums, and legal testimony existed that could cast doubt on the trustworthiness of Von Roll executives. The Union Bank of Switzerland, for a time Von Roll's parent company, had been engaged in stiff negotiations to settle claims against the company for protecting Nazi deposits of the financial assets of Holocaust victims.[142] The connections between the Von Roll affiliate New Jersey Steel and Tommy Petrizzo were well documented. Morever, the standard for libel, especially in the case of public persons, has been a high one in the United States, since the Supreme Court broadened free-speech protections in *New York Times v. Sullivan* in 1964.[143] WTI lawyers would face an uphill battle to prove not only that the comments were intentionally malicious but that the defendants knew them to be false but had stated them publicly anyway. The brief filed by WTI was signed by two lawyers for the firm of Bricker and Eckler, the law firm that had represented WTI from the beginning. One was Charles H. Waterman III, an attorney who had had an intimate relationship with the WTI operations for nearly fifteen years.

Almost a year after filing the initial lawsuit, Terri Swearingen was finally deposed. She was served a subpoena requiring that she supply documents that she had collected over many years related to WTI opposition movements. She held dozens of banker's boxes full of materials that she had filed away. She was required to supply information on Save Our County, Tri-State Environmental Council, Greenpeace, "or [any] other corporation, organization, association or entity that has challenged the construction, permitting, operation or maintenance of the East Liverpool hazardous waste incinerator."[144] WTI lawyers also wanted all her financial records. They were very thorough in their discovery requests.

Acting in good faith, Terri brought all her records to the deposition.[145] She admitted that she was a little worried. She couldn't entirely remember all the contents of everything that was in them. Moreover, she said that she would sometimes sit in meetings with other activists and scribble notes in the margins of press releases that she was holding. Sometimes these might be sarcastic comments or jokes. What, she wondered, if she'd written jokingly on a sheet, "Let's just burn the place down," and then forgotten about it, and eventually thrown that sheet into one of her banker's boxes? Her lawyers told her that it would be a huge savings in the legal fees if she, rather than one of the attorneys, sat with the opposing attorneys as they went through all her material. She agreed to this and sat for several days with them as they did so. At times, they would point at something and become interested and animated. It was, she informed me, extremely nerve wracking.[146] On the positive side, however, her lawyers would now be entitled to discovery as well. They could subpoena documents from the company. Who knew what they might find? Perhaps they would uncover information that would help them in their fight against the facility. They were entitled to all documents by which they might be able to prove that their statements were not defamatory but grounded in facts. WTI lawyers had one year to comply with the discovery requests. On March 24, 2000, the day before they were legally required to turn documents over to the defendants, the company dropped the case.

In a press statement, WTI representatives painted this as a "gesture of good faith." According to the company's press release, "Last year, the company invited the plaintiffs to sit down and talk in an effort to reach common ground and perhaps settle the matter out of court. However, they turned down the company's generous offer." According to Fred Sigg, "It is unfortunate that they declined the opportunity. . . . Now that some of the plaintiffs are keeping company again with Greenpeace and Citizen Action, it is clear they want to keep the needlessly expensive lawsuit afloat in an effort to further their political agenda, which is to embarrass Vice President Al Gore."[147]

It was not clear why WTI would extend good faith to seemingly intransigent opponents. The Hager lawsuit would not be suspended by WTI's actions, only WTI's counterclaim. WTI officials said that they were suspending the counterclaim because the case had slowed "to a crawl" and that it was becoming "unnecessarily expensive." But company lawyers did not waive their rights to "reinstate," so that if they so decided, they could relaunch the suit any time within the next year.[148] While this may have constituted a continuing threat, Hager did not drop his lawsuit, and after the year had expired, the company failed to reinstate its claim. When the suit was suspended, however, the *Morning Journal* had seemed to take WTI officials pretty much at their word, that they were offering an olive branch and trying to speed up the processing of the Hager suit.[149] Alonzo Spencer and Terri Swearingen continued in their vigorous critique of the WTI incinerator.

WTI opponents were not the only defendants in a Von Roll libel suit that took place over the years. Gary Lutin, the owner and manager of Lutin and Company, was also the subject of what turns out to have been a successful lawsuit by Von Roll. In this case, the central issue was Von Roll's relationship with New Jersey Steel Corporation and its alleged ties to the underworld.

As the owner of Advanced Mining Systems Inc., a company that made roof supports for coal mines, Lutin had a dispute with a subsidiary of New

Jersey Steel, Excel Mining Systems. Lutin claimed that Excel had enticed two of his former employees to steal trade secrets and other property from Lutin in order to put him out of business. The strategy succeeded, and AMS filed for bankruptcy. Lutin filed lawsuits against Excel and New Jersey Steel as the parent company. He eventually settled with Excel but continued to pursue litigation against New Jersey Steel. A federal judge pared the case down to the issues at stake and allowed Lutin to replead the case. The judge subsequently found too much extraneous information in the new brief, so that it violated the "short and plain statement rule." This decision was upheld by a higher appellate court as well.[150]

Lutin's offense was to write a letter to an executive vice president of the Union Bank of Switzerland, which at the time was holding most of the shares of Von Roll, which was facing significant financial difficulties. Lutin was presenting a "Proposal for the Disposition of New Jersey Steel Corporation." In the letter, he suggested that New Jersey Steel might be a valuable company for sale on the open market if it was "cleaned up," that is, if it could be disassociated from its alleged underworld connections. It could, he proposed, "attract buyers and be worth $25 to $30 per share, compared with its current $10 per share trading range."[151] He also suggested that "competent management would be expected to generate $10 to $20 million annual operating profit" (3).

Lutin made a number of other statements in the letter, alluding to shady activities associated with the firm: that it had "secretly organized a subsidiary, Excel Mining Systems," that "claims for over $150 million have been filed against NJSC and its affiliates in relation to alleged Excel racketeering activities," and that New Jersey Steel's "failure to establish effective programs to prevent corruption violates established standards of corporate responsibility," especially with regards to its "apparent tolerance of corruption and organized crime relationships" (ibid.).

Lutin was encouraging UBS to take "corrective actions which will allow UBS to satisfy its fiduciary responsibilities in the United States, while simultaneously respecting the protocols of bank and stockholder conduct in Switzerland" (ibid.). Lutin's proposal was to use an Independent Private Sector Inspector General (IPSIG) that would report to a board made up of representatives of UBS, NJS shareholders, and an unspecified government agency (ibid.).

On the basis of this letter, New Jersey Steel filed suit against Mr. Lutin and eventually won a $22 million damage award. Lutin filed various appeals to overturn the award but had no success in doing so.

Resistance and Power

Challenging tightly organized power networks, such as WTI, in which public and private authorities are organized in support of the same set of purposes and interests can be inspiring, energizing, life changing, and fun. The opponents of WTI successfully drew on traditions of collective nonviolent civil disobedience that have roots in the U.S. civil rights movement and the environmental movement as well. They were rhetorically sophisticated, deploying irony to embarrass political leaders and to elicit sympathy and support from journalists and presumably the general public as well. But the costs of challenging the powerful should not be underestimated. The U.S. legal system is not organized to support forces of dissent. Judge Byers-Emmerling's rulings were highly advantageous to WTI opponents, but they were also highly anomalous. The SLAPP lawsuit initiated by WTI, however, was not anomalous and was part of a trend in which corporate authorities used libel law to intimidate critics and suppress political expression. After 9/11, dissent, even nonviolent dissent, faces even more formidable barriers. Insofar as that is the case, the powerful are given ever more discretion, and democracy is threatened.

CHAPTER 5.

Risky Business:
Counting the Costs
of Incineration

The population now represents more the end of government
than the power of the sovereign; the population is the
subject of needs, of aspirations, but it is also the object
in the hands of the government, aware, vis-à-vis
the government, of what it wants, but ignorant
of what is being done to it.
—*Michel Foucault, "Governmentality"*

One in a million,
One in a million,
One in a million,
And we hope that it's you!
—*Anti-incineration chant*

Painting the Kitchen

Paul Connett teaches chemistry at St. Lawrence University. Connett was
among the many people who dedicated time and expertise to WTI opposition. He had special knowledge of risk assessments. Terri Swearingen
received the several-thousand-page WTI risk assessment document one
day before a public hearing on it was to take place in Washington, D.C.
She and Paul spent a day together scrutinizing its findings. A snowstorm
blanketed the East Coast, paralyzing the region. The EPA was, however,
unshakable in its determination to allow citizen input on this day alone.
Terri and Paul drove all night from Chester, West Virginia, to the capital
through a blizzard to make their case.

Paul Connett, originally from Sussex, England, moved to Ithaca in

1963 to study chemistry at Cornell, but he soon became involved in politics. Chemistry's importance to him diminished as the intensity of his interests in peace and antinuclear campaigns intensified. Eventually, however, he returned to chemistry, received his Ph.D. from Dartmouth, and took a job at St. Lawrence. Canton, New York, where St. Lawrence is located, is in the very northern part of New York State, on the western edge of the Adirondacks. Paul had hoped to move there, teach chemistry, and disengage from the activism that had defined his life throughout much of the 1960s and 1970s. He began teaching there in 1983.

After living in Canton for a couple of years, he decided to paint the family's kitchen. Then word drifted through the community that a municipal waste incinerator was going to be sited there. Paul decided to put some time into developing a response to the risk assessment that had been conducted by consultants for the facility's proponents. As was the practice at the time, only an ambient air analysis was undertaken, in this case for PCBs. The calculations are straightforward. The assessment team calculates the amount of PCB that is expected from a plant's operations and averages the amount per cubic meter once dispersion is taken into account. It is relatively easy to calculate the amount of air, and thus the amount of PCBs, that an average-size male (the standard at the time) will breathe over the course of a year. This becomes the basis for the risk calculation. So much PCB breathed over so much time will, according to established models, result in the probability of so many deaths from cancer.

Consultants from Batelle Corporation chose not to undertake a more complicated and costly food chain analysis. It is now widely accepted that food intake is a primary path by which toxics, such as PCBs and dioxin, enter human bodies. In the Canton incinerator case, this set of pathways seemed especially important because of the high concentration of dairy cows in the region. At the time, St. Lawrence County was the highest producer of dairy products in New York State. Cows are high on the food chain, and PCB is easily dissolved by, and concentrates in, fat. Thus some of the heaviest concentrations are found in milk, among both humans and other mammals. Calculating food chain impacts is, however, no easy matter. Investigators have to estimate rates at which PCB will precipitate from the atmosphere, as well as the rates at which it will be broken down by ultraviolet radiation, all before it even gets into the cow's (much less a human's) system. This involves a good amount of work.

Paul asked the city to fund his assessment project. The city refused. He spoke to Tom Webster, a friend and associate of Barry Commoner's. They decided to move the project forward themselves, unfunded. Their expectation was that the analysis would find an approximately two hundred times greater risk of cancer per capita than the ambient air calculations. They were surprised to discover that the risk was actually one thousand times greater than had been predicted by Battelle's consultants. The findings were shocking. If true, they would project that rather than a hypothetical one in a million persons dying from the effects of PCB contamination from exposure to the plant's output, the actual figure would be closer to one out of every one thousand. Those kinds of figures are bound to get people's attention. Further studies followed, each confirming, to one degree or another, much higher risks of cancer than the ambient air study had predicted. The incinerator was never built.

Close involvement with a successful campaign to stop a local incinerator helped establish Paul's reputation as a person with scientific expertise who was willing to challenge corporate power and governmental authorities. His phone began to ring. The incinerator boom of the 1980s and 1990s put people like Paul Connett in demand. Now he has traveled to forty-nine states and forty-seven countries. He's given over two thousand presentations on incineration and the move toward a zero-waste society. He never did get that kitchen painted.

Paul became involved with WTI on the eve of the first Gulf War. He was giving a talk in Charleston, West Virginia, and accepted an invitation to travel to East Liverpool. Terri Swearingen, according to Paul, is a person to whom it's impossible to say no. Moreover, he was aware of the WTI facility's reputation. He would become a key player in the anti-WTI campaign because of his knowledge and his willingness to engage politically. He is one of the "East Liverpool 21." He was arrested with Terri and Alonzo Spencer when the two had themselves welded in place in front of the U.S. EPA building, blocking traffic, so that the police department had to use blowtorches to remove them. He learned, he told me, that if you're going to get arrested, it's best to get arrested with Martin Sheen. The police will be nice to you, and you probably won't spend much time in jail.

Paul Connett had no illusions about challenging an EPA risk assessment document. "They're good at it," he told me. Paid environmental consultants have spent years honing the technical skills that allow them to state with confidence that their estimates are accurate and that risks are low. Given the problems with challenging ambient air and food chain calculations, Paul advised Terri that they focus on accident risks. If a large release of, say, hydrogen cyanide were emitted from WTI by mistake, it could have potentially catastrophic consequences. And given the levels and kinds of activities that were taking place—the loading and unloading of barrels of hazardous materials, along with their mixing and destruction—the potential for accidents was not inconsequential. In fact, at one point, a truck carrying caustic wastes was mistakenly directed to the facility's scrubber. An accident was narrowly averted when it was discovered that a mistake had been made. But if the waste had been substituted for the chemical scrubber, a major accident would have occurred, and lives would likely have been lost.

Paul brought a ruler to the hearing. He wanted to show the short distance that an accidental release would travel from the plant to a neighborhood elementary school. The potential for accidents would be calculated by actuaries, not toxicologists, a potentially more cautious group. The result of this risk assessment, based on similar events at other plants, was seventy accident scenarios, of which thirty were life threatening. The panel's actuaries were impressed, but the assessment team was unwilling to accept the accident risk as enough of an "imminent health threat"—the standard for permit revocation under RCRA—to have the facility's operations suspended.

Paul noted, as have many others, that there seemed to be powerful forces working to protect the WTI plant. Activists could point to tremendous accomplishments. Almost single-handedly, they had put a stop to the building of more hazardous waste incinerators in the United States. They had garnered national publicity and had received editorial support from the *New York Times* and the *Washington Post*. They had been featured on *60 Minutes* and *20/20*. Terri had been a guest on *Nightline*. Activists had done just about everything right in terms of engaging in successful civil disobedience campaigns and drawing attention to their cause. Still, they did not succeed in shutting down WTI. Not only did various regulatory agencies and the Clinton administration do everything possible to keep the facility's permit intact, but the *Wall Street Journal* carried long editorials and full-page ads advocating support for the incinerator's operations. For Paul, it all just seemed "weird." The WTI risk assessment, although

a highly technical and nominally "objective" document, had to be interpreted through the lenses of political power. As with others, a fascination
with the hidden operations of power seemed to have drawn Paul to the
anti-WTI campaign. WTI fascinated as a noir text.

Science, Citizens, and Risk

One of the central conflicts that emerges between citizen activists and
power networks, especially with health and environmental concerns, is
epistemological. Citizen activism represents a democratic challenge to a
positivist and scientific paradigm that supports concentrated public and
private power. Conflict between citizens and experts is one of the defining
features of industrial and postindustrial societies. Such conflicts can be
traced to ideas put forward in the early modern period. The seventeenth-
century philosopher Francis Bacon is a central figure here. Bacon is considered the founder of modern scientific method, primarily because he
systematized the process of experimentation. Bacon was well aware that
science was a field from which power could be asserted over nature as well
as other human beings. He envisioned an ideal society in which a small
scientific elite would rule the rest of humankind.[1] Rule by "experts" has
been a continuous strand of Western social theorizing ever since. John
Dewey, for example, spent considerable effort attempting to resolve the
paradoxes generated by scientific expertise and responsible citizenship.[2]
The citizen-expert binary has been central to contemporary environmental politics.

Conventional approaches to science are mostly grounded in some version of positivism. Positivism posits an independent world of nature that
can be accessed via perception. In Abraham Kaplan's terms, "What we
observe are bare shapes, sounds, colors, and textures, which are then organized and interpreted as the familiar objects and events of experience."[3]
"Scientific method" involves a sophisticated approach to accessing and
organizing this perceptual material. Scientists collect data, conduct experiments, analyze results, and, ideally, repeat the process under a variety
of conditions. What the scientific method is in the abstract and what it
means in practice are matters of great dispute among both philosophers
of science and practicing scientists as well.[4] Whatever the particulars of a
given approach, however, a central supposition among positivists is that

an objective understanding of reality is possible via the proper application of scientific principles. "Objective" means untainted by individual
idiosyncracy or social position. Objective knowledge, in other words,
implies universal access. One person who collects and analyzes a given
set of data via the proper method should arrive at the same findings as
another. If findings differ, then mistakes have been made, which may require additional analysis and testing, but that is to be expected in human
enterprises. The process of testing and retesting is how scientific progress
unfolds over time.

Positivistic science constitutes a double-edged sword within the environmental movement. Environmentalists have embraced scientific findings when they have supported a broad environmental agenda, but they
have been highly skeptical of them when they have been used to minimize
environmental harms. The reverse is also true. Advocates of industrial
interests embrace science when it furthers their advancement, and decry
it as "junk" when it runs contrary to them. In the cases of thinning ozone
and climate change, scientific assessments have been crucial for moving
the policy debate toward taking these problems seriously. In each case,
scientific findings have been used with some effectiveness to challenge industrial interests that have a stake in continuing current systems of production. Government agencies such as the EPA are hardly neutral arbiters
in such disputes or protectors of the "public interest." As often as not, the
EPA is a political instrument. Such has been the case in the Bush administration, and it has long been true in the field of hazardous waste disposal.
The dream, then, of an objectively derived set of valid truths from which
rational policies can be derived seems distant given complex interactions
between science and power. As Ulrich Beck states, "Not only does the industrial utilization of scientific results create problems; science also provides the means—the categories and the cognitive equipment—to recognize and present the problems *as* problems at all, or just not to do so."[5]

Among the most important and most contested scientific methodologies to pervade environmental discourse is that of risk assessment. The
concept of risk, as a technical term, has distinctively modern overtones.
In premodern times, at least in Europe, risk was associated with natural
calamity or divine intervention. Risks were either beyond the control of
human beings, or personal and voluntarily accepted, as when European
explorers willingly risked their lives and fortunes by traveling to the New

World in small sailing ships to conquer and colonize it.[6] The meaning of risk evolved with the development of statistical analysis, which was created to gain understanding and control over rapidly increasing and urbanizing populations during the industrial revolution. Risk thus became "scientized" and cast in terms of probabilities. As this occurred, risk shifted from being the result of "fortune" to being predictable and thus potentially controllable by human intervention. In Deborah Lupton's terms, "The modernist concept of risk represented a new way of viewing the world and its chaotic manifestations, its contingencies and uncertainties. It assumed that unanticipated outcomes may be the consequence of human action."[7] Risk today is a way of policing boundaries, within which are social and scientific order, and beyond which is "chaos."[8] Risks are now global in nature. We face risks that have the potential to destroy human civilization.[9]

Risk assessment is a particular application of scientific methodology. It is oriented not only toward explaining what happens under various conditions; it seeks to predict the future. Prediction is an important element of all scientific methodologies as a mechanism for verification. Famously, part of Einstein's theory of relativity was verified when his predictions about the bending of light rays passing close to the sun's intense gravitation field were demonstrated to be true. With risk assessments, on the other hand, there is no assumption that conventional methods of scientific experimentation will be marshaled to validate them.[10] One reason for this is that evaluating the accuracy of risk assessments, if attempted, would be extremely complicated because of the difficulties of isolating factors of causation. Risk assessments are not used, for example, to predict that one person or another will be diagnosed with cancer. They are used to suggest what the chances are of one person in one hundred thousand or one million being diagnosed with cancer. Attributing specific cases of cancer to a particular cause, given the huge amount of background noise that will be present in any particular case, is virtually impossible. Thus risk assessment draws on positivist models of scientific investigation in only hypothetical terms. In actual practice, risk assessments are neither verified nor falsified.

Whereas positivism proposes the objectivity of scientific claims, in actual practice, scientific investigations are conducted by human beings with social position and interest. Risk assessors are, for the most part, midlevel career professionals who have at least some advanced training in science or engineering. They are essentially a middle layer between policy makers and intransigent citizens. Their role is not to facilitate critical understanding or mediate dissenting views. Most often it is to justify the dominant position predetermined by regulatory authorities. As Frank Fischer notes, "Because of the experts' middle-level position in the social structure, they have too often the basic premises of corporate bureaucratic domination. The professional-client hierarchy has thus been denounced as serving—both wittingly and unwittingly—to impose system imperatives on the intermediate and local levels of the social system."[11] In the case of risk assessments undertaken for hazardous waste and other RCRA-covered facilities, the U.S. EPA chooses the risk assessment team and thus can shape, if not entirely determine, outcomes in advance. In the case of the WTI risk assessment, while there were dissenting views regarding its meanings, the assessment panel did not pose a significant challenge to regulatory authorities, who had, it seems, already decided to authorize its operations. In fact, in the case of WTI, the facility had already been permitted and operating for several years before the completion of what the EPA considered to be the definitive risk assessment.

While a risk assessment allows the EPA and the large corporations that build hazardous waste incinerators to try to shift the debate about their safety to a "scientific" one, certain assumptions are accepted for every risk assessment. It is assumed that at least some of the substances being emitted from the stacks of incinerators are unhealthy and will cause death. The argument, then, is not about *whether* deaths will be caused but about *how many* deaths will be caused, and whether the number of deaths is an acceptable price to pay for the disposal of industrial society's unwanted left-over materials. Every risk assessment is, in essence, a cost-benefit analysis, although a hidden one. The projected deaths are never explicitly balanced against the projected profits generated by a facility. Rather, the projected death rate is presented as so low that it is virtually insignificant. One cancer death in one million over thirty years is the generally acceptable standard for a facility such as WTI. Even assuming, then, the accuracy of a risk estimate, the presumption is that trade-offs between lives and profits are morally acceptable. In taking this approach, Peter Montague notes that EPA has "sanction[ed] the repugnant concept that government can kill citizens without due process of law simply because the names and addresses of those to be killed are not known."[12]

Analysis of the meaning of risk is thus a form of political practice, and arguments regarding what constitutes actual "risk" are ideological. Many on the political Right contend that risk is a necessary aspect of life in modern industrial societies, and that a "risk-free society" is neither possible nor desirable. The potential environmental and health costs from the system of production that creates affluence for some and opportunities for consumption for many are simply "worth the risks." According to this view, Greens and their ilk abuse the concept of risk and invoke it to bite the hands that feed them. This constitutes an irresponsible reaction against legitimate authority.[13] What about people in the affected communities? The argument is often made (with some merit) that individual citizens are not good at calculating risks. Yet risk assessments are always hypothetical, and causation is virtually impossible to determine in specific cases. The presence of higher-than-anticipated harmful effects will be known, if at all, only after the fact. Because of these imponderables, "fear" is not an "irrational" response to siting toxic waste facilities. As Steven Katz and Carolyn Miller note, "The central problem with risky technology is that there is no scientific certainty, only probability. Fear is a psychologically natural and arguably justifiable response to risk that no amount of statistical data or probable argument can rationalize away. . . . When 'neighbors' are faced with the threat of risky technology and scientific uncertainty made all the more suspect by politics, fear may be a more reasonable response to the siting of a waste facility than scientific rationality."[14]

The perception of risk among those affected by a given activity tends to be greatest when they feel as though it is imposed rather than voluntarily accepted, when the imposition is perceived as unfair, and when the threats are invisible and unfamiliar. While experts might argue that such considerations are "irrational," they can also be construed as part of a broader "cultural rationality" that evaluates narrow technical risks in relation to an array of social forces that attempt to control the power relationships within a community. As Frank Fischer puts it, "Citizens want to know how conclusions are reached, whose interests are at stake, if the process reflects a hidden agenda, who is responsible, what protection they have if something goes wrong, and so on. If they believe that the project engineers and managers either don't know what they are talking about or are willing to lie or deceive to serve the purposes of their company, workers or citizens will obviously reject the risk assessment statistics put forth by the company."[15] WTI represents a classic case where risk managers were viewed by many members of the affected community, with justification, as representing a set of obscure yet powerful forces.

The suspicion that powerful forces control the lives of ordinary people is central, as noted, to noir. Noir's persistence and popularity is fostered by deep-seated popular suspicions about the hidden operations of power. When powerful forces marshal scientific expertise to justify policies that further their interests, they confront noir sensibility as a deeply embedded form of cultural resistance. This can be a source of deep frustration to the powerful. No matter how apparently sophisticated the various modeling techniques employed in risk assessment models, they had little credibility with citizen opponents of the WTI facility. The scientific findings could not be disentangled from the narratives structures and cultural tropes through which power's applications are interpreted.

Incineration, Toxic Release, and Human Health

Virtually everyone agrees that hazardous waste incineration, like all waste incineration processes, results in the release of substances that are potentially hazardous to human health.[16] The point of conflict has to do with the standards that are set by the EPA, whether they are sufficient to protect the public's health, and whether incinerators, under regular operating conditions, achieve those standards.

Under perfect laboratory conditions, at least hypothetically, all organic compounds would be destroyed in an incineration process at which ideal temperatures are reached, being converted into carbon dioxide, water, and salt. In the laboratory, one can nearly achieve these results in the burning of a single organic compound.[17] Unfortunately, in the practical world of operating incinerators, where managers are dealing with waste products that are mixtures of various chemicals, it is extremely difficult, even under ideal conditions, to achieve optimal burn temperatures for all chemicals that are part of the mix simultaneously. And temperatures are bound to vary in different parts of an incinerator across time.[18]

Unfortunately, attempts to control some kinds of toxic releases may have negative impacts on the attempts to control others. For example, dioxins are most effectively destroyed at very high temperatures, but those high temperatures also increase mercury volitalization and generate more

nitric oxides, a major element in smog. Ammonia can be injected to control the nitric oxide, but it will control only a little more than one-half
of the toxics released, and it increases the emission of fine particulates.
Lowering temperatures to decrease nitric oxide will generate more dioxins.[19] Carbon particles can be injected into the exhaust system to control
both mercury and dioxin, because the carbon particles provide a cool
surface on which mercury vapors can condense and dioxin particulates
can form. Unfortunately, carbon is also an effective catalyst for generating more dioxin as well, so that total dioxin emissions are increased by
about 30 percent if carbon injection is used.[20] Incineration is then a sort of
"damned if you do, damned if you don't" technology. There are so many
volatile and toxic compounds that react so differently to varying conditions of combustion and control that it is virtually impossible to balance
the many factors involved even under the best of circumstances.

Because regulators recognize the futility of attempting to meet laboratory conditions in the operation of any hazardous waste incinerator, the
standards for destruction and removal efficiency (DREs) are not set at 100
percent. Principal organic hazard constituents standards for DRE are at
least 99.99 percent, or not more than .01 percent of compounds fed into
the incinerator. If PCBs are fed into the waste stream, the DRE requirement is 99.9999 percent. Individual states must meet compliance standards that are at least as stringent as the EPA's.[21] While such standards
appear strict, as Peter Montague has pointed out, a system designed to
destroy 99.99 percent of organic wastes by law is a system that is allowed to
release .01 percent of its organic wastes into the atmosphere by law. Over a
twenty-year period, a hazardous waste incinerator that burns 70,000 tons
per year is allowed to release 14,000 pounds of organic residues into the
ambient environment. Given the persistence of some organics and heavy
metals, long-term deposition is an important consideration.[22] Whether
a given facility meets EPA standards on an ongoing basis will, however,
depend on a variety of intervening factors operating at each individual
facility.

Incinerators do not always operate under ideal conditions. For one
thing, they are subject to periods of what are called "upset," when optimal
burning conditions are not being met. During these upsets, high levels
of toxics can be released. Upset can occur several times a day.[23] A joint
task force of OSHA and the U.S. EPA conducted sixty-two announced

inspections of twenty-nine hazardous waste incinerators during 1990. More than two-thirds of the inspections resulted in detected violations, including 320 OSHA violations and 75 violations of EPA regulations. Two common violations involved waste feed cutoffs and an excessive use of the dump stack. Waste feed cutoffs are initiated when conditions within the incinerator's combustion chamber are not operating at an optimal level. Each time a waste feed cutoff occurs, pollutants are released that would not have been had the system been operating under optimal conditions. One inspected incinerator experienced 13,000 of them.[24] The dump stack issue is even more problematic. The dump stack is an emergency smoke-stack used only when pressure builds in the combustion chamber to the point that it must be released quickly and through a vent. Dump stacks, because they are considered to be for emergencies only, do not have pollution control devices. Nine of the twenty-nine incinerators surveyed by the EPA used their dump stacks in a six-month period.[25] Also, all hazardous waste incinerators also experience "fugitive emissions." These releases do not come from the stack but slip out "between the cracks," so to speak. Fugitive emissions are difficult to track and almost impossible to eliminate. And since they do not flow from the stack, there is no way to monitor them on a regular basis.[26]

Because incinerators cannot operate under ideal laboratory conditions, they generate PICs, or products of incomplete combustion. These can be products of the waste stream that are not entirely burned, or they can be new compounds formed as others are broken down in the incineration process. Some PICs, such 2,3,7,8-tetrachlorodibenzo-p-dioxin (TCDD), are known carcinogens. For others, levels of carcinogenicity have not been established.[27] PICs can be more toxic than the substances that were being burned in the first place.[28] Little is known about the health effects of the thousands of PICs that are generated in the hazardous waste incineration process. The amount of PICs released from a hazardous incinerator is a little less than 1 percent of the total volume fed into a given unit. In the case of an incinerator that burns 70,000 tons of waste a year, that amounts to 700 tons or 140,000 pounds a year.[29]

Dioxin is one of the most notorious substances to be released during the process of hazardous waste incineration. Dioxin entered the public vocabulary in the 1980s, partly as the result of the Love Canal and the Times Beach cases, although scientific analysis of dioxin's toxic effects stretch back to the 1930s. It was not until 1957 that a German scientist discovered that a specific dioxin compound, TCDD, was responsible for chloracne, liver disease, and nervous and immune system disruptions that afflicted people (mostly workers) who were exposed at high levels.[30] Animal exposure tests first conducted in the 1970s established that extremely low levels of dioxin could generate birth defects and liver cancer in rats. These studies led to the conclusion that dioxin was one of the "most toxic synthetic chemicals known to man."[31] In 1985, the EPA published its first review of the health effects of dioxin. Based on its survey of the scientific literature and analysis done by EPA scientists, a level of .0006 picograms per kilogram of body weight per day (pg/kg/day) was set as an "acceptable daily dose."[32]

In 1987, largely, it seems, as the result of pressure from the paper industry, the EPA set up a working group to reassess the 1985 findings. The group, unable to agree on a model for assessing cancer risk from dioxin and dioxin-like compounds, averaged the risk values predicted by all the models in use and came up with a risk value sixteen times higher than the original estimate. The EPA's Science Advisory Board was critical of this approach.[33] In October 1990, the EPA and the Chlorine Institute cosponsored a scientific meeting at the Banbury Center in Long Island. Based on newly developed scientific information about the role of the "Ah receptor" in mediating the effects of dioxin on human cells, industry advocates maintained that there must be a "safe" level below which dioxin could be tolerated by the human body.[34] EPA administrator William Reilly agreed to a second reassessment of dioxin's health effects. That the toxicity of dioxin was being reevaluated by the EPA, because there might be a "safe level" for exposure (an industry concept), was widely reported in the press and became part of a concerted publicity campaign to attack previous scientific findings. The scientific justification for this position hinged on the methodology of cancer risk assessment. L. L. Aylward et al. had proposed a novel approach that indicated a lower sensitivity of humans to dioxin than rats, suggesting that there was a threshold below which dioxin was safe, while also finding that the mean exposure level of the general population was not at the proposed threshold.[35] Since then, several studies have failed to corroborate the "threshold" theory.[36]

The EPA embarked on a third assessment of dioxin, which was released as a "public review draft" in September 1994. The main focus of the review draft document was on health impacts of dioxin other than cancer. A stream of information was coming forward regarding dioxin's effects on the immune, endocrine, and reproductive systems of animals and humans. The EPA was strongly suggesting its support for the idea that the injurious effects of dioxin extended beyond the cancer risks, and that Americans were being exposed at levels that were at or just below acceptable standards, mostly via entry into the body from eating common foods. Even if there were "safe doses" of dioxin, a highly contested idea, exposure levels of Americans put them beyond these levels, even if they were not in high exposure zones or circumstances.[37] (The 1994 report was a draft and subject to public review and criticism. In 2000, a revision was released, finding that the carcinogenic effects of dioxin were ten times greater than stated in the earlier draft.)[38]

Dioxin is insidious. In very small doses, it can cause significant health problems, not only cancer but congenital birth defects, developmental and reproductive effects, diabetes, increased potential for infections, IQ deficits, depression, hyperactivity, and heart disease. In 1998 the World Health Organization (WHO) lowered its recommended Tolerable Daily Intake of dioxin from 10 picograms TEQ per kilogram bodyweight per day (pg/kg/day) to a range of 1 to 4 pg/kg/day, a dose that is close to the EPA's original targets. Unfortunately, the rate of intake for much of the world's population is already above this level.[39] According to the EPA's most recent estimates, members of the general population risk cancer from dioxin exposure at rates of 1 to 100 to 1 to 1,000.[40] Given the dioxin load that populations are experiencing worldwide, people who live near sources of dioxin release, such as incinerators, face especially acute threats. Moreover, incinerators, as in the case of WTI, are often sited in areas that have a history of industrial activity, which means that they likely already have high background levels of dioxin and other toxics.

Dioxin is a by-product of all processes of combustion, but some kinds of combustion are of course more likely to generate significant amounts of it than others. Waste incinerators of all types emit dioxin.[41] Worldwide incineration is a major source of dioxin release.[42] Municipal waste incineration has, for example, been found to be the main source of dioxin contamination of the Great Lakes.[43] Japan, which is home to 70 percent of the world's municipal waste incinerators, is now paying a price with dioxin levels ten times higher than in the United States.[44] Hazardous waste incineration has not contributed as much to the overall environmental load, primarily because the number of hazardous waste incinerators is smaller than municipal waste incinerators.

Measuring the amount of output of dioxin from hazardous waste incinerators is a tricky business. Measurements can be made of outputs from the stack itself, in the ambient air surrounding an incinerator, or in the ground and foliage surrounding an incinerator, where the dioxin will have been deposited over time. While a number of attempts have been made to measure dioxin output from incineration, most striking is the lack of available data. The number of studies that have been undertaken on dioxin release is relatively small, although there are nineteen RCRA-certified hazardous waste facilities and dozens of municipal waste facilities. Hazardous waste incinerators are not continuously monitored for dioxin release. And there is evidence that limited monitoring that takes place over a few hours can significantly underestimate average dioxin releases.[45]

Because of technical improvements, the release of dioxin through stack gases has declined over the last twenty years. Incinerators now burn more efficiently, and technologies are in place in new incinerators that can prevent high levels of dioxin from being released from stacks. Just how effective these new technologies are, however, is not entirely clear, owing to a lack of continuous monitoring. Estimates of improvements are often based on "trial burns" that are designed to determine how well the incinerator is operating under optimal conditions. Studies that have been conducted in the United States to measure dioxin outputs from hazardous waste incineration give evidence of wide variation, but many of those studied would be unable to meet U.S. EPA standards of 0.2 ng TEQ/dscm.[46] Several studies surveying surface areas surrounding incinerators have shown, as one might expect, that dioxin residues present in the ground tend to be proportionate to their distance away from a waste incinerator.[47] Analysis of fruits and vegetables grown near a chemical waste incinerator in Wales revealed their consumption would lead to an additional 3 percent of normal dietary intake for PCBs and 8 percent for dioxins.[48] Analysis of eggs and poultry meat near British and Welsh incinerators revealed that consuming these products would lead to substantial intake of PCBs and dioxins.[49] A comparison of residents near an industrial waste facility versus workers and residents near two municipal waste facilities in Korea

concluded that 70 percent of those living near the industrial waste facility had dioxin TEQs outside of WHO's established tolerable limits.[50] In
the case of an incinerator in western Japan, high concentrations of dioxin
were found in the flue gas and in the area surrounding the plant.[51] In some
cases, however, little or no association has been shown been the operations
of incinerators and increased dioxin levels in a community. Background
levels near a recently built incinerator in Catalonia, Spain, exceeded background levels by only relatively small amounts after two years of operation.[52] A study of dioxin body burdens of residents near a municipal waste
incinerator in Germany revealed no statistically significant differences as
compared to the general population.[53]

   That exposure inside a plant occurs at different rates than outside is not
an unreasonable assumption, often borne out to be true. Thus workers are
not exposed to dioxin in quite the same way as residents of an incinerator
community. Because of workers' close contact with the sometimes toxic
substances being burned, as well as fugitive emissions and incinerator
ash, they would seem likely to experience higher-than-normal exposure
levels. Even within the plant itself, there are differences, with ambient dioxin levels tending to be highest near the kiln.[54] Numerous studies have
shown that plant workers carry higher—sometimes much higher—levels
of dioxin in their bodies than control groups. A recent study of workers at a Japanese municipal waste incinerator found hair measurements
of dioxin TEQs to be 2.5 times higher than in the general population.[55]
A study of workers at six Japanese municipal waste incinerators initially
concluded that dioxin blood levels were not at a statistically significant
higher level than in the general population,[56] but further analysis revealed
a connection between exposure levels within the plant and higher blood
serum dioxin levels.[57] Japanese researchers also found significant exposure of Japanese incineration workers to dioxin at the Nose Bika Center,[58]
as well as at the Tokyo-gun incineration plant.[59] A recent study of workers
at thirteen Japanese municipal incineration plants revealed significantly
higher levels of dioxin in their blood than in that of the general population
(which already has high levels in Japan), probably the result of inhaling
contaminated dust.[60]

   Dioxin is not, of course, the only toxin released into local environments from hazardous waste incineration. PCBs are another by-product
of incineration. PCBs, like dioxins, appear in many varieties. In the case

of PCBs, there are 209 related chemical compounds, about half of which have been detected in the global environment. Like dioxins, PCBs accumulate in the fatty tissue of animals, and they tend to concentrate up the food chain. PCBs, also like dioxins, persist in the environment for long periods of time. They are suspected of being carcinogenic, and some tend to mimic dioxins in their effects on the endrocrinal, immune, and reproductive systems.[61] Waste incineration has been associated with PCB deposition. A study of the Alberta Special Waste Treatment Center in Swan Hills, Canada, for example, showed a pattern of PCB deposition that could be correlated with a plant accident as well as with long-term fugitive emissions.[62]

Chlorinated benzenes are also released from hazardous waste incineration. Among the most worrisome of the chlorinated benzenes is hexochlorobenzene, which is a suspected carcinogen and toxic enough to be used as a pesticide. The liver and the nervous system are most sensitive to HCB exposure.[63] Fifty-three examined workers at a Swiss incinerator had urine with higher-than-normal levels of hydroxypyrene, diclorophenal (DCP), and hexachlorobenzene (HCB).[64]

Polycyclic aromatic hydrocarbons (PAHs) are products of incomplete combustion, generated by many types of combustion and all types of incineration. They constitute a wide variety of chemical compounds (over 10,000), a number of which are believed to be toxic and carcinogenic. They tend to be released during start-ups of incinerators, before facilities have reached maximum levels of efficiency.[65]

Volatile organic compounds (VOCs) are also released from hazardous waste incinerators. Few studies have been conducted on this array of chemical releases. One undertaken at a municipal solid waste incinerator detected 250 compounds, including known toxics and carcinogens such as benzene, substituted phenols, and phthalates.[66] Many of the VOCs released from incinerator stacks are aliphatic hydrocarbons of unknown identity.[67] In 1995, 122 workers at a German industrial waste incineration plant were tested for elevated levels of organic and inorganic substances in their blood. The workers working closest to the incinerator itself had higher levels of toluene in their blood, as compared with other workers in the plant and the general population.[68] An early study (1983) of worker exposure to VOCs at a liquid chemical waste incinerator showed elevated levels only of benzene.[69]

Heavy metals are highly toxic, and some, such as arsenic, are known to be carcinogenic. Up to thirteen kinds of heavy metals are released from hazardous waste incinerators, including arsenic (which damages nerves, stomach, intestines, and skin and affects cardiac function), cadmium (which damages kidneys and lungs), lead (which damages lungs, kidneys, and the nervous system), manganese, chromium (which damages the nose, lungs, and stomach), beryllium (which damages lungs), and mercury.[70] The deposition of heavy metals in local environments has been associated with the operations of municipal waste incinerators.[71] In the case of one sewage sludge incinerator, increased levels of lead and cadmium were found but were considered not to be excessive.[72] Residents of a highly industrialized area of the La Spezia municipality in Italy had increased skin and mucous membrane irritation consistent with reaction to the emissions of a local waste incinerator, along with anemia consistent with exposure to lead emitted from the facility.[73] An analysis of nine incinerator communities, which focused on potential pathways of exposure to heavy metals, found that inhalation and noninhalation pathways both provided means of exposure.[74] A 1989 study of New York City municipal waste incinerator workers found them to have high lead levels (11 pgs) in their blood compared to a control group (7.4 pgs).[75] Analysis of lead levels near a Scottish incinerator showed that lead levels in local soils were highly correlated to the emissions of the incinerator within a radius of five kilometers.[76] A survey of lead and cadmium revealed correlations diminishing according to their distance from a municipal waste incinerator.[77] On the other hand, analysis of ambient air near an Albany incinerator revealed very low concentrations of heavy metals.[78]

With the improvement of technical means for their removal, most heavy metals can be removed, under ideal conditions, to the 95 percent level. Mercury, however, poses special problems because in its elemental form it is highly resistant to absorption in other substances, such as ash. Moreover, it can travel long distances once emitted from a stack. Mercury also combines with chlorine to form divalent mercury, which is water soluable and, when released, is often deposited close to the stack.[79] Waste incinerators are one of the most significant sources of mercury pollution worldwide. One recent study concluded that nearly 10 percent of mercury emissions in eight Great Lakes states came from waste incineration. (In the Midwest, coal-fired power plants are the primary source.)[80] It is estimated that as much as 39 percent of airborne mercury emissions in the United States are generated by waste incinerators.[81] One study found increased concentrations of mercury in the hair of individuals living near a hazardous waste incinerator (although not enough, according to the authors, to pose a health risk).[82] Sphagnum moss and lichens are particularly good bioindicators, and using them to measure deposition has shown that mercury levels decrease with distance from municipal waste incinerators.[83]

Mercury is highly toxic. It attacks the nervous system, and it is especially dangerous for fetuses (since it passes through the placenta) and young children. It can cause a variety of conditions from cerebral palsy to mental retardation, seizures, and blindness. Mercury contamination is high already in the general population. One-tenth of all births in the United States are at risk of developmental problems because of exposure during pregnancy.[84]

The term "particulates" encompasses many different kinds of materials from dust to pollen. Generally, naturally occurring particulates are larger than the fine particulates that result from processes of combustion. The finer particulates are particularly troublesome from the standpoint of public health, because they can be pulled deep into the passages of the lungs, where they can contribute to various lung ailments, including asthma. While modern pollution control methods are capable of limiting the emission of many particulates from hazardous waste incineration, they are incapable of preventing all of them from being released through the stack. In fact, the finer the particulate, the more difficult it is to control, and the more potential damage it can do. Moreover, methods that attempt to control some stack releases, such as ammonia injection, designed to limit the release of nitrogen oxides, may actually increase the levels of fine particulates.[85]

Inorganic gases are also released from hazardous waste incinerators. These include hydrogen chloride, hydrogen fluoride, hydrogen bromide, sulphur, and nitrogen oxides. Sulphur and nitrogen released can both contribute to acid rain. Nitrogen releases contribute to the generation of smog. All of these inorganic releases can combine with ammonia to create what are called "secondary particulates." These in turn can absorb various organic compounds with toxic effects, such as dioxin and PAHs.[86]

While what is deliberately expelled through a stack or accidentally leaked through the seams of an incinerator might be of most interest to those living in a community where one is sited, a mix of highly toxic material is routinely transported from every facility in the form of ash, the unburnable residual material that is a by-product of all kinds of incineration. There are two kinds of ash, fly ash and bottom ash. While the bulk of the volume of ash is the bottom ash (90 percent) the bulk of the toxicity is in the fly ash, where pollution control equipment traps the toxics that would otherwise be released into the surrounding atmosphere. As Neil Tangri notes, "This reveals a central conundrum of incineration: the cleaner the air emissions, the more hazardous the ash."[87] The ash must then be buried in a designated hazardous waste landfill of some kind, where it will, at some distant point, leach into the surrounding surfaces from the containment device within which it has been sequestered.[88] The New York City Department of Health analyzed soil samples at a site that had received incinerator ash from 1954 to 1973, and found that lead levels far exceeded CDC recommendations, leading to increased risk of lead poisoning among children.[89]

The Health Impacts of Incineration

What are the health impacts of releasing toxic substances from incinerators? Given the known connections between dioxin and other chlorine compounds with cancer, there is some expectation that those working in, or living near, waste incinerators would have an elevated risk of being diagnosed with it. Evidence exists that this is the case. Studies attempting to measure the health effects of incinerators on given communities have been done sporadically in the United States. Comprehensive studies are expensive, and neither government nor industry has an incentive to engage in health studies of incineration communities. Epidemiological studies are most useful, since they can give comparative information about disease, but they are especially difficult and expensive to undertake, given the amount of data that must be collected and the variables that must be controlled. Studies that have been completed reveal a mixed record, with many findings troubling enough to cast doubt on claims of incinerator safety.

Given the known connection between dioxin and cancer, elevated cancer rates are a primary focus of interest. A study in Trieste, Italy, found a connection between proximity to an incinerator and higher-than-expected lung cancer rates. People who lived close to the incinerator had a 6.7 times greater chance of dying of lung cancer than those that lived farther away.[90] A massive epidemiological study of 14 million people in England who lived in close proximity to municipal waste incinerators revealed higher rates of stomach, colorectal, liver, and lung cancers. But given intervening socioeconomic factors, and the short lag time (ten years from the time the incinerator began operations), the authors were unwilling to conclude causation.[91] Knox et al. found links between childhood cancer and proximity to 70 municipal and 200 hospital waste incinerators.[92] A Swedish study of four worker cohorts—chimney sweeps, waste incineration workers, gas workers, and bus garage workers—found that exposure to all four sources of combustion was associated with increased risk of esophageal cancer.[93] The lead author, Per Gustavsson, found in his study of a Swedish municipal waste incinerator that workers had 3.5 times the deaths of the national rate from lung cancer and higher-than-average mortality from heart disease.[94] Michelozzi et al. examined the effects of three pollution sources (an oil refinery, a waste disposal site, and a waste incinerator) on Malagrotta, a suburb of Rome. While they found no discernible increase for most cancers, they detected a decline in mortality from cancer of the larynx with increased distance of residence from the plant.[95] Knox and Gillman[96] found higher cancer rates for children who lived near a variety of industrial sources that emitted VOCs.[97] An often-cited study by Bresnitz et al., however, found no adverse health effects from working at a municipal waste incinerator.[98]

Location near an incinerator of some kind is generally associated with living near other industrial facilities, many of which also emit both organic and inorganic gases, heavy metals, and particulates, making it difficult to disentangle effects of an incinerator alone, and thus making it easier for incinerator operators to claim that incinerators themselves are relatively safe. Thus the fact that the worst locations for siting waste incinerators (such as East Liverpool) are the areas most likely now to have them provides a kind of epistemological cover for the industry. Because of the nature of scientific investigation, only relatively small sets of particularities can be analyzed at any given time. Moreover, researchers are understandably cautious when drawing conclusions, especially in terms of attributing causation. This may provide little comfort to residents of places with high concentrations of industrial pollutants. For a family member dealing with the loss of a loved one from cancer, it makes little difference whether an incinerator has been the sole or only a contributing cause of death.

Given releases of polychlorinated hydrocarbons, dioxins, and PCBs from hazardous waste incinerators, changes in sex ratios favoring female to male births might be expected. Only one study, however, has attempted to determine if there is a relationship between proximity to an incinerator and differences in sex ratios, and it showed only limited evidence of such a link.[99] A recent Japanese study found the opposite, that is a slight (not statistically significant) increase in male to female sex ratios for four hundred municipal waste incinerator workers.[100] A study involving a hazardous waste incinerator in Hesse, Germany, found increased frequency of twins among women living near the hazardous waste incinerator there.[101]

Ten Tusscher et al. found a likely relation between a chemical incineration plant in Zeeburg, Amsterdam, and the increased incidence of orofacial clefts.[102] A study of babies born near incinerators in Cumbria, England, from 1956 to 1993 found an increased risk of spina bifida and heart defects.[103] Japanese researchers recently examined birth outcomes for women within ten kilometers of sixty-three municipal waste incineration plants in Japan. They found statistically significant higher levels of both infant death and congenital malformation for residents within 10 km (but not 2 km) of the plants. Peak declines were associated with distance from the plants.[104] A French analysis of seventy incinerator communities found an increased frequency of some abnormalities, such as facial clefts and renal dysplasia in them.[105]

Little doubt exists about the health impacts of particulates. Even short-term increases in the ambient air can have effects on mortality in large cities.[106] As noted, tiny particulates released from incinerators can potentially cause respiratory problems such as asthma. The findings on the respiratory impacts of living near an incinerator are somewhat mixed. Studies of incinerator communities in North Carolina and Taiwan yielded evidence that people living near such sites had a higher likelihood of self-reported respiratory problems (such as cough and wheezing) than those in a nearby control population, although no greater number of physician-reported respiratory diseases or hospital admissions for respiratory ailments.[107] Another study of individuals living near cements kilns, which often burn hazardous wastes in their production processes, found a higher likelihood of respondents to a questionnaire reporting symptoms of respiratory dis-

tress.[108] Wang et al. found that students living near a wire-reclamation facility, within relatively close range of a variety of other industrial facilities,
had some respiratory distress, but the authors confessed to an inability to
disentangle the health impacts of the incinerator from other sources.[109]
Hazucha et al. found in their study of communities with three solid
waste incineration facilities that residents had no decreased pulmonary
function compared to the general population.[110] Shy et al. also found no
evidence of respirator effects on residents living in six incinerator communities.[111] Gray et al. found no connection between the high presence of
asthma symptoms among children in Sydney, Australia, and proximity to
a sewage sludge incinerator.[112] It is worth noting that when the WTI permit was being considered, East Liverpool was a community with air that
already carried a high particulate load.

General surveys of the health of those exposed to incineration have
shown significant impacts in some cases, less so in others. Workers at a
hazardous waste incinerator in Lenoir, North Carolina, suffered multiple
health problems that resulted in financial losses of $3 million and potential
wage losses of $14 million. One worker died after settling with the state's
workers' compensation board.[113] An analysis of workers at three French
municipal waste incinerators found statistically significant increases in
white blood cells and lead levels, increases in skin irritation and coughing,
and slightly reduced lung function, but concluded that workers suffered
few adverse health effects.[114] Comparing incineration workers with workers at municipal water treatments plants, Scarlett et al. found higher levels
of mutagenic changes in the urinary tracts of the incinerator workers,[115]
although in a two-year follow-up, the differences were no longer statistically significant.[116] Recent research suggests that incineration worker exposure to PAHs is associated with immune system damage.[117]

Humans are not the only species whose health is affected by incineration. A study of prefledgling black kites that were nested near a municipal waste incinerator in Madrid, Spain, found that higher-than-normal
levels of cadmium, resulting from plant emissions, adversely affected the
immune systems of the birds.[118] Studies of dairy cattle in Scotland have
shown higher twinning rates and a higher ratio of female to male births in
an area where two waste incinerators operate.[119]

It is always possible to raise doubts about the significance of any individual study; so many variables are at play in any given case. Populations

are mobile, so it is not always easy to track them. Medical conditions are difficult to determine accurately, especially when one is considering things such as "general respiratory distress" with questionnaires. Moreover, incinerators vary in their outputs. Municipal and medical waste incinerators emit a different mix of effluents than hazardous waste incinerators. And there is variation between individual incinerators. Incinerators brought online in the 1990s have better pollution abatement technologies than those used in the 1960s and 1970s. Some incinerators are managed better than others. The types of waste being burned differ as well, resulting in variations from year to year or even week to week. Given all these complicating factors and the dearth of systematic scientific studies, it is difficult, if not impossible, to say with certainty that a particular incinerator in a given community is causing particular health effects. Yet the evidence that does exist is more than suggestive. Enough studies have been conducted that citizens living in incinerator communities of all kinds need not be apologetic about feeling threatened by the incinerators emitting hazardous chemicals in their communities. A vast experiment is being conducted on them, the findings of which may never be entirely reported, but enough facts are now known to legitimize citizens' concerns.

Unfortunately, in the case of the incinerators now operating, the decision to permit was made not on the basis of epidemiological analysis but on the basis of risk assessments. Those risk assessments, measured against the medical evidence that has accumulated, have often turned out to be wrong. In every case that a risk assessment was undertaken, it concluded that the risks of cancer and other health impacts were infinitesimal, roughly one in a million; but epidemiological analysis has shown that in numerous places the health consequences have exceeded predictions. Yet, as Allsopp et al. note, "Nearly all . . . risk assessments from the 1980s through the 1990s have concluded that contaminants from incinerators do not pose a significant health risk to populations living within their vicinity. This is direct contrast to human epidemiological studies, some of which have found evidence of health impacts."[120]

Monitoring processes for hazardous waste incinerators are, even under ideal conditions, crude measures of the materials that are being emitted from the waste stack.[121] The actual toxics are not measured. Rather, the amount of oxygen and carbon dioxide coming out of the stack is measured, and from this information, problems with the incinerators operations can be estimated. The monitoring devices are therefore indirect. The people doing the monitoring can tell if something is wrong, but they cannot tell exactly what it is.[122] Dioxins are typically monitored twice a year, with each test involving just a six-hour sample. Most dioxins, however, are produced during the start-up and shutdown periods, when the incinerator is not burning at maximum efficiency. In fact, it is estimated that standard dioxin testing will make estimates that reflect only 2 percent of the total in dioxin emissions.[123]

It is one thing to monitor emissions; it is another to control them. By monitoring, if it is done properly, managers and regulators may be able to get some sense of past mistakes, but the process does not necessarily give adequate information to correct for them. To control emissions there must be real-time monitoring, so that adjustments can be made to prevent excessive releases. Unfortunately, such real-time monitoring is highly problematic for dioxins, and it is virtually unheard of for mercury releases.[124]

The WTI Risk Assessment

The first risk assessment that the U.S. EPA made of the WTI facility, not unlike the one in the Canton, New York, case that Paul Connett was involved with, examined only the impacts of inhalation on residents in the area. The study found the impact from WTI to be within acceptable EPA standards for cancer risk. After Clinton's election in 1992, however, activists attended a meeting in Washington at the office of the new EPA administrator Carol Browner. Browner opened the meeting by stating that she would have to recuse herself from any participation in the WTI case, because of a conflict of interest involving her spouse, who had worked for Citizen Action in Florida. She then left the office, leaving Terri Swearingen, Alonzo Spencer, and others alone there. Being both curious and enterprising, they began looking around for potentially useful information. Somewhat unbelievably, they found, in a wastebasket, a copy of a memo written by Richard Guimond, a senior EPA employee and public health expert, that was meant to be circulated only inside the EPA. According to the memo, based on preliminary analysis of food chain pathways for dioxin, the EPA's Office of Research and Development had concluded that regular consumption of beef and milk local to the East Liverpool area would result in cancer risks one thousand times higher than had been predicted in the inhalation study. The memo had been prepared for a lawsuit that had been filed in U.S. District Court to have the facility's permit revoked. Guimond and the U.S. EPA had never intended the memo to be made public, and when plaintiffs in the lawsuit attempted to have it introduced at the trial, the EPA attempted to have it suppressed. Judge Aldrich, however, allowed the memo to be entered into the court record after it was made public and eventually found in favor of the plaintiffs, although her ruling was ultimately overturned on appeal (on procedural grounds). The EPA then initiated a second risk assessment, more comprehensive than the first, this time involving food chain analysis. This became known as the "Phase II" risk assessment.

The Phase II risk assessment document for WTI is impressive. It consists of several thousand pages. What first catches the attention of someone with knowledge of the history of WTI is the date. The cover document from David Ullrich, at the time acting regional director for the U.S. EPA Region V, to Donald Schregardus, director of the Ohio Environmental Protection Agency, is dated April 22, 1998. This date reveals that at the point of delivery of the final document, fifteen years had elapsed since the WTI permit had been issued by the Ohio Hazardous Waste Facilities Board, and nearly five years had elapsed since WTI began regular operations. Suppose the findings had been troubling enough that the U.S. EPA would have had to reevaluate its position favoring operation of the facility? Would the WTI permit have been suspended or revoked? While the risk assessment could have an impact on the parameters of the facility's operations, in terms of matters such as the volume and characteristics of the waste feed, it is difficult to imagine a scenario in which scientific findings would be forthcoming that would place WTI's continuing operations in actual jeopardy. Given this backdrop, the assessment could legitimately be viewed by skeptical citizens as a post hoc rationalization, rather than as an "objective" inquiry into the risks posed by the facility.

A risk assessment is long chain of estimates, with uncertainties existing and judgments being made about their meaning at innumerable junctures along a path that extends from the point at which wastes enter the facility until their burned residues make their way back outside and into the ecosystem and human bodies. The pieces of the chain are then linked together via both explicit and hidden assumptions and complicated scientific calculations. A risk assessment such as WTI's is both a tremendous technical accomplishment and a very expensive roll of the ecological dice. Four million dollars was spent on the WTI Phase II risk assessment, but in the end, in terms of regulatory policy, only one conclusion counted. That conclusion was that for "most of the population, including students who attend the nearby elementary school, the potential increased lifetime cancer risk would be less than 1 in 1 million from stack emissions, and less than 2 in 1 million from fugitive emissions."[125] In other words, the findings concluded that, for the purposes of U.S. EPA regulatory rules, the increased cancer risk from WTI's operations was negligible to the point of nonexistence.

It would be virtually impossible to expose all of the complexities, uncertainties, and hidden assumptions of a document as weighty as the WTI risk assessment, but it is worth considering some of them in detail to gain insight into the processes by which risk analyses are conducted and the particular meanings in this case. Analysis of important aspects of the WTI risk assessment reveals the conjectural character of such documents. A perhaps simple, but useful, way to think about the vast amount of information contained in the document is in terms of the what, where, how, and who of the facility's operations. *What* is being emitted from the plant? To *where* are these substances dispersed? *How* do they interact with various environments? *Who* is affected by them?

What Is That Stuff?

Without having some reasonable sense of what is being released from an incinerator—or any industrial facility, for that matter—it would be impossible to determine its various impacts. The characteristics and quantities of these substances, however, are far from certain. When highly complex materials such as hazardous wastes are burned at very high temperatures, all sorts of transformations occur. Thousands of new chemical substances are generated. The levels at which these substances are released are not subject to continuous monitoring. Levels must be estimated based on data collected during trial burns, analysis of waste feed inputs, continuous monitoring of carbon dioxide and other gases being discharged, and ambient air monitoring (at sites near the facility). The meaning and

value of information collected from each of these sources are highly contested. A trial burn, for example, is a highly controlled experiment, and
the extent to which it represents the actual operations of a facility can be
questioned. Feed rates under actual conditions are bound to vary over
time, as the authors of the WTI risk assessment recognized. In their words,
"The estimation of emission rates for metals and certain organic chemical
residues (for which stack testing was not conducted) is highly dependent
upon the feed rate. Limited data, which might not be fully representative
of long-term operations, are used to estimate feed rates."[126] And even data
collected during the trial burn involve estimates that may include inaccuracies. As the Greenpeace chemist Pat Costner pointed out in her analysis
of the WTI risk assessment, the "quantification of PCDD/Fs in stack gases
suffers from great uncertainty." She also noted that PIC emissions were
measured in "grams per second," rather than "grams per cubic meter," as
is conventionally done, thus making it impossible to draw direct comparisons between WTI and other trial burns.

Even if an incinerator is well managed and maintained, it will undergo
periods of "upset," when it is not operating at optimum efficiency. The EPA
did not include an analysis of the impact of upsets in the final quantitative risk assessment. They did estimate the amount of organic compound
releases to be 30 percent greater with upsets included in the analysis by
comparing monitoring data that included upsets with baseline data that
did not.[127] But these additional emissions were not included in the final
risk assessment, either for nondioxin or dioxin compounds (66).

Even the best-run facilities also release so-called fugitive emissions. Pat
Costner argued that these were a potentially larger problem than emissions
that actually came out of the stack, and this was not fully recognized in the
risk assessment. Moreover, risk assessors ignored what Costner believed
to be the most important source of fugitive emissions: the kiln (66).

The test burn also raised the issues of "expected" versus "permitted"
rates of emission. Risk assessment calculations were based on mean emissions measured during the trial burn, the performance test, and comparisons to other facilities. But under WTI's RCRA permit, the facility was
legally entitled to higher emissions than were indicated in those figures.
The permitted emissions were not, however, included in the final risk assessment, even though such a calculation was promised in the 1993 project

plan for the risk assessment (71–72). Ashley Schannauer points out that the omission was particularly important for metals, especially lead, which, if emitted at a rate allowed under the permit, would result in levels of release that would exceed EPA standards (72).

Problems with determining the "what" of the WTI facility crystalized with a scandal that erupted over the North Ohio Valley Air Authority (NOVAA). NOVAA was hired by the Ohio EPA in 1994 for $847,000 a year to conduct air quality monitoring in Ohio River valley. The agency had primary responsibility for overseeing compliance issues involving WTI. As such, the agency oversaw monitoring equipment and collected and analyzed data from continuous stack emissions testing, ambient air testing, and quarterly stack emissions testing. NOVAA employees were also actively involved in overseeing the WTI trial burn. Unfortunately, the agency's operations were riddled with improprieties, to the point that it was disbanded in 1997.

Robert J. Martin, the EPA ombudsman appointed by the Clinton administration to review the operations of WTI, confirmed three central allegations made against NOVAA that cast considerable doubt on its monitoring activities. First, NOVAA employees were being paid, on the side, by WTI officials during the same period that they were monitoring the facility. Second, at some time during the period when NOVAA was supposed to be monitoring WTI, the highly sophisticated ambient air monitoring equipment was "gutted," and the computers on which the accuracy of readings depended "disappeared." Finally, the stack monitors, designed to give continuous emissions data, "had been programmed in a way that prevented them from providing regulators with correct data."[128] In other words, virtually none of the information that was supposed to be indicating WTI's compliance with the parameters laid out in the risk assessment was reliable; neither the data that was coming from the stack, nor the data from the ambient air surrounding the facility.

Perhaps even more important than the lack of continuous monitoring were problems with data related to the trial burn itself, information on which calculations for the risk assessment were based. Vincent Zumpano, one of the key figures at NOVAA involved with WTI monitoring, revealed problems with the trial burn analysis in a deposition for his trial on bribery and tax evasion charges:

Q. Was there ever a time when you noticed that monitoring equipment or things of this nature [were] not functioning properly or not turned on properly at WTI?

A. Yes, there was one time when me and Mike Walosky Jr. went up to change the filters the machines were turned off. So, at that time, when we can back into the office at NOVAA, when Dan Zorbini was, you know, the technician—not the technician, the engineer in charge, we told him about it. And he said, "Don't worry about it."

Q. Now who said that?

A. Dan Zorbini. So that meant that there was no air sampling that day, and they were doing a trial burn . . .

Q. If there was a trial burn—I mean to the best of your knowledge, I realize you are not an engineer, if there was a trial burn, then that type of equipment should have been on it; am I correct?

A. Yeah, from the way I understood it, it should have been on, but it wasn't.

Q. And are you indicating that you don't know why it was off?

A. No, they didn't give me an explanation.[129]

Compliance testing apparently involved similarly egregious kinds of problems. Tammy Hilkens of the Ohio EPA told Robert Martin that "the company has not exactly been forthright in using data to establish compliance under worst case scenarios. " When they underwent their quarterly lead testing "three quarters of testing went by before we realized that they were not feeding any Pb [lead] into the incinerator during the compliance testing and then they had the nerve to brag about their 'low' Pb emission rates once the tests were submitted." Hilkens's conclusion based on his own experiences with WTI is rather astonishing: "I suspect," he said, "that in most of the situations, the compounds in question were below the detectable because waste being fed into the incinerator during the tests did not contain any of the compounds being sought."[130] As Martin pithily put it to me, "No lead in, no lead out."

The scandal involving NOVAA extended beyond WTI. Onetime director 'Patsy' DeLuca, along with his cohort Zumpano, had, it turned out, spent years pressuring local industries to provide kickbacks and bribes in order to avoid regulatory oversight. Their activities seemed to reach toward Governor Voinovich's office. In 1997 Zumpano was convicted of attempting to bribe a Jefferson County commissioner in connection with a jail construction project. He had been trying to secure the contract for a construction firm known as the V Group that was directed by the governor's brother Paul.[131] Representatives of the V Group denied any connection to Zumpano, but federal authorities investigating the case said that there was a record of phone calls from NOVAA to the V Group's headquarters in Cleveland.[132]

The connections between Voinovich, WTI, and NOVAA are even more disturbing. Early on, WTI officials said the relationship between the firm and NOVAA had been "antagonistic," so they hired Anthony Fabiano, a campaign consultant for Mamais and Associates, a firm with ties to the V Group, to "improve" the relationship with NOVAA. Fabiano was paid $27,000 a month for his services. WTI officials stated that they hired Fabiano "to manage downward politically toward better relations with the local agency." Apparently at the suggestion of Paul Voinovich, Fabiano then hired Anthony Gallagher, a union representative with long-running connections to the governor, on a "retainer" of $6,000 a month. Moreover, the governor's chief of staff, Paul Mifsud, may have helped Fabiano gain his position with WTI. According to grand jury testimony by the governor's campaign manager Vincent Panichi, Paul Voinovich was "furious" that the V Group's consulting fee was reduced to pay Gallagher's salary. He then asked his brother, the governor, for reimbursements, to be made through Mamais and Associates.[133] The governor denied all of this and was never indicted on any charges related to it. Still, when the dust settled, it was clear that WTI had been paying friends of the governor's brother and others associated with the governor to improve their relationship to the agency that was supposed to be providing state and federal regulators with monitoring data.

WTI also acknowledged paying NOVAA for unnecessary monitoring studies. In one case, the company paid the agency $100,000 for a study that was never completed. While WTI officials contended that these payments were to go the "extra mile" toward monitoring, critics charged that they were essentially kickbacks. Zumpano also claimed that Paul Voinovich had pressured NOVAA to "go easy on Waste Technologies Industries hazardous waste incinerator," and that he "threatened to have the state funding pulled for the North Ohio Valley Air Authority if it didn't cooperate."[134] It is perhaps not surprising, then, that when the U.S. EPA, at the petition of several Ohio citizen groups, conducted a review of files in the Northeast Ohio EPA Office, they discovered that NOVAA inspection reports were often inadequate. For example, one entry from the U.S. EPA review stated with regard to several inspection reports, "These reports are on a standard form, but offer little information. They are conclusory in nature. It's extraordinary that the brief 12/7/94 report apparently presents the results of a week-long inspection."[135]

DeLuca and Zumpano both eventually pled guilty to charges associated with Ohio's unlawful gratuity law and tax evasion. DeLuca was sentenced to six months in prison and fined $10,000, while Zumpano received fifteen months and a $8,000 fine. Fabiano pled guilty to tax evasion charges. The V Group filed for Chapter 11, and NOVAA was dissolved. George Voinovich soon became U.S. senator from Ohio, a position that he holds as of this writing.

Based on his analysis of the various procedures used for trial burns and subsequent monitoring activities, Robert Martin concluded that it was "clear that there are significant data problems surrounding the trial burn for the WTI facility and compliance with the testing thereafter" and that the EPA "was most likely not aware of those problems during the trial burn itself or the subsequent compliance testing for lead required by the RCRA permit for WTI." These problems, he judged, strike at "the very heart of how safe the WTI facility is and whether it is protective of human health and the environment." Since the data from the trial burn were "inconclusive at best," the validity of the entire risk assessment had to be cast into question, making it almost totally dependant on stack testing.[136] For example, Martin noted, "predictions relating to blood lead levels in the community were made in the risk assessment relying upon [trial burn stack testing] data: and ambient air monitoring equipment data as well."[137] Because of the significant concerns that Martin had regarding the quality of all of the monitoring, his recommendation, never followed by the Bush administration, was to stop operations for six months in order to conduct a new trial burn.[138]

On April 22, 2002, Robert Martin resigned from his position at the EPA. The office of Ombudsman as it related to hazardous waste and Superfund programs had been dissolved by the recently appointed EPA administrator Christy Todd Whitman, effectively terminating Martin's position. Martin's files were, according to him, "seized," the locks on his office were changed, and he was transferred to the Inspector General's Office. He objected to the transfer on the grounds that as an employee of the IG's office, he would have less independence than as an ombudsman.[139] He had clearly raised the hackles of some in the hazardous waste and chemical industries, Von Roll managers, no doubt, being among them. In reporting on his resignation, the *Washington Post* observed that "his investigations have made him a folk hero in several communities."[140] Martin had also questioned the EPA's determination to minimize the potential health threats from atmospheric contamination at Ground Zero in New York. He further claimed that he was being disciplined for investigating possible favorable EPA findings involving businesses with connections to Whitman's spouse, John.[141] Martin had clearly become persona non grata in the new Bush administration.

Unfortunately, the NOVAA scandal did not turn out to be the end of monitoring problems at the plant. The report of an investigation into the work habits of Christine D'Amico, a technical services employee of the Ohio EPA's Northeastern District Office of the Department of Air Pollution Control, is a fascinating document. It paints a picture of a completely incompetent employee, who did a terrible job of monitoring the air quality in the area in which WTI is located. She was apparently a troubled person who had some significant personal issues that made her incapable of fulfilling her duties. That kind of thing, of course, can happen to someone in almost any position. But how could a person be that incompetent and not be exposed for a period of at least two years? Various claims about the safety of facilities such as WTI often tend to focus on the technical accomplishment of such enterprises. Unfortunately, these extremely complex and technically impressive facilities have to be run and monitored by fallible human beings.

As a member of a technical team working for DEPA (Department of Air Pollution Control), Christine D'Amico was responsible for overseeing and gathering data from monitors at three sites around East Liverpool. One was at the Columbiana County Port Authority building (within a stone's throw of the WTI facility), one at the town's wastewater treatment plant, and one at the East Liverpool City Schools administration building.

The Port Authority building monitor is what's known in the business as total suspended particulates (or TSP) monitor, designed, as the name implies, to detect total amounts of particulates in the ambient air in the city. She was also assigned to a TSP and a PM-10 monitor at the water treatment plant. A PM-10 monitor is designed to measure various particles in the ambient air. She also had responsibility for two TSP, two PM-10, and two sulfur dioxide monitors at the school administration building.[142]

The type of monitors used and their placement had itself been a matter of some controversy. As early as 1993, EPA toxicologist Dave Nuber had written a confidential memo to the director of the Ohio EPA's Division of Air Pollution Control. In it, he noted that EPA's risk assessment had made no attempt to pinpoint where the monitors could be most effectively placed. They appeared "to be chosen without concern for high human exposure receptor areas." He stated that he was "left to wonder why somebody didn't run a new model (possibly HEM II based on the most recent census data) showing high exposure areas." If this had been done, he asked, "Couldn't we have placed more confidence in the monitoring data of WTI?"[143] Nuber was also concerned that chemical releases were not being properly monitored by the Ohio EPA. "It is my understanding that we will not be monitoring for any other chemicals beyond lead, mercury and VOCs.[144] From a toxicity standpoint, I am much more concerned with PAHs,[145] dioxins and benzene emissions than VOCs." He argued, further, that any risk analysis based upon the collected data would be "highly suspect, at best."[146]

Air pollution monitoring devices are highly sensitive and must be carefully checked to make sure that they are operating correctly. The SO2 monitors, for example, must be kept in air conditioning, because fluctuations in temperature can affect their accuracy. The PM-10 monitors use a quartz filter, which is "a soft, flexible and somewhat fragile piece of paper containing quartz fibers."[147] The filters trap particles. Weighing them before and after they have been deployed yields a measurement of various kinds of particulates in the air. Air flow can affect the levels of particulates that wind up in the filters, so the amount of air flowing into the devices is also recorded, either with a hand-held meter or with is called a "Dioxon chart recorder" (3). Finally, the TSP monitors also have glass filters. Strips of these are cut, once the filters have been used, and are sent to an Ohio EPA lab where they are analyzed for mercury and other metals (4).

Because of the sensitivity of these devices, they need to be properly and routinely maintained. Charts that track read-outs for the SO2 monitors need to be replaced. Diagnostic tests need to be run. Filters must be removed and weighed, with records kept of weight data as well as dates for replacements. Data are sent to central offices and are eventually entered into national databases. The U.S. EPA depends on technical service workers to do their jobs properly, because air pollution data across the United States are highly dependent on their work. The investigative report of the D'Amico case sums this up quite well, stating, "The various maintenance steps and data recording requirements and backup systems are all designed to generate data which is accurate and reliable and in which the Ohio EPA, US EPA and the public can have a degree of confidence" (6). Given the circumstances that were discovered in the audit of Ms. D'Amico's work, it would be difficult to understand how such confidence could be maintained.

Ms. D'Amico was apparently not making timely reports of her PM-10 data, and this was brought to her attention in the summer of 2002. David Ambrose, from the Ohio EPA Department of Air Pollution Control, had not received any data for the entire year. Neither had Phil Downey, who was responsible for gathering data from TSP monitors in the state, received any 2002 data by the summer of that year, and he was even missing data from late 2001. Also, that same summer, fellow tech service workers reported seeing exposed filters in the back of Ms. D'Amico's state vehicle. In September, Ms. D'Amico missed an audit with John Barnett, the official charged with auditing state pollution monitors.

By October 4, the central office had still not received data regarding the PM-10 monitor, but two weeks later, 2002 data were sent up through March of that year. Toward the end of the month, Sam Richey, a monitoring expert from the DAPC, checked the SO2 monitor and found significant problems. Specifically, "the strip chart recorder had been turned off, the strip chart paper had run out, and the recorder equipment had burned out because the end of the strip chart was taped to the reel and had prevented the gears from turning" (8). For at least two months, the data at the site were completely useless. Moreover, the 2002 data on metal from the TSP monitors had still not been received. On November 5, a scheduled audit at the Port Authority building had to be canceled, because Ms. D'Amico told her supervisor, Jennifer Kurko, that the key to the door leading to the roof where the monitors were place was broken off in the lock, and the door could not be opened. On November 19, Ms. D'Amico was assigned to another job (8–9).

With Ms. D'Amico in another position, a detailed audit was conducted. It revealed dirty filters and monitors. Chart recorders had run out of ink. The intake device for the S02 monitor was lying in the gravel on the roof of the Port Authority Building. John Barnhart, the state auditor, reported that he found charts and filters that had been thrown into a wastebasket (13). Log books seemed to have had a number of entries added at the same time (9). Ms. D'Amico was unable to produce numerous data cards, and she admitted to discarding many filters. Of the forty-one that she turned over, more than half had significant tears. For seven of the data cards submitted, identification numbers were recorded that were identical to identification numbers that had been submitted for the previous year (2001). It seemed as though most, if not all, of the monitoring data for the year 2002 had been compromised.

Barnhart was worried not only about the 2002 TSP data but about the 2001 data as well. In 2001 TSP monitors had been down three times when audited and had failed audits twelve times (out of sixteen), or 75 percent of the time. Barnhart stated that he had seen monitors fail by more than 25 percent only twice in his twenty-five-year career. He had never seen "similar blocks of data lost" (14).

When confronted with these facts, Ms. D'Amico confessed that she had made numerous mistakes and had essentially faked data in some cases. She noted that ongoing monitoring of the WTI stack was undertaken on a regular basis, and the computerized results were directly transmitted to Columbus, making many of her activities redundant. She had significant personal problems that put her in a "fog" and made it difficult for her to do her job properly. She did not have a good relationship with the other "lab rats," so that she tended to avoid the lab, making it harder for her to keep accurate records. She also noted that she had done better at her new job in the permitting department, and in 1996 she was chosen as the Northeastern Ohio Department of Operations "Outstanding Employee of the Year" (18). When the information about D'Amico's conduct became public, she resigned from the Ohio EPA and did not make public comments about her case.

A spokeswoman for the Ohio EPA, Patricia Madigan, dismissed claims made by critics of the plant that this provided evidence of continued failure of regulatory agencies to fulfill their mission to carefully monitor the plant's operations. Madigan stated, "There probably was not an air-quality problem in Columbiana County during this period because the 'before' and 'after' numbers are so similar."[148] What Madigan meant by "before" and by "after" is not entirely clear from her comment, but given auditor Barnhart's analysis, she could very well before referring to before 2001 and after 2002. She seemed, in other words, to be suggesting that officials could extrapolate for an entire two-year period and simply assume that ambient air quality had not fluctuated in any significant way during that time. But if you can assume that, then you have to wonder why the elaborate system of monitoring exists in the first place. Moreover, the assumption seems to be a rather large one and hinges on the supposition that there were no spikes in the release of any of the heavy metals or other contaminants that the monitors are designed to detect. Given that the monitoring agent since 1998 had been Christine D'Amico, the possibility of corruptions of the data stretching before 2001 had to at least be entertained as a possibility.

Madigan also argued that stack monitors had been in compliance for the period in question, from which one could surmise that ambient air quality had not been compromised by the plant.[149] This was, of course, very close to the argument put forward by Ms. D'Amico. There are really two problems with it, however. First, there are other sources of pollution in the area that affect the ambient air quality of East Liverpool, and what affects the health and well-being of residents is the total impact of all pollution sources over time. Stack monitors could not detect the total contamination load in the area. Second, the stack monitors are designed to measure different pollutants than ambient air monitors.

In response to the findings regarding the lack of monitoring, Fred Sigg, general manager of the facility, stated, not without some justification, that this was not a facility problem but a state regulatory problem, and WTI managers could not be held accountable for the state's deficiencies. Madigan agreed, stating, "It really doesn't have anything to do with them. . . . We had an employee who messed up."[150] True that WTI was not responsible for the problem, but where did that leave the citizens of East Liverpool? They were, as usual, caught in a web of regulatory incompetence and blame shifting. As Teresa Mills, director of the Buckeye

Environmental Network, put it, "They've been telling us for years that this
is the most heavily monitored and scrutinized facility in the country. . . .
Where's the proof?"

Where Is That Stuff Going?

The "where" of the WTI effluents also poses significant uncertainties.
When minute quantities of highly toxic substances flow from the stack of
a facility such as WTI, it is not easy to determine where they will end up.
Wind currents are difficult to predict, especially over long periods of time.
The determination of what models to use to predict wind patterns was
subject to considerable internal dispute among members of the risk assessment panel. Wind currents are especially difficult to predict in a place
with the varied topological features of the Ohio River valley. In WTI's
case, many of the wind measurements used for WTI were taken at the
Pittsburgh airport, because data are available there. Other meteorologi-
cal matters also can impact where toxic residue may end up. Rain, for
example, can have an impact, as it washes effluents out of the atmosphere
into surrounding environments. Weather data for only one year were collected and used in the risk assessment, thus ignoring the considerable
variation that can occur in weather patterns over longer periods of time
and their potential effects on dispersion of WTI stack emissions.

The potential for accidents attracted some of the most intense scrutiny
in the risk assessment. Accident analysis, according to the document and
peer reviewers, is a more difficult domain to make predictions about than
others where risk analysis has a relatively well-recognized set of methodologies. Dispersion models, which might be acceptable for routine operations, for example, were seen by some as inadequate to address accident
risks.[151] The peer reviewers of the risk assessment had several suggestions
for the EPA, including developing more quantitatively satisfying estimates of accident likelihood. "Likely" or "unlikely," "moderate" to "catastrophic," seemed inadequate (2–5). Some attempts were made to answer
the criticisms, but the EPA resisted one important suggestion, that made
by Paul Connett, to undertake a comparison of WTI with a toxic waste
incinerator in Biebesheim, Germany. The Germany facility is similar in
many respects to the WTI facility, and it had experienced some significant

accidents (2–5). EPA officials argued that the differences between the two facilities made such comparisons virtually meaningless, and they refused to undertake a serious set of comparisons.

Critics also pointed out that the risk assessment's prediction of "one emergency incident involving hazardous waste release for every 25 or 30 years of operation" was questionable given that two releases of hazardous waste had already occurred, and that there was "frequent occurrence of kiln overpressures" (3–19). As one critic of the risk assessment process pointed out, "Use of the term 'moderate risk' to describe an accident involving 10 fatalities is 'insensitive' to impacted residents" (4). Peer reviewer Thomas McKone suggested that, based on the presented data, it appeared that the community would experience one death every ten years from activities at the plant. In early 2004, a worker died when he fell into one of the chemical scrubbers at the facility. The circumstances of the death were not immediately disclosed by WTI, and the U.S. and Ohio EPAs turned the investigation over to OSHA.

Accidents can be large and catastrophic, but they can also be more mundane, and less dramatic. While the former might grab national headlines, the latter are potentially more insidious, because their impacts can be minimized or ignored. But, if common, the cumulative effect can be significant over time. The Ohio EPA list of "Reported WTI Equipment/ Procedural Failures and Incidents," from the earliest trial burns in January 1993 covering all operations through mid 2003, contains references to 115 episodes where problems arose at the plant. When I visited the WTI plant, the managers and operators that I talked to minimized these problems, pointing out that a number of them involved such things as fires in the solid waste pit, fires that are soon put out by an automatic sprinkler system, the fumes of which are contained by the negative air pressure under which many of the facility's buildings operate. In fact, waste pit fires are among the most common of the incidents reported. It is difficult to know with certainty what the environmental impact of these fires is, given the lack of properly working ambient air monitors. Other incidents were more troubling or more noticeable or both. Several times odors from released gases permeated the town. On one occasion the substance was mercaptan, a chemical used to lend natural gas its smell.[152] The odor was detectable all the way to Weirton, West Virginia, almost twenty miles away. On two other occasions, thiophenol was released, inundating the town with the smell of cat urine.[153] Twice exceeded limits on arsenic release were reported.[154]

The WTI Risk Phase II Assessment alluded to oversight and operations problems at the facility, stating, "One concern expressed has been that all the recurring fires, fugitive releases, waste feed cutoffs, etc., at WTI indicate negligent management operations." The assessment clearly states that "there have been compliance problems at this plant." The recommended response was "that both the U.S. EPA and the Ohio EPA continue to enforce the regulations and permit requirements, and work to ensure that problems involving releases are investigated and solved."[155] Compliance problems have, however, continued to dog the facility. In June 2005, the U.S. EPA leveled a more than $600,000 fine against WTI for, among other things, exceeding dioxin limits by five times during the most recent test burn.

While the case of Donna Trueblood did not involve an accident per se, it indicated a set of practices that might further undermine the confidence of local residents and others in the continued safe operations. Trueblood had been an employee for Von Roll America since January, 1999. She had worked as a service technician at the plant and had been a member of the drum crew. As such, her duties included sampling waste containers to check their contents, reviewing the manifests, determining whether the contents of the drums corresponded to statements on the manifest, signing the manifests and then handling the drums themselves. Trueblood contended that in the course of attempting to do her job responsibly, she had been subjected to harassment by management, that she had been subjected to a layoff, that she was prevented from applying for new positions within the facility, that she had been subjected to unwarranted disciplinary actions, and that she was eventually discharged on October 25, 2002.[156] As noted in chapter 3, the Trueblood case led to some interesting findings regarding the ownership of facility. Here, however, I want to focus on the operational problems at the facility that the Trueblood case revealed.

Initially hired under contract for services, Donna Trueblood was soon put on the drum crew as a full-time employee. Some of her fellow workers considered her be a conscientious employee, but one, Curt Cox, believed Trueblood to have a "big mouth," and "he foresaw that her views would conflict with the corporate culture" (7). As a member of the drum crew,

Trueblood was intimately involved with the handling of wastes that came into the facility. Examining manifests and checking their accuracy is an important part of this process, due to legal requirements under RCRA that wastes be tracked "from cradle to grave." Trueblood found numerous daily inaccuracies in the manifests. Sometimes waste containers were not labeled properly, at other times concentrations of wastes were incorrect, and at times the shipping name of the waste was wrong. Waste generators were not always careful at specifying the wastes that they were sending to the facility. Given these circumstances, it is the obligation of the facility to make appropriate corrections so that a final accounting of all wastes can be made (8).

Trueblood would carefully check the wastes against the manifests and record any discrepancies that existed. Customers, however, were unhappy with this practice, because it would generate red flags that might be noticed by state and federal regulators, resulting in requirements for further accounting of what wastes were being generated and how they were being disposed. Because of this, employees were encouraged, if not required, to change the actual manifest rather than note discrepancies on a separate report. Management instructed drum crews to mark discrepancies from Heritage Environmental Services on a separate sheet and not to change the manifests themselves. Trueblood resisted these practices and complained about them. She testified that her relationship with her supervisor began to deteriorate when she started to complain that the company was not following practices that were required by law (9).

Because of Trueblood's practices of noting manifest discrepancies, she was instructed to contact customer service before she noted any. Customer service would attempt to contact the customer to resolve the issues. Unfortunately for Trueblood, her attempts to keep accurate records didn't stop with the wastes that she checked. She also noted mistakes in manifests that were being examined by her coworkers and her supervisor, Juanita Kuhn. Trueblood felt as though the practices that the company was engaged in violated the law governing hazardous wastes disposal. Apparently, because of her resistance to following management directives, performance reports on her work on the manifests was rated average or below average. On April 2001, she was given a written warning by her supervisor about mistakes that she had made on manifests (9).

Trueblood sent an e-mail to Pat Natali at the Ohio EPA noting that she believed VRA to be violating RCRA compliance rules. She continued to communicate with Ms. Natali about ongoing problems that she perceived to be occurring at the site. As a result of this, and charges made by a former employee, Terry Lancaster, the Ohio EPA conducted an investigation of the WTI facility in the winter of 2002. According to the OEPA, Trueblood's information was helpful in dealing with a variety of compliance issues at the plant.

Rumors, however, were now apparently swirling that Trueblood had contacted the Ohio EPA on her own, without telling management of her decision to do this. David Cuppett, Von Roll's on-site environmental manager, informed Fred Sigg, the plant's manager, of these rumors. Sigg, troubled, he said, about possible health and safety issues at the plant, took an interest. Sigg in turn informed the company's president, Rudolph Zaengerle, concerned that Trueblood "may have conveyed information to the EPA without telling management." Zaengerle informed Sigg that VRA had a right to know what kind of information was being communicated. He told Fred Sigg to "defend our right" (10).

Partly in response to this meeting, Sigg called Trueblood to his office and advised her that he had knowledge about "health and safety" complaints that she had made to the Ohio EPA without first informing the management of her concerns. He wanted to see her communications with the agency. Trueblood said that she was frightened by the meeting and was worried that she would lose her job. She was somewhat evasive with her answers. She did not say that she had made "health and safety" complaints, because she believed her complaints to be "environmental." And with regard to communications with the Ohio EPA, she simply said that she had always been "cooperative" with them (10). Sigg testified during the trial that he understood that such communications were protected under whistle-blower statutes.

After the meeting, Sigg sent Trueblood a letter (dated March 11, 2002). In it he stated that he'd become aware that Trueblood had communicated with the Ohio EPA, that he was "disappointed" and "concerned" that she had not first notified the VRA management regarding the "health and safety violations," and that if employees encountered such violations, they should notify the management. He then requested that Trueblood do two things. "1. Provide VRA with any and all documents, including all e-mails sent to the Ohio EPA inspector, regarding or referring to any alleged health and safety violations at the VRA facility in East Liverpool, Ohio. 2. Report any and all concerns regarding any alleged health and safety violations occurring at the VRA facility in East Liverpool, Ohio first to VRA management. We expect that you will notify VRA management of any alleged health and safety violations immediately upon becoming aware of the alleged violations" (11). He concluded with the statement that "we expect our employees to fully comply with our requirement to immediately notify VRA management of any potential or existing health and safety violations at the facility" (11).

While VRA management maintained that the meeting with Trueblood wasn't "disciplinary," she was quite upset by it and took sick leave on March 13 for "acute anxiety" (12). Soon thereafter, Sigg wrote a follow-up letter to Trueblood (March 18), in which he was "reiterating my concern regarding your alleged health, safety, and environmental compliance violations" at the facility. He again asked for e-mails and any notes with which she had communicated with the Ohio EPA, and he also again noted that "We expect all of our employees to fully comply with our requirement to immediately notify VRA management of any potential or existing health, safety, or environmental violations at our facility" (12). Sigg then called Trueblood at home and requested her communications. She said she didn't have them. She also said that she had notified her supervisor of problems that she had encountered. In response, Sigg sent her another letter, confirming her statements that "no such communication took place and that all potential compliance issues you were aware of had been communicated to a management person." He then noted that he considered this "non-disciplinary" matter to be "closed" (12). Pat Natali considered VRA's reactions to Trueblood's actions to be "surprising" and "out-of-the-ordinary" (12).

After this series of meetings and exchanges, Donna Trueblood's health began to deteriorate. She had acute anxiety and stress reactions. She was depressed and was unable to return to work. Her doctor diagnosed her as having "major depressive disorder-moderate-single-episode; occupational problems" (12). She wouldn't return to work until early May. In the meantime, she attempted to move within the company to become a customer service representative, although she was not offered the position. When she asked for vacation time for a day off (feeling sick), she was given sick time and then given a warning for exceeding her allotted sick leave. She was given a "minor offense" for "excessive absenteeism by the disciplinary committee" (15–16).

On May 22, Trueblood was working with her supervisor, Ms. Kuhn, on the drum crew unloading drums onto a conveyor belt. Trueblood used a knife to jam the fail-safe mechanism on the conveyor belt. Kuhn, observing this, warned her not to do it, although Trueblood said that it was a common practice by the drum crew, and it was done openly, with no previous warnings issued by supervisors. During the disciplinary investigation, two other employees admitted to doing this as well. The knife incident, along with the minor offense for excessive absenteeism, led to a one-week suspension without pay (16). Upon returning to work, Trueblood continued to have problems. She was hospitalized for withdrawal from her medications. She missed work because she was stranded in Texas at one point, at another because of menstrual cramping. She eventually exhausted all of her disability and leave time. She was again disciplined for absenteeism. The cumulative record led to her dismissal on October 25, 2002, two days after she sent another e-mail to Natali at the EPA with concerns regarding the proper cleaning of empty hazardous waste containers (17–18).

The administrative judge in the case, Richard Morgan, wrote an opinion extremely sympathetic to Donna Trueblood. While he conceded that some, including her supervisor, Ms. Kuhn, may have found her to be something of a "know-it-all," who was at times "argumentative," he believed that the actions taken against her were largely the result of her communications with the Ohio EPA, communications that were protected under a variety of federal environmental statues. He found her meeting with Fred Sigg to be intimidating, in spite of Mr. Sigg's contention that it was not intended to be disciplinary. In the judge's words, "Mr. Sigg not only wanted to know the substance of what she had told the OEPA, but must have known the manner in which Ms. Trueblood was approached would be intimidating" (32). Von Roll's policy, which most employees apparently followed (a problem in and of itself), of requiring consultation with the management before approaching EPA was illegal. Under whistleblower protection statutes that covered Donna Trueblood, "an employee may not be disciplined for failing to observe an established chain of command when making safety complaints" (40). The judge found, in fact, that "Mr. Sigg's actions had a devastating psychological and physiological impact on Ms. Trueblood. In essence, "Her work environment became hostile." From the meeting onward, the actions that the company took to discipline Ms. Trueblood "were motivated by the desire to eventually discharge [her]." They had a "retaliatory animus" and as a result constituted an awful form of discrimination (24). Moreover, in spite of the legal separation that existed between Heritage Environmental Services and Von Roll, the judge found that that HES/VRA president Zaengerle, in effect, "pulled the strings" with regard to actions taken against Trueblood. He was intimately involved in many of the decisions that eventually led to her discharge (33).

The judge questioned the credibility of plant managers, especially Fred Sigg. There appeared to be much forgetfulness. The judge found Sigg to be a very intelligent and focused manager who was "unusually 'forgetful' for a man of his ability." His testimony also seemed to contradict itself (26).

Judge Martin found Trueblood's request for $50,000 in compensatory damages to be quite reasonable. He ordered her reinstatement, the expungement of her disciplinary record, back pay and benefits, and exemplary damages of $125,000, along with attorney's fees. Liabilities were split 90/10 between VRA and HES. He also required VRA and HES to post notices in all of their facilities that stated, in part, "There is no requirement for employees who wish to or do contact federal agencies, such as the Environmental Protection Agencies, with their concerns over environmental compliance matters to first report such matters to either a supervisor or to management. Any policy stating or suggesting otherwise is unlawful" (50–51).

The decision was a complete and total rebuke of not only the HES/VRA's actions in the Trueblood case but both companies' policies, which had been operating in violation of number of federal whistle-blower statutes. A spokesman for Von Roll refused to comment on the case pending an appeal. Donna Trueblood returned to work to be reinstated, but the company refused to allow her into the facility.

What Are the Impacts?

Given the imponderables associated with the "what" and "where" of WTI's effluent emissions, any determination of the effects on the surrounding ecologies must be considered as indeterminate. Yet even the estimates given by U.S. EPA regarding emissions reveal potential problems. One of the primary tools that U.S. EPA uses to estimate the impacts of toxic substances is via established "toxicity values" for a variety of inorganic and organic chemicals. Toxicity values are expressed as Toxic Equivalents (TEQs) of TCDD (tetrachlorodibenzo-p-dioxin), which is assigned a value of one. Each analyzed compound is then rated in terms of its equivalence to TCDD. These values are the primary references to be used by risk assessors in their analysis of cancer risks.[157] As of January 2004, this list included 728 organic and inorganic elements and compounds for which some kind of reference dose as been established (a reference dose being the point beneath which toxic effects do not, according to the EPA, occur). Reference doses are set for dermal contact, oral ingestion, and inhalation. Each listed substance does not, however, have a reference dose for each potential pathway into the body. In other words, there are numerous gaps in the EPA's database. More important, perhaps, in the case of WTI and other hazardous waste incinerators, there are thousands of released substances that have not even been chemically characterized, much less analyzed for potential health impacts. The strategy taken with regard to these substances in the WTI risk assessment was to ignore them.

The EPA's 1994 Draft Risk Assessment Guidelines recommended that 236 chemicals be included in future risk assessments. Partly in response to this, the WTI risk assessment began with a list of two hundred substances, and included all with toxicity values in the inhalation study, but included fewer in the food chain analysis. According to Schannauer, "the lack of EPA-approved toxicity values was the major factor prompting the shortening of the list."[158] And he goes on to state: "The lack of information about toxicities and likely emissions rates was most influential in narrowing the list of compounds to be addressed. Seventy-seven compounds were deleted from the food chain analysis due solely to the lack of EPA-determined toxicity values for cancer and seventy-two other compounds (including the seventeen dioxins and furans) were deleted due to the lack of EPA-determined reference doses for noncancer effects. The EPA deleted thirty-one additional compounds because the agency could not estimate its emissions rates."[159] In the end, then, the WTI risk assessment included only 15 of 174 organic residues, seventeen dioxin-furan congeners, and 13 metals. The rest were ignored, not because they were safe, but because information about them was unavailable.

This list was narrowed even further for noncancer risks, because the EPA has no officially established toxicity values for noncancer risks for dioxins and furans and many metals.[160] This is in spite of the fact that the 1994 Dioxin Reassessment lists several potential noncancer effects, including immune system disruptions (which can increase disease susceptibility as well as encourage autoimmune disorders), alterations in hormonal activity, elevated gamma glutamyl transference activity (resulting in possible liver damage), endometriosis, and increased risk of diabetes.[161] In fact, the Dioxin Reassessment suggests that "subtle changes in biochemistry and physiology . . . are seen with TCDD exposures at or just several fold above these average TEQ levels." As a result, and given the estimated distribution of TCDDs throughout the population, it can be inferred that "some more highly exposed members of the general population or more highly exposed, special populations, *may* be at risk for a number of adverse effects" such as those listed above. The reassessment states further that "this inference that more highly exposed members of the population may be at risk for various noncancer effects is supported by observations in animals, by some human information from highly exposed cohorts, and by scientific inference."[162]

The WTI Risk Assessment recognized the potential for noncancer effects, particularly endocrine disruption, stating, with apparent reference to the reassessment, that "the U.S. EPA is aware of the growing body of scientific research that indicates a number of synthetic chemicals may interfere with the normal functioning of human and wildlife endocrine systems." Yet the authors argued that since dose-response data were not available, it could not be included in the risk analysis. As the U.S. EPA put it, "Without this type of information, a quantitative risk assessment cannot be performed for these effects at this point in time."[163]

In response to this claim, Tom Webster, an environmental health specialist at Boston University, observed, "This is at best a half truth and has the appearance of hiding unpleasant information." While the EPA may not have promulgated official guidelines, the EPA's own dioxin reassessment had concluded that any standard for dioxin-like compounds would be below current "background levels." In fact, the EPA's reassessment of dioxin risk states that reference doses for dioxin and dioxin-like compounds should be set at levels 10 to 100 times below current intake levels. And the results of EPA's analysis were widely known.[164] Ten years after the

reassessment, the U.S. EPA still had not implemented standards for exposure related to noncancer effects, probably because a standard below current background levels would, if strictly applied, force the conclusion that
any additional point sources of dioxin-like compounds would pose unacceptable health risks. To address the issue in the WTI risk assessment,
EPA simply compared the dose exposures expected from WTI, compared
them with national average background levels, and concluded that the
additional risk was tolerable.[165] Yet the Dioxin Reassessment makes clear
that even within the general population, exposure levels necessarily vary
below and above the national average, so the assumption that any particular
community experiences "average" exposure is itself a matter of conjecture.
Beyond that, however, it would be expected that a community such as East
Liverpool, with a long history of industrial activity, would be likely to have
above the national average of exposure even without the presence of a hazardous waste incinerator. While the risk analysis makes claims to "conservative" estimates at many points, such a set of assumptions regarding
noncancer effects of dioxin-like compounds in a community such as East
Liverpool, seems to be wildly optimistic.

Who Is Most Affected?

The effects of toxics when they enter into the atmosphere and the food
chain are not evenly felt. The most vulnerable segments of the population
are the very young, those in the earliest stages of development, especially
breast-feeding infants, and those that experience the highest rates of exposure through consumption of local food sources. In many communities in the United States the local farmers' market is a place where community members congregate to buy fresh, often organic, produce, tastier
and healthier than that available for purchase in the area's Wal-Mart
Superstore. In the East Liverpool area, however, a person would be wise
to avoid a regular diet of local produce, because it is grown in soil and air
that has small but potentially hazardous levels of dioxin, dioxin-like compounds, and heavy metals. At even higher risk is someone who eats "up
the food chain," for example, a local resident who consumes locally grown
beef. Joy Allison, one of the earliest and most determined opponents of
WTI, lived directly across the Ohio River from WTI, on a hill where she

raised cattle that she slaughtered and consumed. According to assistant administrator Richard Guimond's 1993 internal EPA memo, a hypothetical person in Joy Allison's position would be most likely to die from cancer as a result of toxics emitted from the plant. In a grim irony, nonsmoking Joy Allison died of lung cancer in 1998.[166] The Phase II risk assessment did not calculate the impacts of WTI emissions on breast-feeding infants, even though this would be the population group at highest risk.[167]

The WTI risk assessment relied on "national statistics in lieu of site-specific demographic information" with regard to demographic information. Specifically, it assumed that people "generally only live in an area for nine years." This hardly seems to be a legitimate assumption given stability of a community such as this, which is hardly comparable to, say, Palo Alto or Madison. One of the reasons that opposition to the facility was able to take root in the community was because of the commitment of longtime residents to protecting what they felt was the safety and environmental integrity of their community.

The standard of an increase in one cancer death per million in a given population is, according to U.S. regulatory standards, an "acceptable" risk. Advocates of the current trajectory of industrialization and the forces of capital that it represents are quick to point out that other risks of life in the modern world are much greater. The risk of dying in an automobile accident, for example, is higher than this, as is the risk of dying of cancer from smoking cigarettes, which millions of people do every day, willingly, to satisfy pleasure or addiction. Still, the comparisons help to disguise what is happening in any particular case. In this case, regulatory bodies have arrived at the conclusion that sacrificing two to three people who live in a particular area to a potentially deadly disease is a fair sacrifice, because the benefits of hazardous waste disposal via incineration make it so. Moreover, every risk assessment chooses one or more anonymous persons in each hypothetical sample population as a sacrificial lamb. The social and moral acceptability of the risk assessment depends utterly on the anonymity of these persons. If the actual person being targeted were known, then the acceptability the risk assessment's findings would be seriously undermined or would collapse outright. Suppose, for example, that EPA officials were to go to the nearby elementary school with the names of two of the students and tag them as the future cancer patients who would be chosen as a necessity for the facility's operations. They would no longer be "two in a million"; they would now represent two actual human beings. Ignorance fosters tolerance for sacrificing the innocent, but are the consequences acceptable from any reasonably standard of fairness or decency? "Well," starts the familiar response, "we close our eyes every day to these sorts of sacrifices, and have to or the modern order would disintegrate." Roll the dice, hope for the best. The proposition holds a certain undeniability, or maybe inevitability, but the social cost of willful denial is bound to take its toll over time. What are we actually getting in return. Comfort? Security? Wealth? Some are, and others aren't.

A risk assessment is a chain of uncertainties. And each link in the chain is forged by experts in that particular field of inquiry. Chemists analyze the properties of materials that enter into the facility and consider their transformations as they are intermixed with one another and then burned at high temperatures. Physicists estimate the wind currents and how they will carry and deposit the trace amounts of chemicals that flow from the stack. Biologists study the effects of chemical contamination on human health. Ecologists study the effects on larger natural systems. At each stage, complicated technical arguments occur regarding measurement, estimate, and meaning. The links in the chain are then pulled together in impressively massive documents that, when closely examined, turn out to be a set of loosely connected particulars, because no one person has the expertise or the mental capacity to survey and effectively understand and criticize each step along the way. Any attempt to target one piece will lead to the legitimate contention that another important piece has been ignored. And since the risk assessment is grounded in a complex regulatory regime, any valid criticism can legitimately be ignored as long as it is interpreted by authorities to be beyond the borders of regulatory control. In the case of WTI, one peer reviewer concluded, "The risk assessment has a general tendency to bury the bad news or split it up into smaller perhaps more 'acceptable' pieces."[168] According to the official story, the findings of a risk assessment are "sound science," but citizens can hardly be blamed if they view them with caution that is grounded in reasonable skepticism and common sense.

In truth, the determination of risks, no matter how impressive the documents and studies involved, devolves to the central question of "how do we live?" "Risk calculations," as Ulrich Beck notes, "never lead to what they are supposed to lead to produce, namely acceptance." How could they? Establishing and sustaining the life of a community involves much more than avoiding risk. For one thing, in a democratic community, questions of power are central. Who controls the life of a community? Experts, regulators, and business managers, or the extraordinary people who live there? In matters of risk, "No one is an expert."[169]

Conclusion:
Where Do We Go from Here?

The future is inevitable and precise, but it may not occur.
—*Jorge Luis Borges*, Other Inquisitions

Under the productive regimes and power networks of the twentieth century's chemical industrial economy, huge amounts and varieties of goods have been generated for consumption, but the external costs have been massive and yet to be fully counted. Industrial systems have been richly productive, while also being dirty, exploitative, and inefficient. In time, as the ecological accounting books move toward balance, the wasteful and destructive tendencies of industrial production may undermine the material and cultural foundations that make its productivity possible in the first place. Hazardous waste is only one example of the environmental and efficiency failures of the industrial system, but it crystallizes them in clear, definite terms.

Within hazardous waste is concentrated the wasteful and inequitable practices that pervade current systems of production and consumption. Around it have been organized complicated networks of power, for good reason. A commitment to hazardous waste incineration implies commitment to the industrial economy itself with the inequalities that are endemic to it. Those that benefit most from consumer society tend to waste the most, while those that benefit the least tend to waste the least. Material possession, in general, is highly correlated with high levels of external costs, one of which is the generation and disposal of waste. At the same time, those that benefit most directly from consumer society harm those that benefit the least by either implicitly or explicitly encouraging hazardous and other wastes to be dumped in their communities. Wastefulness and inequality are in this sense inseparable. It is no accident that the environmental justice movement organized itself around issues of waste disposal, because waste disposal sits at the heart of deep structural inequalities that exist in the United States and globally. How or whether the waste problems can be solved, then, needs to be considered in light of existing structures of political power.

Reduce, Reuse, Recycle

Even without disturbing current industrial practices, there have been and probably will continue to be innovations that will reduce the amounts of toxic wastes that are generated. The decline in hazardous waste production in the 1990s was largely the result of decisions by waste producers to find mechanisms to reduce, reuse, and recycle materials that became hazardous waste. This was partly, at least, in response to market and political forces, which drove up disposal costs during the period.[1]

More could be done. If, for example, chemical wastes were kept separate from one another, in some cases they can be recycled and used again. Unfortunately, however, waste chemicals are usually mixed together, making some disposal method inevitable.[2] Given industry practices, the waste disposal problem becomes more intractable, but that does not mean that waste has to be burned or buried. Phase separation and component separation techniques are designed to allow for reuse of many chemical wastes by returning substances to a manageable state. Chemical transformation techniques can detoxify hazardous substances. Biological transformation techniques use microorganisms to break complex hydrocarbons and heavy metals into component parts.[3] Many of these alternatives to incineration have been available for decades. From a purely technical standpoint, there are, in other words, already available means to deal with hazardous waste without burning it. Incineration may be less expensive than other techniques, but that is only true if external costs generally shifted to the less affluent and powerful are not taken into account.

In 2002, TDP, or thermal depolymerization, emerged as a potential "magic bullet" to solid and hazardous waste disposal problems. Discovered by Paul Baskis, TDP is a process by which organic matter is cooked at 500 degrees Fahrenheit under 600 pounds of pressure, turning it into a partially depolymerized soup that is then dehydrated via depressurization. The result is steam, which is used to heat the first phase of the process, solid material (that can be used for a variety of purposes), and the remaining organic goop. The highly concentrated liquid is then distilled via the same process that is used to refine oil. The result, hypothetically at least, is high-grade heating oil, powdered carbon, and solids. What constitutes the residual solid material depends on what is fed into the process. At a plant in Carthage, Missouri, ConAgra Foods processes the waste material left from turkey slaughter, yielding oil, minerals that can be used for fertilizer, and fatty acids that can be used for soap, tires, and lubricants. Feeding polyvinyl chloride into the process yields hydrochloric acid—which has multiple industrial uses—and heating oil.[4] If an infrastructure of such plants were fully established and operating according to plan, Superfund sites could literally become repositories of materials that would be "mined" for industrial use.

Initially TDP generated a good deal of excitement. *Discover* magazine did a feature story on it. Baskis turned his patents for the process over to Changing World Technologies, whose CEO, Brian Appel, put together a group of private investors who invested $40 million to build TDP facilities. Appel is not an engineer but a businessman with strong ties to the Republican Party. He was able to bring CIA director James Woolsey and former Bush Sr. science adviser Alf Andreassen onto the CWT board.[5] The Carthage plant has, by all accounts, been successful, disposing of the waste of 30,000 turkeys a day, and another plant is being built near Philadelphia to deal with the city's sewage. Warren Buffet is one of the primary investors.[6] CWT has continued to receive accolades. *Scientific American* named the company as one 2003's top fifty new technologies.[7] It has even been the subject of a question on the television program *Hollywood Squares*.[8]

Yet things have not been entirely smooth sailing for the company. In November 2003 the U.S. Public Interest Group (PIRG) reported on its Web site that CWT would be receiving $95 million in tax write-offs. This led to press accounts of CWT as a leading beneficiary of energy-bill pork.[9] CWT denied the claim, arguing that it received only $148,000 over a four-year period, hardly making the application for it worth the time and effort involved.[10] More significantly, perhaps, a pilot plant in Philadelphia has had its share of problems. The oil that was generated from sewage conversion was contaminated with acids and dioxin, making it unusable. The promise of a relatively simple "technical fix" does not, then, seem to be on the horizon at this point.

While changes in disposal and recycling practices themselves significantly decrease or eliminate the need for hazardous waste incineration, equivalent if not greater impacts could be achieved by altering practices of production. Generating large volumes of hazardous waste is not an economic necessity. Substitutes exist for virtually all the products that are now manufactured with the use of chlorine, one of the primary constituents of nearly all forms of hazardous waste. The widespread use of chlorine in industrial production is mostly a post–World War II phenomenon. As Joe Thornton notes: "Chlorine chemistry has been a widespread part of modern life since about 1950. Before chlorine, we had food, cars, electricity, telephones, airplanes, refrigeration, radios, films, antibiotics, vaccines, beautiful clothing, and sturdy heated homes. Chlorine chemistry has penetrated today's production technologies, but it is hardly the foundation of modern life as we know it."[11]

Ninety percent of chlorine production goes to a relatively limited number of major applications, some of which could be minimized or eliminated, and some of which could be replaced. For example, pesticide use can be drastically limited or eliminated with organic farming techniques, and non-chlorine-based pesticides are available. Paper does not have to be bleached a blinding white, and non-chlorine-based bleaching agents are available. Sulfuric and nitric acids can be used in place of hydrochloric acid. A combination of agents can be used in lieu of chlorine-based solvents. Drinking water can be treated with filters and ultraviolet light. A variety of other materials, from wood to chlorine-free plastics, are available as PVC plastics substitutes (365–67). The difficulties involved with eliminating chlorine from industrial production should not, however, be underestimated, and it would be "of magnitude equal to or greater than the post–cold war demilitarization of the civilian economy in the United States" (365). In the long run, there are economic benefits from doing so, benefits that are overwhelming when balanced against current external costs. Moreover, while entirely eliminating chlorine use would be expensive, a drastic reduction could be achieved for a relatively modest price.

A report that the Chlorine Institute commissioned from Charles River Associates projected that a 95 percent reduction in chlorine use could be achieved for approximately $17 billion a year, and a 97.6 percent reduction could be achieved for about $22 billion a year (368–69).

Politics and Markets

The presence of technical means for eliminating hazardous waste does not, of course, guarantee their use. How and whether they are implemented is obviously crucial. Historically environmental protection in the United States has depended heavily on complex regulatory regimes. Imperfect as they may be, they have resulted in some control over release of various pollutants, along with protection of ecosystems and wildlife.

POPs

In the case of hazardous waste, the most important recent regulatory development has occurred at the international level. In May 2002, 127 national governments signed the Stockholm Convention on Persistent Organic Pollutants (POPs), an agreement that proposes bans or significant restrictions on the so-called dirty dozen petrochemical agents. A number of pesticides are banned under the treaty: aldrin, chlordane, DDT,[12] dieldren, endrin, heptachlor, mirex, toxapene, and hexachlorobenzene. Given that most of these pesticides are already prohibited in the United States and Western Europe, the convention can be criticized for simply ratifying current practices. Nevertheless, it is symbolically important, reflecting an international consensus regarding reductions in production and use of toxics. The primary impact of the pesticide provisions of the treaty will be on Third World nations, many of which continue to use them. Given that the world's less-affluent economies are tied to U.S. chemical producers through a "circle of poison," the POPs treaty has the potential to decrease dependency.

Under the treaty, dioxins, furans, and PCBs are slated for elimination. Given that PCBs are no longer produced in the United States, the impact here will be modest. Dioxins and furans are not, nor have they ever been, manufactured for any industrial use but are the unwanted by-products of combustion of chlorinated hydrocarbons. To bring their release under strict controls would be an important regulatory move. Substantial restrictions on the release of furans and dioxins would put an end to hazardous and other waste incineration anywhere in the world. Under the POPs convention, signatories are required to develop plans for reducing emissions of dioxins and furans, but the imposed restrictions are at this point so indefinite as not to pose a serious threat to any industrial activities, including incineration, for the foreseeable future. In fact, the convention was adopted with the support of the chemical industry.[13]

Under the convention's regime, new substances can be added to the list of banned chemicals, but only after scientific proof of toxicity has been established. Environmentalists had pushed for incorporating the less-restrictive precautionary principle that would shift the burden to proving the safety of potentially toxic chemicals. The chemical industry successfully resisted these efforts.[14] Between the convention's first draft and its enactment as the Protocol on Persistent Organic Pollutants, four other substances were added to the list of banned chemicals: lindane, chlordecone, hexabromobiphenyl, and polycyclic-aromatic hydrocarbons.[15]

The Bush administration made a commitment to support rapid ratification of the treaty. The Senate, however, has yet to act more than six years after President Bush assumed office. The Bush administration proposed legislation to Congress in April 2002 that would have amended the Federal Insecticide, Fungicide, and Rodenticide Act (FIFRA) and the Toxic Substances Control Act (TSCA) to bring the United States in line with the current POPs protocols. Still, within this proposal was a provision that any future chemical bans be subject to congressional approval, a provision widely seen as violating the spirit of the treaty.[16] The POPs treaty is certainly a step in the right direction, and part of a whole set of international environmental agreements that have broad global support, but which are undermined by U.S. intransigence.

Natural Capitalism

Over the past decade, a transition has occurred in environmental policy thinking in which markets, rather than regulatory structures, are conceived of as having a central, if not *the* central, role. There are multiple reasons for this, some of which are quite pragmatic, such as the continued withdrawal of the public sector from its role in environmental protection. Market-based systems for environmental protection are part of larger trends toward deregulation and privatizing that which was once a public responsibility. Moreover, attractive and sophisticated proponents of the market system have emerged who have argued persuasively that markets will inevitably align themselves to the ecological contexts within which they are seated.

Natural Capitalism, by Paul Hawken, Amory Lovins, and L. Hunter Lovins, has been a central text in market-based environmental thinking. It is a fascinating and in many respects compelling book. The central premise is that industrialized societies are on the verge of, as the book's subtitle suggests, "the next industrial revolution." The book is part Buckminster Fuller, part Francis Taylor, and part Alvin Toffler: Fuller in its attention to sustainable technology; Taylor in its attention to efficiency; and Toffler in its optimistic presentation of a brighter and seemingly inevitable future.

One of the central figures in *Natural Capitalism* is Taiichi Ohno, the father of the Toyota production system. Ohno was obsessed with the elimination of waste, defined as "any human activity which absorbs resources but creates no value." Ohno was opposed to "every form of waste." Waste, for Ohno, carried a kind of existential significance. The Japanese term *muda* incorporates "waste," "futility," and "purposelessness." In the business world, it includes everything from improperly inspecting products for defects to generating demand slack with overproduction. Ohno believed in "lean thinking," and he was the developer of the concept of "just-in-time production." Ohno sought radical efficiency and favored ongoing assessments of productive processes to reveal hidden *muda.*[17] He favored simplicity in the processes of production as well as the products produced. The Nissan Micra, for example, has one mirror style with four parts, whereas the VW Golf has four styles, each with eighteen or nineteen moving parts. As such, the Nissan Micra eliminates *muda* (130–31).

The authors of *Natural Capitalism* give Ohno's thinking an ecological turn. Nothing, seemingly, is wasted in nature. Radically efficient production can mirror nature in this regard. Under a regime of natural capitalism, service-based industries that favor durability over obsolescence would become the norm. Consumers would buy contracts for the use of goods that, when they have reached the end of their useful life, will be reacquired by producers and recycled into new products. Ray Anderson's company Interface Carpets is the model. Interface leases floor coverings that are exchanged for new ones when they are worn out, the old ones then being recycled (17). Again, the emphasis is on eliminating waste. Efficient production techniques organized around the delivery of services draw on natural capital while not drawing it down. The system is thus self-sustaining and "perfectly attuned to what customers want, the environment deserves, labor needs, and the economy can support" (19).

Hawken and the Lovinses see themselves as charting a fourth path between "Blues," mainstream free marketeers, "Reds," socialists, and "Greens," who "see the world primarily in terms of ecosystems, and thus concentrate on depletion, damage, pollution, and population growth." "Whites," on the other hand, "are the synthesists," who develop a "middle way of integration, reform, respects, and reliance. They reject ideologies . . . argue that all issues are local," recognize market imperfections, favor social solutions that "naturally arise from place and culture," and favor the "Taoist reminder that good rulers make their subjects feel as if they succeeded in themselves" (312). Rejecting "ideology" always has a certain appeal in American political culture, but it is important to keep in mind that Taoism holds no democratic imperatives. Moreover, capitalism is not simply a system of markets but a system of power. Ignoring this central feature of capitalist development may lead one toward overly optimistic predictions about its potentialities to be both humane and ecologically sustainable. Moreover, a principled aversion to ideology may result in confusing a series of interesting, yet disparate, green practices with social and ecological transformation. Just-in-time production, for example, is not necessarily humane or environmentally friendly. One of its most effective corporate practitioners is Wal-Mart.

Green building practices offer concrete evidence of natural capitalism's progress for Hawken and the Lovinses. Examples include a Lockheed building in California, a mail-sorting office in Reno, a Boeing lighting system, and Wal-Mart's "Eco-Store" in Lawrence, Kansas. According to *Natural Capitalism*, "These and other well-measured case studies now show consistent gains in labor productivity of around 6–16 percent when workers feel more comfortable thermally, when they can see what they're doing, and when they can hear themselves think" (89). The emphasis on worker productivity, one of the long-running obsessions of America's business elite, is telling, as is the silence regarding the products made by Lockheed and Boeing (military hardware) and the labor practices of Wal-Mart (horrendous). As long as a business organizes its workplace to generate more satisfaction for at least some of its employees, then an advance in "natural capitalism" has apparently been made. But should Ford Motor Company, the corporation primarily responsible for the fashion in sports utility vehicles, receive kudos because managers built a "green building"? Hawken and the Lovinses even give credit to Shell Oil as an environmentally friendly company, after its deplorable actions in the death by hanging of the Nigerian environmental activist Ken Saro-Wiwa, because in response to boycotts and even the bombing of its stations in Holland, "Shell has begun to re-examine all its racial, economic, and environmental policies" (319).

While sustainable business practices are certainly laudable, the likelihood that capitalism will evolve into a humane and ecological system "naturally" seems unlikely. External costs of industrial production, which are nothing more than Ohno's *muda,* have existed in capitalist economies from the start. If capitalist-oriented systems have not eliminated them at this point, then what reason have we to believe that they will do so in the future without massive and persistent political intervention? Capitalism is not, unfortunately, a rational system. The irrationalities of capitalism are reinforced by the desire of many humans to assert control and power over other humans and the natural world. Transformations can occur, but general systems of political power can be converted into more humane and democratic ones only via the application of democratic opposition and resistance. The true costs of waste disposal are made explicit when brave people in local communities demand that their neighborhoods and cities not be waste respositories.

The citizens of East Liverpool have made, and will continue to make, an incalculably significant contribution to a sustainable future by resisting the powerful forces that have profited from the system's current organization. They have increased the costs of hazardous waste disposal and thus moved producers closer to more benign forms of production. In the process, they have helped to expose the networks of power that influence all of our lives, and in doing so, they have made contributions that extend beyond any narrow definition of environmental protection.

A Continuing Story

One of the defining characteristics of artists' works—novels, stories, and films—is that, by necessity, they must end, even if the ending is unhappy, indeterminate, or confusing. The story of WTI, however, is a narrative without a clear end. Problems have continued to plague the facility while government regulators have continued to support its operations.[18]

Billy Joe Cole, a fifty-one-year-old man from Perryville, Missouri, fell into his tanker truck while delivering a load a lime slurry to the WTI site in February 2004. Cole apparently called for help, and two other employees at the plant entered the tanker to try to save him. Cole was taken to a local hospital. Neither East Liverpool's police or fire departments were called in response to the problem. According to assistant police chief Gary Cornell, "There was some sort of mix-up."[19] The trucker died soon thereafter. Finding information beyond that, however, became exceedingly difficult, continuing a phenomenon that seems endemic to the WTI narrative.

An e-mail exchange between Terri Swearingen and Gary Victorine, the U.S. EPA Region V administrator, exemplifies the frustrations of a bureaucratic process that seems to have been organized to foster the withholding of information from citizens concerned about the environmental health of their community. In an e-mail to Mr. Victorine, Terri noted that the only information that had been received had been through a press release in the local newspaper, the *East Liverpool Review,* which stated only that an "unidentified driver" inside the tanker truck had died. The press release also stated that the lime slurry, into which the man fell, was a "non hazardous waste."[20] The determination to list lime slurry as non-hazardous seemed odd, or perhaps not so, given the history involved. Terri had a series of specific questions for Victorine. "Why was the driver alone, unsupervised by a WTI employee while on the WTI property?" Terri suggested that leaving a driver alone indicated some potentially serious security problems at the plant. She wanted to know what the protocol was for such accidents, and what protections were offered to other WTI employees. Why was the lime slurry even being brought into the plant in the first place? She asked, "What kind of 'lime slurry' was the driver hauling to WTI? Why was the driver hauling a load of lime slurry to WTI? Was it spent lime slurry—slurry that had been used in some air pollution control device or flue gas cleaning system to remove acid gasses and/or mercury? Were there any other constituents in the lime slurry?" All of Terri's questions were legitimate and on target, a reasonable set of queries to a tragic, if not horrifying, event.

The U.S. EPA, however, had apparently decided that it wanted as little to do with the case as possible. In fact, the determination that lime slurry "was not a hazardous waste" was sufficient to get the EPA entirely off the hook. Thus, in Mr. Victorine's response to Save Our Country, he stated the following:

> Thanks for your message regarding the tragic death of the truck driver at WTI on Monday, January 26. From the information that the Ohio EPA has provided, it seems that the material into which the driver fell was not a waste or a hazardous waste, and was not released into the environment. Based on this, the accident does not appear to be within RCRA authority. It would, however, appear to fall within the authority of the Occupational Safety and Health Agency (OSHA), and the information from Patricia/Michelle indicates that OSHA has already been on site investigation the event.
>
> Even though the event appears to be outside of the RCRA regulations and authority, we will be very interested in reading OSHA's findings on this matter, to determine whether any of its findings and recommendations (with respect to trucks of product) might also be applicable to the handling of hazardous waste.[21]

Terri was not, however, willing to give up on the matter. In a follow-up letter, she responded: "Corrosive waste is *hazardous* waste! How do you know that the waste in the truck tank was not hazardous? Were samples of the waste taken and split for testing with EPA and OSHA? What are the results? Why would a hazardous waste generator send non-hazardous waste to an expensive hazardous waste permitted facility? Who generated the waste? Do you have a copy of the manifest?"[22] All legitimate questions. If the U.S. EPA's entry into the case hinged on whether the material was hazardous, then a determination of how this was arrived at seemed like a reasonable set of queries.

Victorine's response is that the question is "not whether or not the material was hazardous, but whether or not it was waste. The information we have received to date indicates that the lime was a commercial product, and not waste. Regulations under Subtitle C of RCRA, which cover HW management facilities, seem to specifically apply only to wastes, and not to products. . . . Because the regulatory issue is whether it was a waste, not whether it was hazardous, testing is not relevant."[23] In other words, the U.S. EPA would have nothing further to say or do about the case. This left the citizens of East Liverpool where they had generally been: in the dark. Eventually, however, OSHA did find the plant managers to have been negligent, a finding that was upheld throughout the appeals process. This was the second time that WTI had lost an OSHA appeal. Word got out that the drivers' family was planning a wrongful-death suit against Von Roll.

Throughout much of 2003 and 2004, WTI had been seeking a permit renewal under Title V of the Clean Air Act. When I visited the facility in 2004, the public relations person with whom I spoke, Raymond Wayne, told me that WTI had been seeking such compliance, and when it received it, it would be the only hazardous waste incinerator in the United States to have done so. But WTI's attempts to gain the Title V permit were hardly smooth sailing. To achieve Title V compliance, WTI had to pass a test burn. Test burns, it is worth reiterating, take place under highly controlled conditions. They are not done in a random fashion to test the ordinary daily operations of a facility. There is some question whether, even under the best of circumstances, they give an accurate reading of what is generally flowing from the stack, leaking from the seams, and in general being deposited in the local community. The first test burn was undertaken in September 2003. WTI failed. Another was undertaken in December 2003. Again WTI failed. In January 2003, Mr. Cole was killed at the WTI site when he fell into a tanker truck. In February 2004 the Title V permit was authorized by the Ohio EPA. In March, WTI failed another test burn. In April, a fourth test burn was undertaken, and WTI finally passed. Thus the already-accepted permit was legitimized by a fourth test.

In May, another accident occurred at the plant. Sandy Estell, who lives above the incinerator in the East End, said that she saw a ball of fire rising from the plant. "At first you could see some flames, then there was a huge loud explosion and a giant ball of fire shot up in the air. I've never seen anything like it before," she stated in the local paper.[24] The fireball was just to the right of one of the kilns. Raymond Wayne downplayed what he described as an "incident" that "resulted in a brief discharge of smoke." Estell, however, said it generated a noise that rattled her windows and that "the plant was lost in smoke for awhile." Whatever the different accounts, there was little doubt that something had happened. Upon inspection, the fire chief noted that a steel door providing access into the combustion chamber had been blown open.

Terri and Alonzo each decided that they would appeal the Title V permit authorization. The appeal would be heard before the state's Environmental Review Appeals Commissions. It costs nearly $100 to become a party to such an appeal. Applications had to be sent to all of the parties, with five copies going to the board itself. The appealing parties must appear in Columbus for any hearings that would be held (more than 150 miles from East Liverpool). If a party misses even a single meeting, this can be grounds for exclusion from the process. In regulatory parlance, this is known as "citizen participation." WTI, it turns out, was appealing the permit as well, opposing objections to restrictions imposed by the permit on their operations. For WTI, representation at the hearings posed little problem. Charles Waterman, the attorney representing WTI for more than a decade, represented the company. His firm, Bricker and Eckler, has an office in Columbus.

On June 29, a mere two months after the permit was renewed, the U.S. EPA imposed a $643,908 fine on WTI. The EPA complaint pointed to four compliance problems: WTI had (1) "failed to route air emissions through an EPA-approved air pollution control device," (2) "failed to replace absorbing carbon boxes which control air emissions from waste storage tanks," (3) "failed to meet incinerator stack emissions permit (levels) by releasing *five times the dioxin limits allowed during a test*," and (4) "failed to prepare a written manifest for hazardous waste shipped off-site."[25] These violations, while worthy of a more than one-half-million-dollar fine, were not sufficient, of course, to undermine the U.S. EPA's support for the facility's permit. That the U.S. EPA was assessing fines while the Ohio EPA was granting a permit seemed to Terri Swearingen to be simply another irony associated with the WTI story, or, as she put it, "same old, same old." Terri believed the original objections to the facility had been entirely vindicated, especially in terms of the release of dioxin and mercury, which had been continuous problems, problems that had been predicted by opponents and now demonstrated to be true.

Alonzo now seemed to be feeling somewhat optimistic about the possibilities for stopping the facility's operations. For one thing, the U.S. EPA had recently declared the East Liverpool area to be an Environmental Justice site. This meant that special scrutiny would be given to pollution sources there. Not only that, but the NAACP was looking into the case. They were considering putting some resources into the area, and perhaps providing legal counsel to help with the permit appeal. Alonzo saw the permit appeal as an opportunity to raise issues that had been ignored the first time around, for instance, the siting of the facility so close to an elementary school, something that was now prohibited under Ohio law.

Moreover, opponents of the plant had received a document that an anonymous source from within the Ohio EPA had sent to Ohio Citizen Action. It listed hundreds of violations of the Maximum Achievable Control Technology standards. The MACT standards were promulgated by the EPA in September 1999. EPA has touted these as bringing about significant reductions in emissions from hazardous waste incineration combustion sources: dioxins and furans by 70 percent, mercury by 55 percent, cadmium and lead by 88 percent, and particulates by 42 percent.[26] Continuous violation of MACT standards can lead to a facility becoming listed as a High Priority Violator (HPV), moving it to the top of the EPA's enforcement list. Even one violation of MACT standards is enough to make a facility a HPV. In WTI's case, there were hundreds, and WTI exceeded MACT standards 2 percent of the time in 2004.[27] That such information was made available to the public only via a leaked source was, in itself, very troubling.

In the meantime, a human interest story had been circulating through the town regarding a young girl who had been born with hydroma. While her birth weight was five pounds, she had an eight-pound growth attached to the side of her head. The growth was swelling associated with blockages in her lymphatic system. The sac had to be drained, and one of her ears reattached to her head. She was being treated at Children's Hospital in Pittsburgh. Of course, there was not, nor could there be, any direct evidence connecting the girl's condition to WTI, although she did live in the East End. But as Terri told me, when something like that occurred in the area, it was very difficult, if not impossible, not to think about the incinerator. Worrying about such things is in itself one of the external costs imposed on communities.

On July 8, 2005, WTI was recertified as a wildlife habitat. The company held a barbeque to celebrate the event. The current mayor of East Liverpool was on hand for the occasion. Native plant species had been planted on a six-acre area of the facility that had been designated as habitat. Twenty-six species of wildflowers appeared there. Tree swallows were nesting in the bird boxes that had been placed through the area. According to Raymond Wayne, "The ground was prepared by being mowed, treated with herbicide and covered with two inches of topsoil from West Virginia." Not all the efforts at habitat generation had been successful, however. Green ash and river birch, planted in 2002, died "probably," according to Raymond, "because of a dry period." "Bluebirds nested in past years," but this year they did not return.[28]

Acknowledgments

As a matter of propriety and form, academic authors will sometimes state in a preface that a book would not have been possible without the help and support of certain individuals. Sometimes this might be a mentor, a colleague, a friend, or perhaps a spouse. In the case of *Toxic Burn*, the statement is not simply a matter of propriety. This book would literally not have been possible, and would more than likely not have been written, if not for the help of Terri Swearingen and Alonzo Spencer.

Terri is the person who is primarily responsible for drawing me into this project. Had I not had the good fortune of having her answer the phone when I called the number I found on the Web for the Tri-State Environmental Council, I would probably have moved on to another project. Within the first two or three minutes of talking to her, I was convinced that WTI was fertile ground for at last one case study. Moreover, to be given access to the trove of documents related to the history of WTI that Terri has in her basement was as generous a gift as a scholar can hope to receive. Had Terri simply led me to this material and then left me to sort through it, it would no doubt have taken me months, if not years, to make sense of it all. But Terri was not only the provider; she also acted as interpreter and guide. She filled in contexts from which I could begin my own tasks of reconstructing and reinterpreting the WTI story.

Alonzo, who also provided me with numerous documents, was exceedingly generous with his time. If a relevant meeting was taking place when I happened to visit East Liverpool, he was sure to invite me. As far as I can tell, he knows everyone in town, and he made a point of introducing me to whomever we might run into when I was with him. (One of the people I met through Alonzo was Virgil Reynolds, Alonzo's longtime friend and colleague in the opposition. Virgil is another one of those decent and determined people who have long resisted the presence of a hazardous waste incinerator in the community.) Alonzo gave me the idea of thinking about WTI (and perhaps public policy in general) as a kind of noir text. In fact, if there is a private eye in the WTI story, it is no doubt Alonzo Spencer. As much as Alonzo would like to see the plant's operations curtailed or terminated, he seems equally motivated by the desire to *know*—to know why a facility with so many problems and so much opposition has been politically protected for so long. Some people choose to spend their retirements in Florida playing tennis, while others wander the country in an RV. Alonzo has spent his as an environmental activist. As far as I can tell, he attends every meeting that has some relevance to the incinerator, and he never seems to lose his optimism about the capacity of the opposition to succeed.

I would also like to thank Raymond Wayne, the public relations officer for WTI, and others in the plant who talked to me. Raymond gave me an extensive tour of the WTI plant. He read and made comments on a paper that I had written about WTI. He is smart, articulate, and committed to the facility. He has been with the company for many years and is one of WTI's greatest assets. He will no doubt find much in this volume to disagree with, but I respect his commitment to his job and his belief in the environmental benefits of the incinerator.

I presented early drafts of some of the work here to the American Political Science Association Workshop on Myth, Rhetoric, and Symbolism, organized each year by John Nelson. The half-day workshop brings together scholars from a variety of backgrounds with eclectic interests. Unlike some conference formats, paper presentations are brief, with an emphasis on critical exchange. I have always found the resulting dialogue to be extremely fruitful. Moreover, John has been commenting on my work since I was his graduate student at the University of Iowa. His insightful criticisms are always welcomed, and they continue to make my work better. I found John's knowledge of, and interest in, the politics of noir especially helpful for this particular project.

Ithaca College provided support money through summer research and travel grants for my trips to East Liverpool.

Finally, I would like to thank the staff at the University of Minnesota Press. This is the second book of mine that the Press has agreed to publish. Moving a book from manuscript to acceptance to publication can sometimes be a difficult process, but that has not been my experience with the editors at Minnesota. Working with them has been a pleasure. I would especially like to thank Carrie Mullen, Pieter Martin, Jason Weidemann, and Laura Westlund.

Appendix:
WTI Ownership Patterns

WTI Early Partnership Configurations

July 26, 1981

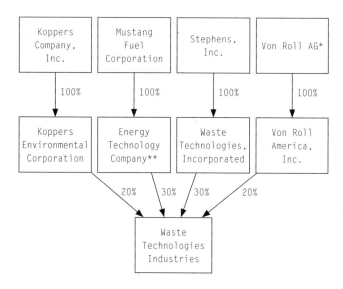

July 1, 1982

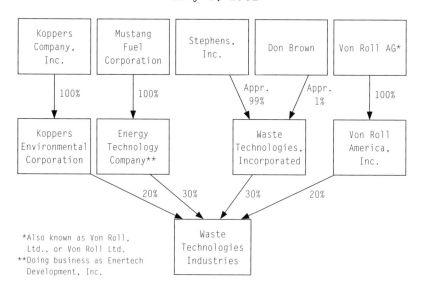

*Also known as Von Roll,
Ltd., or Von Roll Ltd.
**Doing business as Enertech
Development, Inc.

Figure A1. Ownership of WTI was originally a partnership constituted by four entities. Koppers Environmental Corporation was a subsidiary of the Pittsburgh construction firm Koppers Company, Inc. Energy Technology Company was a subsidiary of the energy firm Mustang Fuel. Waste Technologies, Inc., originally incorporated as Stephens Consultant Services Inc., was a subsidiary of the Arkansas investment firm Stephens, Inc., run by Jackson Stephens and undoubtedly the most important entity involved in the deal. Von Roll America, Inc., was a subsidiary of Von Roll AG, a Swiss construction company with experience building (although not managing or operating) hazardous waste facilities.

East Liverpool native Don Brown knew Jackson Stephens and may have suggested to him the idea of bringing the facility to East Liverpool. Brown had been roommates at Kent State University with East Liverpool mayor John Payne, who became an early and enthusiastic supporter of the project. In 1982, Brown was made vice president of the WTI operation and given approximately 1 percent share in the ownership of the facility. *Source:* Ohio Attorney General's Report, Appendix N.

WTI Ownership Changes, 1981–1986
(Koppers side of original partnership)

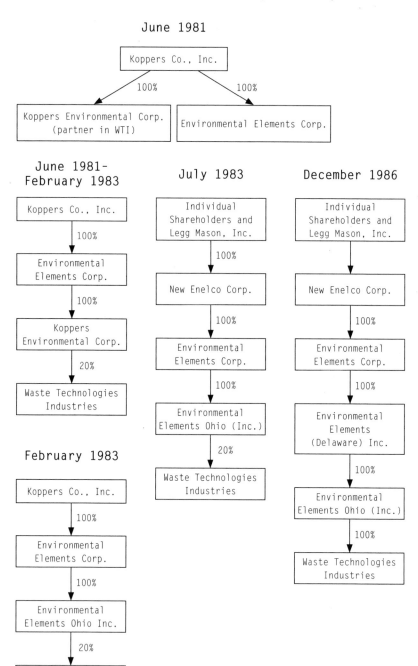

June 1981

Koppers Co., Inc.

100% → Koppers Environmental Corp. (partner in WTI)

100% → Environmental Elements Corp.

June 1981–February 1983

Koppers Co., Inc.
↓ 100%
Environmental Elements Corp.
↓ 100%
Koppers Environmental Corp.
↓ 20%
Waste Technologies Industries

February 1983

Koppers Co., Inc.
↓ 100%
Environmental Elements Corp.
↓ 100%
Environmental Elements Ohio Inc.
↓ 20%
Waste Technologies Industries

July 1983

Individual Shareholders and Legg Mason, Inc.
↓ 100%
New Enelco Corp.
↓ 100%
Environmental Elements Corp.
↓ 100%
Environmental Elements Ohio (Inc.)
↓ 20%
Waste Technologies Industries

December 1986

Individual Shareholders and Legg Mason, Inc.
↓ 100%
New Enelco Corp.
↓ 100%
Environmental Elements Corp.
↓ 100%
Environmental Elements (Delaware) Inc.
↓ 100%
Environmental Elements Ohio (Inc.)
↓ 100%
Waste Technologies Industries

Figure A2. WTI was originally owned by four partners. (See Figure A1.)
This figure shows the ownership transformations that were undertaken by
one of the partners, Koppers Co., Inc., over five years. Koppers Co., Inc.,
created two wholly owned subsidiaries, Koppers Environmental Corp.
and Environmental Elements Corp., one of which had a 20 percent share
of WTI. Environmental Elements Corp. bought Koppers Environmental
Corp., making it a wholly owned subsidiary of a wholly owned subsidiary.
Environmental Elements Corp. then created the wholly owned subsidiary
Environmental Elements Ohio (Inc.).

In July 1983, New Enelco Corporation was formed to buy the stock
of Environmental Elements from Koppers Co., Inc. Legg Mason, Inc., a
mutual fund, also bought New Enelco stock, and the rest was sold publicly to shareholders. Environmental Elements Corp. and Environmental
Elements Ohio, Inc., were now wholly owned subsidiaries of New Enelco.
Environmental Elements Corp. then formed a holding company (a firm
with no assets), Environmental Elements (Delaware).

As a result of these actions, 20 percent of WTI was owned by Environmental Elements Ohio, Inc., in turn owned by Environmental Elements
(Delaware), in turn owned by Environmental Elements Corp., in turn
owned by New Enelco Corp., in turn owned by shareholders and Legg
Mason. Six ownership layers thus existed between the parent company
and any potential liability judgments. WTI received a permit to operate from the Ohio Hazardous Waste Facilities Board on April 27, 1984.
Source: Ohio Attorney General's Report, Appendix N.

WTI Ownership Changes, 1981-1986
(Von Roll side of original partnership)

June 1981   October 1986

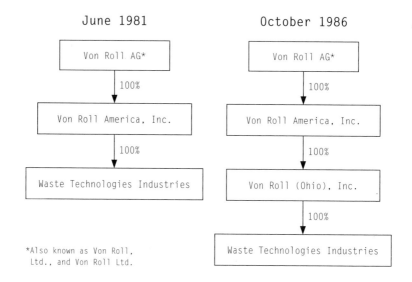

June 1981	October 1986
Von Roll AG*	Von Roll AG*
100%	100%
Von Roll America, Inc.	Von Roll America, Inc.
100%	100%
Waste Technologies Industries	Von Roll (Ohio), Inc.
	100%
	Waste Technologies Industries

*Also known as Von Roll,
Ltd., and Von Roll Ltd.

Figure A3. Von Roll AG is a Swiss construction firm that had experience in building (but, at the time, not operating) hazardous waste incinerators. Von Roll America, Inc., was a wholly owned subsidiary organized by the parent company to manage its share of the WTI facility. (Oddly, Von Roll America, Inc., was not mentioned in the company's annual reports from 1980 to 1989. The 1990 and 1991 reports, however, did state that Von Roll AG owns Von Roll, America, Inc.)

In 1986, the parent firm, Von Roll AG, set up a subsidiary, Von Roll (Ohio), Inc., wholly owned by its subsidiary Von Roll America, Inc. All of Von Roll AG's interest in the WTI facility was transferred to this new entity. While the various transfers of ownership here were not as complex as with the Koppers side of the partnership, they no doubt served much the same purpose: to shield the parent corporation from liabilities that might be associated with the operations of the plant. *Source:* Ohio Attorney General's Report, Appendix N.

WTI Ownership Changes, 1986
(Mustang Fuel Corp., Stephens Inc., and Don Brown as original partners)

October 31, 1986

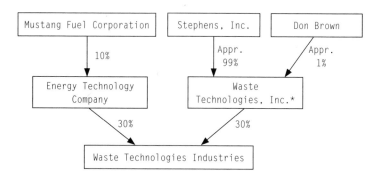

Mustang Fuel Corporation →(10%) Energy Technology Company →(30%) Waste Technologies Industries

Stephens, Inc. →(Appr. 99%) Waste Technologies, Inc.* →(30%) Waste Technologies Industries

Don Brown →(Appr. 1%) Waste Technologies, Inc.*

December 1, 1986

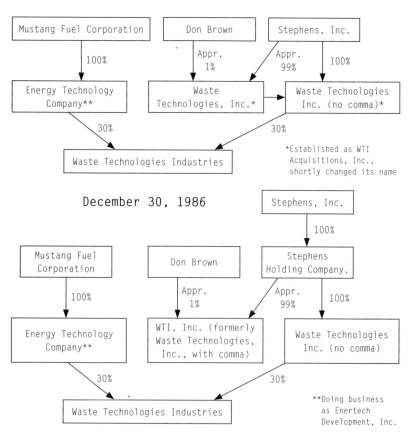

Mustang Fuel Corporation →(100%) Energy Technology Company** →(30%) Waste Technologies Industries

Don Brown →(Appr. 1%) Waste Technologies, Inc.*

Stephens, Inc. →(Appr. 99%) Waste Technologies, Inc.* ; Stephens, Inc. →(100%) Waste Technologies Inc. (no comma)* →(30%) Waste Technologies Industries

Waste Technologies, Inc.* → Waste Technologies Inc. (no comma)*

*Established as WTI Acquisitions, Inc., shortly changed its name

December 30, 1986

Stephens, Inc. →(100%) Stephens Holding Company.

Mustang Fuel Corporation →(100%) Energy Technology Company** →(30%) Waste Technologies Industries

Don Brown →(Appr. 1%) WTI, Inc. (formerly Waste Technologies, Inc., with comma)

Stephens Holding Company. →(Appr. 99%) WTI, Inc. (formerly Waste Technologies, Inc., with comma)

Stephens Holding Company. →(100%) Waste Technologies Inc. (no comma) →(30%) Waste Technologies Industries

**Doing business as Enertech Development, Inc.

Figure A4. Stephens associate Don Brown became a part owner of the Stephens, Inc., subsidiary Waste Technologies, Inc., in 1982. (Waste Technologies, Inc., was briefly named WTI Acquisitions, Inc., a name that may have too obviously connected it to the incinerator project.)

In early December 1986, Stephens Inc. created another wholly owned subsidiary, with a name nearly identical to the first—Waste Technologies Inc. (without a comma), in which Brown had no ownership interest. Later that same month, Stephens created a holding company (a firm with no assets) and positioned it between Stephens, Inc., and Waste Technologies Inc. (no comma). At the same time, the name of Waste Technologies, Inc. (with comma) was changed to WTI, Inc.

The Ohio attorney general's report summarized this succinctly: "The Waste Technologies, Incorporated parent company first allowed an individual to acquire stock in the subsidiary, then sold the quasi subsidiary's partnership interest to a wholly owned subsidiary, with a name very similar to the first partner" (50). Soon thereafter, WTI, Inc., would be dissolved, leaving Don Brown with a 1 percent interest in a liquidated firm. *Source:* Office of the Attorney General, State of Ohio, *Statutory Criteria Discussion, Waste Technologies Industries,* June 1993.

WTI Ownership Changes, 1990

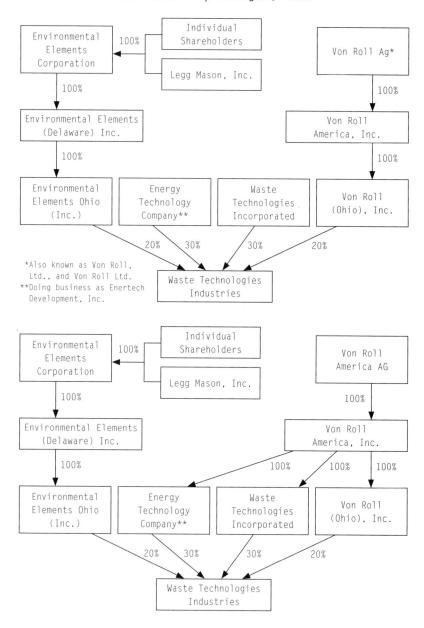

Figure A5. On May 7, 1990, New Enelco Company and its subsidiary, Environmental Elements Corporation, merged under the name Environmental Elements Corporation. Von Roll AG bought Energy Technology Company and Waste Technologies Incorporated. Later in 1990, Von Roll AG also bought the stock of Environmental Elements (Delaware) Inc., making it the sole owner of each of the WTI partners. *Source:* Ohio Attorney General's Report, Appendix N.

Notes

Introduction

1. Terri told me that she was very frustrated at first trying to contact Kaufman. His answering machine seemed to always be full. Eventually she realized that it emptied out at 2 a.m. each morning, so she waited to call him at that time. After she left a dozen messages, her persistence paid off, and he agreed to make a trip to East Liverpool.

2. Browner stated a conflict of interest, on the grounds that her husband worked for Florida Citizen Action.

3. Robert Greene, *The 48 Laws of Power* (New York: Penguin Books, 2000).

4. David R. Hawkins, *Power v. Force: The Hidden Determinants of Human Behavior* (Carlsbad, Calif.: Hay Books, 2002), 42.

5. Norman Peale, *The Power of Positive Thinking* (New York: Ballantine Books, 1996); *Positive Imaging: The Powerful Way to Change Your Life* (New York: Ballantine Books, 1996); *Stay Alive All Your Life* (New York: Ballantine Books, 1996); *Enthusiasm Makes the Difference* (New York: Ballantine Books, 1996).

6. Dale Carnegie, *How to Win Friends and Influence People* (New York: Pocket Books, 1990); *How to Stop Worrying and Start Living* (New York: Pocket Books, 1990).

7. For a sobering look at current income distributions in the United States, see, David Cay Johnston, "Richest Are Leaving Even the Rich Far Behind," *New York Times,* June 5, 2005, 1.

8. See David Truman, *The Governmental Process: Political Interests and Public*

Opinion (New York: Knopf, 1951). Also see Robert Dahl, *Preface to Democratic Theory* (Chicago: University of Chicago Press, 1956); Dahl, *Who Governs? Democracy and Power in an American City* (New Haven: Yale University Press, 1971); and Dahl, *Polyarchy, Participation, and Opposition* (New Haven: Yale University Press, 1971).

9. In reading the debates between pluralists and power elite theorists, one can't help being struck by a central argument of the pluralists: if power elites and the business classes rule, then why has the regulatory state been so successful in curbing their power? The question seems archaic, almost quaint, seen through the prism of twenty-first-century global economies.

10. C. Wright Mills, *The Power Elite* (New York: Oxford University Press, 1958).

11. Jacques Ellul, *The Technological Society*, trans. John Wilkinson (New York: Knopf, 1964).

12. Lewis Mumford, *Technics and Civilization* (New York: Harcourt, Brace, 1958).

13. William Kornhauser, *The Politics of Mass Society* (Glenco, Ill.: Free Press, 1959); Philip G. Olson, ed., *America as Mass Society: Changing Community and Identity* (Glenco, Ill.: Free Press, 1963); Robert M. Stein, Arthur J. Vidich, and David M. White, eds., *Identity and Anxiety: Survival of the Person in Mass Society* (Glencoe, Ill.: Free Press, 1960).

14. William H. Whyte, *The Organization Man* (New York: Simon and Schuster, 1955).

15. Ibid., 7.

16. Ibid., 39.

17. Ibid., 44–45.

18. Paul M. Sweezey, *Modern Capitalism and Other Essays* (New York: Monthly Review Press, 1972). The antagonism of the old Left to Mills's ideas is one of the things that made him attractive to, and important for, the student movements of the 1960s. See James Miller, *Democracy Is in the Streets: From Port Huron to the Siege of Chicago* (Cambridge: Harvard University Press, 1994).

19. Robert Dahl, "A Critique of the Ruling Elite Model," in *The Power Elite in America,* ed. Norman L. Crockett (Lexington, Mass.: D.C. Heath, 1970), 38.

20. Ibid. In response, "institutionalists," most notably Thomas Dye, attempted to shift emphasis away from the need to demonstrate individual control of one over another in a given case to the "potential" for such control. Thomas R. Dye, *Understanding Public Policy* (Englewood Cliffs, N.J.: Prentice Hall, 1972); Dye, *The Politics of Inequality* (Indianapolis: Bobbs-Merrill, 1971); Dye, *Politics in State and Local Communities* (Englewood Cliffs, N.J.: Prentice Hall, 1985).

21. G. William Domhoff, *Who Rules America? Power and Politics* (New York: McGraw Hill, 2001), *Who Rules America? Power and Politics in the Year 2000*

(New York: McGraw Hill, 1998), *Who Rules America Now? A View for the 1980s* (New York: Simon and Schuster, 1986).

22. James Ring Adams, *The Big Fix: Inside the S&L Scandal: How an Unholy Alliance of Politics and Money Destroyed America's Banking System* (New York: John Wiley and Sons, 1989); James Ring Adams and Douglas Frantz, *A Full Service Bank: How BCCI Stole Billions around the World* (New York: Pocket Books, 1992); James Adams, *Dangerous Ambition: The Assassination and Life of Gerald Bull* (New York: Atlantic Monthly Press, 1991). Adams is an interesting character. While his exposés of power relationships and critiques of the upper reaches of the business world make his books attractive to left-oriented readers, he wrote for the very conservative *American Spectator* in the 1990s. At that time, it was the Clintons who were the targets of numerous scandal rumors and investigations. To a certain extent, there is no contradiction here, because if one takes Adams's arguments seriously, then there is really little difference between the leaders of the Democratic and Republican Parties. They are all connected to one another through complicated networks of power.

23. Kevin Phillips, *American Dynasty: Aristocracy, Fortune, and the Politics of Deceit in the House of Bush* (New York: Viking Press, 2004); Craig Unger, *House of Bush, House of Saud: The Secret Relationship between the World's Two Most Powerful Dynasties* (New York: Scribner, 2004).

24. Directed by Michael Moore (New York: IFC Films, 2004).

25. On Enron, see Sherron Watkins and Mimi Swartz, *Power Failure: The Inside Story of the Collapse of Enron* (New York: Doubleday, 2003); Bethany McLean and Peter Elkind, *The Smartest Guys in the Room: The Amazing Rise and Scandalous Fall of Enron* (London: Portfolio, 2003); and Robert Bryce and Molly Ivins, *Pipe Dreams: Ego, Greed, and the Death of Enron* (New York: Public Affairs, 2002). On Halliburton, see Dan Briody, *The Halliburton Agenda: The Politics of Oil and Money* (New York: John Wiley and Sons, 2004).

26. Jeff Gerth, "Washington Talk: The Study of Intelligence; Only Spies Can Find These Sources," *New York Times,* October 6, 1987, A32.

27. Mark Hand, "Searching for Daniel Brandt," *Counterpoint,* January 3, 2003, http://www. counterpunch.org/hand01032003.html.

28. Ibid.

29. http://www.namebase.org.

30. His most recent project involves challenging the hegemonic power of Google. A name entered into the Google search engine might yield a very different set of connections than those found on Brandt's NameBase, something that he has been trying to correct. See Hand, "Searching for Daniel Brandt."

31. http://www.namebase.org/cgi-bin/nb06?_STEPHENS_JACKSON_ THOMAS.

32. Stanley Aronowitz, "A Mills Revival?" *Logos* 2, no. 3 (Summer 2003), http://www.logosjournal.com/aronowitz.htm.

33. Michel Foucault, *Discipline and Punish: The Birth of the Prison* (New York: Pantheon Books, 1977).

34. Michel Foucault, *Power/Knowledge: Selected Interviews and Other Writings, 1972–1977* (New York: Pantheon, 1980), 55.

35. Ibid.

36. John Caputo and Mark Young, "Institutions, Normalization, and Power," in *Foucault and the Critique of Institutions,* ed. John Caputo and Mark Young (University Park: Penn State University Press, 1993), 6.

37. On this aspect of Foucault's thought, see Richard A. Lynch, "Is Power All There Is? Michel Foucault and the 'Omnipresence' of Power Relations," *Philosophy Today* 42 (Spring 1998): 65–71.

38. Todd May, *Between Geneaology and Epistemology: Psychology, Politics, and Knowledge in the Thought of Michel Foucault* (University Park: Penn State University Press, 1993), 44.

39. Michel Foucault, "The Subject and Power," in *Michel Foucault: Beyond Structuralism and Hermeneutics* (Chicago: University of Chicago Press, 1982), 208.

40. Michel Foucault, *Politics, Philosophy, Culture: Interviews and Other Writings, 1977–1984* (New York: Routledge, 1988), 103.

41. Ibid., 104.

42. For an analysis of Foucault's concept of "geneaology," see Michael Mahon, *Foucault's Nietzschean Genealogy: Truth, Power, and the Subject* (Albany: SUNY Press, 1992).

43. Murray Bookchin, *Remaking Society* (Montreal: Black Rose, 1989); Bill Duvall and George Sessions, *Deep Ecology* (Layton, Utah: Gibbs Smith, 1987).

44. John S. Nelson, "Noir and Forever: Politics as If Hollywood Were Everywhere," paper presented at the Annual Meeting of the American Political Science Association, August 2003.

45. *Panic in the Streets* is a classic film directed by Elia Kazan, in which Richard Widmark plays a New Orleans public health official, attempting to stave off an outbreak of bubonic plague. Directed by Elia Kazan (Los Angeles: 20th Century Fox, 1950). *Frightened City* (London: Zodiac Productions, 1962) is very loosely based on a smallpox outbreak in New York City in 1946. In the film, the National Guard is called in to quell a potential epidemic. In truth, the outbreak was "brief, well-controlled, and not very sensational." Eddie Muller, *Dark City: The Lost World of Film Noir* (New York: St. Martin's Press, 1998), 17.

46. *The Asphalt Jungle,* directed by John Huston (Hollywood: MGM Studios, 1950), is a cautionary tale about city life. Dix (Sterling Hayden) seeks only to return to Kentucky to buy back the family farm. His compulsive gambling prevents him from fulfilling his dream. Desperate for the money, he participates in a

jewelry heist organized by the criminal mastermind Doc Reidenschneider (Sam Jaffe). Dix tells his sometime girlfriend Doll Conovan (Jean Hagen), "First thing I'm going to do is take a bath in the creek and wash this city dirt off me." After things go terribly wrong with the heist, he escapes town with Doll. Shot in the belly and hemorrhaging badly, Dix drives with Doll to Kentucky, where he dies in a field of beloved bluegrass.

47. In *Night and the City,* directed by Jules Dassin (Los Angeles: 20th Century Fox, 1950), Richard Widmark plays Harry Fabian, a small-time hustler done in by greed, impatience, and emotional immaturity.

48. Paula Rabinowitz, *Black and White and Noir: America's Pulp Modernism* (New York: Columbia University Press, 2002), 5.

49. Eddie Muller, *Dark City: The Lost World of Film Noir* (New York: St. Martin's Press, 1998).

50. Ibid., 16.

51. Nicholas Christopher, *Somewhere in the Night: Film Noir and the American City* (New York: Henry Holt, 1997), 67.

52. James Naremore, *More than Night: Film Noir in Its Contexts* (Berkeley: University of California Press, 1998), 9, 10.

53. Nelson, "Noir and Forever," 3.

54. Ibid., 10.

55. Ibid., 2.

56. Christopher, *Somewhere in the Night,* 179–80.

57. Nelson, "Noir and Forever," 12.

58. Mills, *The Power Elite,* 92–93.

59. Camile Paglia, *Sex, Art, and American Culture* (New York: Vintage, 1992), 230.

60. See, for example, Lutz P. Koepnick: "Film noir can be understood as a heterotopia in Michel Foucault's sense: a site that differs from most other spaces but that allows us to better understand how society organizes human relations across space and time." Koepnick, *The Dark Mirror: German Cinema between Hitler and Hollywood* (Berkeley: University of California Press, 2002), 165.

61. Naremore, *More than Night,* 13.

62. Raymond Borde and Etienne Chaumeton, *Panorama du film noir americain, 1941–1953* (Paris: Editions de Minuit, 1995). Quoted in Naremore, *More than Night,* 21.

1. Past as Prelude

1. "The Carnegie Libraries of Ohio," http://www.andrewcarnegie.cc.

2. Herman J. Daly and John B. Cobb Jr., *For the Common Good: Redirecting*

the Economy toward Community, the Environment, and a Sustainable Future (Boston: Beacon Press, 1994).

3. William C. Gates, *The City of Hills and Kilns: Life and Work in East Liverpool, Ohio* (East Liverpool: East Liverpool Historical Society, 1984), 1.

4. William B. McCord, *History of Columbiana County, Ohio, and Representative Citizens* (Chicago: George Richmond Press, 1905), 17.

5. W. S. Potts, "Geological History of Columbiana County," in *History of the Upper Ohio Valley*, vol. 2 (Madison: Brent and Fuller, 1891), 61.

6. Gates, *City of Hills and Kilns*, 1.

7. Judge Gibson L. Cranmer, "The Ohio Valley," chapter 1 of *History of the Upper Ohio Valley with Family History and Biographical Sketches*, vol. 1 (Madison: Brent and Fuller, 1891), 17. Another historian of the same period, Horace Mack, writing specifically about Columbiana County, would note that the wealth that exists there "lies not alone in her rich surface-soil which yields so bountifully of grass and grain and fruit, but also of those other treasures which, at varying depths and in wonderful profusion, Nature has stored for her needs, and which have proven to be the foundation of a prosperous activity in trade, in art, and in manufacture." Horace Mack, *History of Columbiana County, Ohio* (Philadelphia: D. W. Ensign, 1879), 51.

8. The judge was certainly less hostile to Native American culture than Charles D. Dickinson, the author of a latter chapter in the same volume. In Dickinson's view, "The Indian character, as a whole, was not without some redeeming points of humanity, but the acts of generosity, the absence of murderous tendencies, the examples of human feelings are so few and far between in the history of the tribes who occupied this state, that they shine like a very few bright stars on the black scene of unprovoked outrage, not giving enough light to redeem the scroll from almost total darkness." "Indian History of Columbiana County," in *History of the Upper Ohio Valley*, vol. 1 (Madison: Brent and Fuller, 1891), 369.

William McCord, perhaps having read Dickinson's account, was more admiring of Native peoples: "To have lived at such a time [the ice age] and to have successfully overcome the hardships of that climate and the fierceness of the animal life, must have called for an amount of physical energy and practical skill which few of this generation possess. Let us not therefore speak of such people as inferior. They must have had all the native powers of humanity fully developed and are worthy ancestors of succeeding generations." William B. McCord, *History of Columbiana County, Ohio, and Representative Citizens* (Chicago: George Richmond Press, 1905), 20.

9. Cranmer, "The Ohio Valley," 17.

10. Ibid., 18.

11. Mack, *History of Columbiana County*, 173.

12. McCord, *History of Columbiana County*, 40.

13. Ibid., 41.

14. Mack, *History of Columbiana County*, 52.

15. Ibid., 52.

16. Gates, *City of Hills and Kilns*, 145–48.

17. Ibid., 150. In fact, the pottery industry, in general, was highly supportive of protective tariffs. Marc Jeffrey Stern, *The Pottery Industry of Trenton: A Skilled Trade in Transition, 1850-1929*, (New Brunswick, N.J.: Rutgers University Press, 1994), 20–26.

18. Gates, *City of Hills and Kilns*, 259.

19. "Charles 'Pretty Boy' Floyd: Public Enemy Number One," August 15, 1997, http://www.geocities.com/CapitolHill/Lobby/3935/#Folk%20Stories%20and%20quotes%20about%20his%20life.

20. Ibid.

21. Joseph Geringer, "Wrong Place, Wrong Time," *Court TV's Crime Library*, http://www. crimelibrary.com/gangsters/prettyboy.

22. Ibid.

23. Woody Guthrie, "Pretty Boy Floyd," in *The Legendary Woody Guthrie* (Los Angeles: Tradition, 1967).

24. "Charles 'Pretty Boy' Floyd."

25. See "Charles Arthur Floyd: Alias 'Pretty Boy Floyd,'" Memorandum for the Director, Federal Bureau of Investigation, Department of Justice, April 13, 1933, http://foia.fbi. gov/floydsum /floydsum.pdf.

26. "Charles 'Pretty Boy' Floyd."

27. Gates, *City of Hills and Kilns*, 331.

28. Quoted in Gates, *City of Hills and Kilns*, 366–67.

29. Gates, *City of Hills and Kilns*, 400.

30. Terry F. Buss and F. Stevens Redburn, *Shutdown at Youngstown: Public Policy for Mass Unemployment* (Albany: State University of New York Press, 1983), 1.

31. Dale A. Hathaway, *Can Workers Have a Voice? The Politics of Deindustrialization in Pittsburgh* (University Park: Penn State University Press, 1993), 27.

32. Buss and Redburn, *Shutdown at Youngstown*, 15.

33. Ibid., 16–19.

34. Barry Bluestone and Bennett Harrison, *The Deindustrialization of America: Plant Closings, Community Abandonment, and the Dismantling of Basic Industries* (New York: Basic Books, 1982), 36.

35. Ibid., 35, 33, 31. A good analysis of regional job loss through the late seventies and early eighties is provided by Candee S. Harris in "Magnitude of Job Loss," in *Deindustrialization and Plant Closure*, ed. Paul D. Staudohar and Holly E. Brown (Lexington, Mass.: Lexington Books, 1987), 89–100.

36. Bluestone and Harrison, *The Deindustrialization of America*, 152.

37. Buss and Redburn, *Shutdown at Youngstown*, 137.

38. Bluestone and Harrison, *The Deindustrialization of America*, 66.

39. For a detailed discussion, see Jim Cullen, *Born in the U.S.A.: Bruce Spring-steen and the American Tradition* (New York: Harper Perennial, 1998), 1–5.

40. Marie Jahoda, foreword to *The Magic City: Unemployment in a Working-Class Community*, by Gregory Pappas (Ithaca: Cornell University Press, 1989), xii.

41. Pappas, *The Magic City*, 189.

42. Katherine S. Newman, "Deindustrialization, Poverty, and Downward Mobility: Toward an Anthropology of Economic Disorder," in *Diagnosing America: Anthropology and Public Engagement*, ed. Shepard Forman (Ann Arbor: University of Michigan Press, 1997), 122.

43. For a concise introduction to some proposed policy options, see Edward J. Blakely and Philip Shapira, "Public Policies for Industry," in *Deindustrialization and Plant Closure*, ed. Paul D. Staudohar and Holly E. Brown (Lexington, Mass.: Lexington Books, 1987), 139–53. For a good analysis of several local government responses to plant closings, see John Portz, *The Politics of Plant Closings* (Lawrence: University Press of Kansas, 1990).

44. Hathaway, *Can Workers Have a Voice?* 21.

45. For a comparison of American approaches to deindustrialization versus those in other industrialized nations, see Philip L. Martin, "Displacement Policies in Europe and Canada"; Gregory Hooks, "Comparison of the United States, Sweden, and France"; Bennett Harrison, "European and American Experience"; and Tadashi A. Hanami, "Policies in Japan"; in Staudohar and Brown, *Deindustrialization and Plant Closure*, 237–44, 245–58, 259–66, 267–73.

46. J. R. McNeill, *Something New under the Sun: An Environmental History of the Twentieth-Century World* (New York: W. W. Norton, 2000), 29.

47. Eckardt C. Beck, "The Love Canal Tragedy," *EPA Journal*, January 1979, http://www. epa.gov/history/topics/lovecanal/01.htm.

48. Allan Mazur, *A Hazardous Inquiry: The Rashomon Effect at Love Canal* (Cambridge: Harvard University Press, 1998), 19–21.

49. Numerous books have been written about Love Canal. Lois Gibbs, who became a nationally known antitoxics activist as a result of her actions in the case, wrote *Love Canal: My Story* (Albany: State University of New York Press, 1982). Paul Brown, who covered the story for the *Niagara Gazette*, also wrote a book about toxics, which included his analysis of the controversy, *Laying Waste: The Poisoning of America by Toxic Chemicals* (New York: Pantheon Books, 1980). The definitive academic history of Love Canal is probably Adeline Levine's *Love Canal: Science, Politics, and People* (Lexington, Mass.: Lexington Books, 1982). Mazur's *A Hazardous Inquiry* looks at the events at Love Canal from the perspectives of a variety of participants and draws some conclusions based on a synthesis

of them. A good short summary of the site's history can be found at "Love Canal History," *The Hazardous Web Site,* http://www. globalserve.net/~spinc/atomcc/ history.htm.

50. Mazur, *A Hazardous Inquiry,* 159, Jeffrey G. Miller and Craig N. Johnston, *The Law of Hazardous Waste Disposal and Remediation: Cases—Legislation—Regulations—Policies* (St. Paul: West Publishing, 1996), 8–9.

51. Melinda Beck et al., "The Toxic Waste Crisis," *Newsweek,* March 7, 1983, 20.

52. Joseph L. Galloway and Ronald A. Taylor, "When the U.S. Plows Under a Poisoned Community," *U.S. News and World Report,* July 4, 1983, 57.

53. Joseph F. Dunphy and Alan Hall, "Waste Disposal: Settling on Safer Solutions for Chemicals," *Chemical Week,* March 8, 1978, 28.

54. Greg Johnson, "Ever Felt Like Shouting 'NIMBY' to a 'LULU'?" *Industry Week,* April 18, 1983, 28.

55. For a concise history of the development of the chlorine industry, see Joe Thornton, *Pandora's Poison: Chlorine, Health, and a New Environmental Policy* (Cambridge: MIT Press, 2000), 233–58.

56. "Community Relations: A Higher Profile at the Grassroots," *Chemical Week,* July 27, 1983, 31.

57. Ibid., 33.

58. Elizabeth M. Whelan, *Toxic Terror: The Truth about the Cancer Scare* (Ottawa, Ill.: Jameson Books, 1985), xv, 105.

59. Miller and Johnston, *Law of Hazardous Waste Disposal,* 43–44.

60. Dunphy and Hall, "Waste Disposal," 30.

61. Ibid., 31.

62. Ibid., 29.

63. "Toxic Waste Cost Rises Again," *Engineering News-Record,* March 14, 1985, 16.

64. Quoted in Eddie J. Girdner and Jack Smith, *Killing Me Softly: Toxic Waste, Corporate Profit, and the Struggle for Environmental Justice* (New York: Monthly Review Press, 2002), 38.

65. Ibid.

66. *Statistical Abstract of the United States, 2000* (Washington, D.C.: U.S. Government Printing Office, 2000), 241.

67. Ibid., 239.

68. Michael B. Gerrard, "Fear and Loathing in the Siting of Hazardous and Radioactive Waste Facilities: A Comprehensive Approach to a Misperceived Crisis," *Tulane Law Review* 68 (May 1994): 1058.

69. Ibid., 1059–60.

70. Ibid., 1059.

71. WasteAge Staff, "Waste Age 100," *WasteAge.com,* June 1, 2002, http://

wasteage.com/ar/waste_waste_age/index.htm. The vast majority of toxic releases are still generated by two industries, chemicals and petroleum (*Statistical Abstract of the United States, 2000,* 239). What constitutes the "chemical industry" is largely a matter of convention. Petroleum refiners, mining operations, and primary metals industries could all be considered producers of chemicals, often highly toxic ones. Yet these industries are not included as such by the Standard Industrial Classifications Codes. Taking the narrow definition of SIC Code 28 (Chemicals and Allied Products), the chemical industry still accounts for almost one-half of all Toxic Release Inventory chemicals. Maureen Smith and Robert Gottlieb, "The Chemical Industry: Structure and Function," in *Reducing Toxics: A New Approach to Policy and Industrial Decisionmaking,* ed. Robert Gottlieb (Washington, D.C.: Island Press, 1995), 221, 211. The Toxic Release Inventory is itself considered an inadequate measure of released toxics due to its "rather narrow and idiosyncratic list of reportable chemicals, extremely high reporting thresholds, SIC code problems, and the exclusion of important sectors such as mining, agriculture, and, until 1993, federal agencies" (230).

72. World Waste Staff, "The Sixth Annual WasteAge 100," September 1, 2001, http://wasteage.com/ar/waste_sixth_annual_wasteage/index.htm.

73. Although energy shortages did not become a material reality until 1973, in the years leading up to it, the nascent environmental movement and the work of "Malthusians" such as the authors of the Club of Rome Report predicted future difficulties. See Donella H. Meadows, *The Limits to Growth: A Report for the Club of Rome's Project on the Predicament of Mankind* (New York: Universe Books, 1972); Congressional Quarterly, *Energy Crisis in America* (Washington, D.C.: Congressional Quarterly, 1973). Moreover, supporters of nuclear power, threatened by public opposition that had begun to materialize in the late 1960s and early 1970s, were predicting shortages of oil and natural gas. See Richard S. Lewis and Bernard I. Spinrad, eds., *The Energy Crisis* (Chicago: Educational Foundation for Nuclear Science, 1972).

74. Joe Stark, *Middle East Oil and the Energy Crisis* (New York: Monthly Review Press, 1975); Michael Tanzer, *Energy Crisis: World Struggle for Power and Wealth* (New York: Monthly Review Press, 1974).

75. "An End to the Trash Burden," *AHSRAE Journal,* March 28, 1986, 34–35.

76. As the report graphically stated: "Middle and higher-socioeconomic strata neighborhoods should not fall at least within a one-mile and five-mile radii of the proposed site." Cerrell Associates, *Political Difficulties Facing Waste-to-Energy Conversion Plant Siting* (Los Angeles: California Waste Management Board, 1984), 43.

77. Ibid., 1–2.

78. William H. Holmes, "Converting Waste to Energy," *Plant Engineering,* March 21, 1991, 120.

79. "Power from Sludge," *Power*, February 15, 1984, S9.

80. Rudy G. Novak, William L. Troxler, and Theodore H. Dehnke, "Recovering Energy from Hazardous Waste Incineration," March 19, 1984, 146.

81. Johnson, "Ever Felt Like Shouting 'NIMBY' to a 'LULU'?" 28.

82. "A New Breed of Environmentalists Puts the Heat on Industry," *Business Week*, March 19, 1984, 86B.

83. Ibid., 88B.

84. Ibid., 89B.

85. Miller and Johnston, *Law of Hazardous Waste Disposal*, 52.

86. Girdner and Smith, *Killing Me Softly*, 44 (quoting "Incineration News," *Rachel's Democracy and Health News*, no. 592, April 2, 1998.)

2. Be Careful What You Ask For

1. Frances Richard, "Obsessive—Generous: Toward a Diagram of Mark Lombardi," *wburg.com* 2, no. 2 (Winter 2001–2), http://www.wburg.com/0202/arts/lombardi.html.

2. Ibid., 5.

3. Ibid., 4.

4. Terri Swearingen, e-mail to Tom Shevory, June 24, 2003.

5. Mickey Cartin, quoted in Richard, "Obsessive—Generous," 9.

6. Richard, "Obsessive—Generous," 10.

7. Memorandum in Support of a Criminal Investigation into the WTI Incinerator Permitting Process, Environmental Crimes Project, April 8, 1994, 1, 2.

8. Jonathan Turley, letter to Willam J. Hotop, Special Agent, Federal Bureau of Investigation, April 12, 1994.

9. Ernst and Ernst, *Analysis of Economic Factors and Market Potential Related to River Port Development in Columbiana County, Ohio*, April 12, 1978.

10. Am. Sub. HB. No. 204, sec. 217.

11. Site Plan, Columbiana County Port Authority River Transfer Facility.

12. Ashley Schannauer, memo, "Port Authority Ownership Issues—Development Plan," April 30, 1992.

13. Office of the Attorney General, State of Ohio, *Statutory Criteria Discussion, Waste Technologies Industries*, June 1993. The attorney general's office saw no problem with this change of strategies by the CCPA, since using revenues generated from the incinerator's operations could still, hypothetically at least, be used to "enhance the use of Ohio rivers," as required of the CCPA by the Ohio legislature (ibid., 14). This requires a generous interpretation of the meaning of the term "enhance." Over time, few "enhancements" were actually made. A flood wall was built, and some improvements were made to a railroad crossing on the

CCPA property. Beyond the incinerator's construction and operation, no significant economic development has been generated by the CCPA after more than twenty years in existence.

14. Ibid., 16.

15. Ibid., 17.

16. Ibid., 18.

17. The attorney general's report found fault with the CCPA, not WTI. "The deficiency in the CCPA's plan, however, does not appear to be a negative reflection on WTI's reliability, competence, or expertise. It was the duty of the CCPA, not WTI, to ensure that the plan was adopted in accordance with legal procedures" (ibid., 19).

18. L. J. Davis, "The Name of Rose: An Arkansas Thriller," *New Republic,* April 4, 1994, 14.

19. Ibid., 15.

20. Ibid., 15–16.

21. Gore spoke at the event, where Buddhist nuns were reportedly given wads of cash and told to write checks for the Clinton campaign. As a result of this scandal, John Huang was suspended from fund-raising activities for the party. Howard Fineman et al., "The Asian Connection," *Newsweek,* October 28, 1996, 24–25.

22. John M. Broder and James Risen, "Little Rock Law," *Los Angeles Times,* April 3, 1994, 22.

23. Ibid., 22.

24. Davis, "The Name of Rose," 16.

25. Kate Kelly, "Arkansas Couple (Not the Clintons!) Buys $8 Million House on East 65th Street," *New York Observer,* August 30, 1999, 4.

26. "A WTI Sit-In at the White House: Activists Want Gore to Keep Promise," *Cleveland Plain Dealer,* March 19, 1993, 3B.

27. Waste Technologies Industries, *Permit Application Document,* September 4, 1981, 5.

28. Regulation 45 CFT 33074, May 19, 1980.

29. WTI, "Waste-to-Energy: Direct Answers to Some Hard Questions about the Future of the Tri-State Area," September 1981.

30. Ibid.

31. "Applegate Officers Aid to Help Get Port Grant," *East Liverpool Review,* January 8, 1982, 3.

32. "Payne Expects Second Term Bid," *East Liverpool Review,* January 8, 1982, 1.

33. "ELO Mayor Takes Stand at Hearings," *East Liverpoool Review,* March 29, 1983, 1.

34. Tom Giambroni, "East Liverpool Drops UDAG Application," *Morning Journal*, May 6, 1982, 3.

35. "Waste Plant Permits Possible by September," *East Liverpool Review*, January 15, 1982, 1.

36. Ibid.

37. "WTI and the Treatment Plant: Q's and A's," *Morning Journal*, June 28, 1982, 2.

38. Ibid., 2.

39. Ibid., 4.

40. Tom Giambroni, "ELO Votes to Oppose Treatment Plan, 4–3," *Morning Journal*, January 4, 1983, 4.

41. Ohio Administrative Code 3745-50-41 (B).

42. Fred Miller, "WTI Technical OK Seen," *East Liverpool Review*, December 29, 1982, 1.

43. Richard J. Maloy, "Area Faces EPA Action," *Evening Review*, January 3, 1983, 12.

44. The ordered stated: "In order to avoid to the extent possible the long and short term adverse impacts associated with the occupancy and modification of floodplains and to avoid direct or indirect support of floodplain development wherever there is a practicable alternative, it is hereby ordered as follows: Section 2(a)(2). If any agency has determined to, proposed to, conduct, support, or allow an action to be located in a floodplain, the agency shall consider alternatives to avoid adverse effects and incompatible development in the floodplains. If the head of the agency finds that the only practicable alternative consistent with the law and with the policy set forth in this Order requires siting in a floodplain, the agency shall, prior to taking action, . . . (ii) prepare and circulate a notice containing an explanation of why the action is proposed to be located in the floodplain." Codification of Presidential Proclamations and Executive Orders: Executive Order 11988, Floodplain Management, 42 FR 2695, 3 CRF, 1977.

45. Codification of Presidential Proclamations and Executive Orders: Executive Order 11099, Floodplain Management, May 24, 1977.

46. Waste Management Inc. proposed a one-million-gallon above-ground hazardous waste storage tank in Mobile, Alabama, in 1983. The permit was, however, denied because of the location of the tank on a floodplain.

47. Tom Giambroni, "ELO Votes to Oppose Treatment Plant, 4–3," *Morning Journal*, January 4, 1983, 4.

48. Mary Makatura, "Commissioners Stand 2–1 against WTI Waste Plant," *Morning Journal*, January 21, 1983, 1.

49. "City Council Instructs Payne to Cease His Support for WTI," *East Liverpool Review*, February 15, 1983, 10.

50. AP, "EPA Chief Quits Post," *Morning Journal,* March 3, 1983, 6.

51. UPI, "Turmoil Spread in EPA Dispute," *East Liverpool Review,* February 18, 1983, 1.

52. "WTI May Give Up ELO Site," *Morning Journal,* March 21, 1983, 1.

53. "WTI Hearing Ruling Due Monday," *East Liverpool Review,* March 18, 1983, 1.

54. Glenn Clark, "WTI Foes Rap Permit Process," *East Liverpool Review,* March 29, 1983, 1.

55. Jim Davis, "WTI Site a Concern to ODNR," *Morning Journal,* April 7, 1983, 10.

56. Jim Davis, "More Information Sought for WTI Permit," *East Liverpool Review,* June 16, 1983, 12.

57. Fred Miller, "WTI Gets U.S. Permit, but Faces Appeal Moves," *Morning Journal,* June 25, 1983, 1.

58. "Brown Exits Waste Technologies," *East Liverpool Review,* June 16, 1983, 8.

59. Fred Miller, " WTI Gets U.S Permit, but Faces Appeal Moves," *Morning Journal,* June 25, 1983, 10.

60. 45 FR 333169.

61. "Koppers Sells Subsidiary," *Evening Review,* July 29, 1983, 6.

62. U.S. Congressman Doug Applegate, letter to U.S. EPA Administrator William Ruckelshaus, July 24, 1983 (italics mine).

63. Ohio Siting Criteria 3734.05(D)(6).

64. *West Virginia v. Ohio Hazardous Waste Facility Approval Board,* 28 Ohio St. 3d, 2–7.

65. U.S. EPA Air and Radiation Branch Chief Steve Rothblatt, memo to Deputy Regional Counsel Dave Ullrich, "WTI's Air Pollution Permit," March 25, 1987.

66. Alonzo Spencer, interview with the author, June 11, 2004.

3. The Center of the Onion

1. *Chinatown,* directed by Roman Polanski (Hollywood: Paramount Pictures, 1974).

2. PBS, "William Mulholland," *New Perspectives on the West,* http://www.pbs.org/weta/thewest/people/i_r/mulholland.htm.

3. *Corporation of Kingston-upon-Hull v. Horner,* 98 Eng. Rep. 807, 815 (1774).

4. E. Merrick Dodd, "The Evolution of Limited Liability in American Industry: Massachusetts," *Harvard Law Review* 61 (1948): 1351.

5. Richard S. Farmer, "Parent Corporation Responsibility for the Environmental Liabilities of the Subsidiary: A Search for the Appropriate Standard," *Journal of Corporation Law* (Summer 1994): 773.

6. *United States v. Milwaukee Refrigerator Transit Co.*, 145 F. 1009 (1906).

7. *United States v. Milwaukee Refrigerator Transit Co. et al.*, 142 F. 249 (1905).

8. *United States v. Milwaukee Refrigerator Transit Co.*, 142 F. 255 (1905).

9. Farmer, "Parent Corporation Responsibility," 773.

10. Ibid., 774n22.

11. The controlling case in Ohio is *Belvedere Condominium Unit Owners' Assn. v. R. E. Roark Companies, Inc.*, 617 N.E.2d 1075 (1993), which has a three-prong test: "(1) control over the corporation by those to be held liable was so complete that the corporation has no separate mind, will, or existence of its own, (2) control over the corporation by those to be held liable was exercised in such a manner as to commit fraud or an illegal act against the person seeking to disregard the corporate entity, and (3) injury or unjust loss resulted to the plaintiff from such control or wrong." *Ashley v. Ashley*, 393 A. 2d. 637, 641 (1978). Quoted in Farmer, "Parent Corporation Responsibility," 779.

12. *Miles v. American Telephone and Telegraph Co.*, 703 F.2d 195 (1983).

13. *Ashley v. Ashley*, 393 A. 2d. 641 (1978).

14. *Kilduff v. Adams, Inc.*, 593 A.2d 478 (1991).

15. *BEC Corporation v. Department of Environmental Protection*, 256 Conn. 602.

16. Farmer, "Parent Corporation Responsibility," 779.

17. M. Casey Jarman gives the example of a case that he worked on as an attorney in California involving a cement kiln operation on a large ranch. He relates it as follows: "The story of the plant follows an all-too familiar pattern. Local residents' health complaints were virtually ignored, and reports of violations of the plant's air pollution permits were routinely trivialized by state agencies charged with protecting public health and the environment. Our strategy was to derail the fast track permitting by using the law and community action. We took part in the RCRA permitting process. Luke and I submitted written testimony supporting the EPA's 'intent to deny' the plant's RCRA permit for lack of the landowner's signature. Local residents presented the oral testimony. The ranch owner and cement kiln operator attempted to reach a compromise on the signature issue that would satisfy EPA. They failed, and EPA denied the kiln's RCRA permit." The plant, however, continued to operate under an interim permit. Jarman, "Essays on Environmental Justice: A New Approach to Expanding Resources for Environmental Justice: The Professor-in-Residency," *West Virginia Law Review* 96 (Summer 1994): 1170.

18. Office of the Attorney General, State of Ohio, *Statutory Criteria Discussion, Waste Technologies Industries,* June 1993.

19. Alan Block, "Into the Abyss of Environmental Policy: The Battle over the World's Largest Commercial Hazardous Waste Incinerator Located in East Liverpool, Ohio," *Journal of Human Justice,* November 1993, 45–47.

20. *Martin v. Schregardus,* 1 (1996).

21. Keith Schneider, "Ohio Orders New Public Review of Hazardous-Waste Incinerator," *New York Times,* July 4, 1992, 18.

22. Ibid.

23. Scott Powers, "Ohio EPA Order Owners to Update Burning Permit," *Columbus Dispatch,* July 1, 1993, D1.

24. Ibid., 2–3.

25. Ibid., 14–15.

26. *Greenpeace Inc. v. Waste Technologies Industries,* 9 F.3d 1177, 1993.

27. "Challenge to WTI Permit Status Fails: Matter Pending before Ohio Permit Board," *BNA Chemical Regulation Daily,* February 8, 1996, 1.

28. Quoted in James Adams, *Bull's Eye: The Assassination and Life of Supergun Inventor Gerald Bull* (New York: Times Books, 1992), 15.

29. Ibid., 243.

30. Ian Rodger, "Five Swiss Charged over Iraqi 'Supergun,'" *Financial Times,* September 6, 1994, 2.

31. Ken Ward Jr., "Employee of WTI Parent Convicted of Exporting War Materials to Iraq," *Charleston Gazette,* February 7, 1996, 5B.

32. "A Supergun for Saddam?" *Swiss Review of World Affairs,* March 1, 1996, 3.

33. Ward, "Employee of WTI," 5B.

34. Adams, *Bull's Eye,* 253, 254.

35. Selwyn Raab, "Double Portrait of a Man on Trial Astounds Friends," *New York Times,* April 11, 1995, 1B.

36. Ibid., 3B.

37. Ibid., 3B.

38. Helen Peterson, "Alleged Mobster Is Nailed in Fraud," *New York Daily News,* May 2, 1996.

39. Raab, "Double Portrait," 3B.

40. "Challenge to WTI Permit Status Fails," 2.

41. Diana B. Henriques, "New York City Builds a Better Watchdog: Agency May Be a Model for Business," *New York Times,* March 14, 1996, 1D.

42. *Greenpeace Inc. v. Waste Technologies Industries,* U.S. 2d Case No. 4:93CV0083, 1993, 1.

43. Ibid., 31–38.

44. 42 U.S.C.A. sec. 6972(a)(1)(B) (West Supp. 1992).

45. Joseph J. Santoleri, Joseph Reynolds, and Louis Theodore, *Introduction to Hazardous Waste Incineration* (New York: John Wiley, 2000).

46. T. C. Brown, "Memo Says Incinerator Food-Chain Risk Studied," *Plain Dealer,* February 9, 1993, A1.

47. *Greenpeace Inc. v. Waste Technologies Industries,* U.S. 2d, 60–61.

48. *Palumbo v. Waste Technologies Industries* 989 F.2d 159, 1993.

49. "Comments on the Draft Title V Permit For: Waste Technologies Industries, Inc.," May 9, 2003.

50. Charles Waterman III, letter to Gary Victorine, November 10, 2000.

51. Alonzo Spencer, letter to Terence Branigan, September 20, 2001.

52. Terence Branigan, letter to Alonzo Spencer, February 1, 2002 (italics mine).

53. Mr. Branigan also professed to have no knowledge of Alonzo Spencer's allusion to Waterman's providing false information. In response, Alonzo sent him a 1997 letter, written to him by David Sholtis, then assistant chief of hazardous waste management for the Ohio EPA, in which Sholtis agreed that the information submitted was false and was determined to have been so by the Ohio attorney general's office.

54. Terence Branigan, letter to Charles Waterman III, January 18, 2002.

55. *Trueblood v. Von Roll America, Inc.,* 2002-WPC-3 to 6, 2003-WPC-1 (*Administrative Law Judges: Initial Decisions and Orders,* March 26, 2003).

56. Alonzo Spencer, letter to Bill Skrowronski, Frank Popotnik, September 16, 2002.

57. Alonzo Spencer, letter to Patricia Natali, March 6, 2003.

4. Don't Give Up the Fight

1. Rachel Carson, *Silent Spring* (Boston: Houghton Mifflin, 1962).

2. Rachel Carson, *The Sea around Us* (Oxford: Oxford University Press, 1991).

3. See Giovanna Di Chiro, "Environmental Justice from the Grassroots: Reflections on History, Gender, and Expertise," in *The Struggle for Ecological Democracy,* ed. Daniel Faber (New York: Guilford Press, 1998), 104–36. Di Chiro grounds her claim in interviews that she conducted with women leaders involved in the environmental justice movement.

4. As Bill Lawson stated: "Environmentalists have not given due consideration to negative attitudes about cities and how these attitudes influence their environmental policies. . . . When negative attitudes about cities combine with certain racial attitudes, there is an adverse impact on the lives of poor black people who live in cities." Lawson, "Living for the City," in *Faces of Environmental Racism: Confronting Issues of Global Justice,* ed. Laura Westra and Peter S. Wenz (Lanham, Md.: Rowman and Littlefield, 1995), 41–42. Two significant exceptions to the neglect of cities in environmental thought stand out. Lewis Mumford began his career as an architectural critic for the *New Yorker.* His voluminous and often brilliant work on technology and human history lamented the decline of urban

life and proposed solutions for its revitalization. Mumford was an early and prescient critic of automobility. See, for example, *The City in History: Its Origins, Its Transformations, and Its Prospects* (New York: Harcourt, Brace, and World, 1961) and *The Culture of Cities* (New York: Harcourt, Brace, Jovonovich, 1970).

5. Dane Alston, quoted in Roger C. Field, "Risk and Justice: Capitalist Production and the Environment," in *The Struggle for Ecological Democracy: Environmental Justice Movements in the United States* (New York: Guilford Press, 1998), 83.

6. A good collection of environmental justice perspectives can be found in Paul Bryant, ed., *Environmental Justice: Issues, Policies, and Solutions* (Washington, D.C.: Island Press, 1995).

7. Di Chiro, "Environmental Justice," 109.

8. The commission presented five major findings: (1) "Race proved to be the most significant among variables tested in association with the location of commercial hazardous waste facilities. They represented a consistent national pattern"; (2) "Communities with the greatest number of hazardous waste facilities had the highest composition of racial and ethnic residents"; (3) "In communities with one commercial hazardous waste facility, the average minority percentage of the population was twice the average minority percentage of the population in communities without such facilities"; (4) "Although socio-economic status appeared to play an important role in the location of commercial hazardous waste facilities, race still proved to be more significant. This remained true after the study controlled for urbanization and regional differences"; and (5) "Three out of the five largest commercial hazardous waste landfills in the United States were located in predominantly Black or Hispanic communities." United Church of Christ Commission for Racial Justice, *Toxic Wastes and Race in the United States: A National Report on the Racial and Socioeconomic Characteristics of Communities with Hazardous Waste Sites* (New York: United Church of Christ, 1987), xiii.

9. A considerable body of research has accumulated since the 1987 study first appeared, not all of it confirming a correlation between race and the presence of waste disposal facilities. For findings that challenge the UCC Commission's findings, see Douglas Anderton et al., "Environmental Equity: Evaluating TSDF Siting over the Past Two Decades," *Waste Age*, July 1994, 83; and Douglas L. Anderton and Andrew B. Anderson, "Environmental Equity: Hazardous Waste Facilities: 'Environmental Equity' Issues in Metropolitan Areas," *Evaluation Review* 123 (1994). (Both studies were funded by Chemical Waste Management Inc.) For a critique of Anderton et al., see Vicki Been and Francis Gupta, "Coming to the Nuisance or Going to the Barrio? A Longitudinal Analysis of Environmental Justice Claims," *Ecology Law Quarterly* 24 (1997). The UCC Commission study was updated in 1994. The more recent analysis supported many of the claims of the

earlier one. See Benjamin Goldman and Laura Fitton, *Toxic Waste and Race Revisited: An Update of the 1987 Report on the Racial and Socioeconomic Characteristics of Communities with Hazardous Waste Sites* (Center for Policy Alternatives, NAACP, United Church of Christ Commission for Racial Justice, 1994).

10. Cerrell Associates, *Political Difficulties Facing Waste-to-Energy Conversion Plant Siting* (Los Angeles: California Waste Management Board, 1984), 1–2.

11. Ibid., 18–19.

12. Ibid., 19–22.

13. Ibid., 42–43.

14. Gregory E. McAvoy, "Partisan Probing and Democratic Decision-Making: Rethinking the Nimby Syndrome," *Policy Studies Journal* 26 (Summer 1998): 2. As Daniel A. Mazmanian and David Morell put it: "The good news for many, especially those living near a proposed site, is that most projects can today be stopped through concerted action by local citizens working with environmental and health advocates from within or outside the community. The bad news is that society often pays a high price for those local vetoes, harming the economic viability of those communities and eventually weakening the nation's economy." "The 'NIMBY' Syndrome: Facility Siting and the Failure of Democratic Discourse," in *Environmental Policy in the 1990s,* ed. Norman J. Vig and Michael E. Kraft (Washington, D.C., 1994), 234.

15. Myra Piat, "The Nimby Phenomenon: Community Residents' Concerns about Housing for Deinstitutionalized People," *Health and Social Work* 25 (May 2000): 127–38.

16. Terrance Sing, "Lanikai Residents on Cellular 'Antenna Farm,'" *Pacific Business News,* June 22, 2001, 26–27.

17. Dan Sandoval, "Surviving in a Nimby World: While Most People Favor Recycling as a Practice, Recycling Operations Are Considered Unwelcome Neighbors by Many," *Recycling Today,* March 1, 2003, 44–50. An excellent account of the environmental inequalities generated by the placement of recycling centers among the neighborhoods of the less affluent can be found in David Naguib Pello, *Garbage Wars: The Struggle for Environmental Justice in Chicago* (Cambridge: MIT Press, 2002).

18. NIMBY was followed by a whole series of acronyms that attempted to capture resistance to community intrusions of various kinds: LULA (Locally Unwanted Landuse), GOOMBY (Get out of my backyard), CAVEs (Citizens Against Virtually Everything), BANANAs (Build Absolutely Nothing Near Anyone), and NOPE (Not on Planet Earth). The acronyms are designed, so it seems, to undermine the idea that there may be a legitimate grievance at stake. The acronym NIMBY has now even been trademarked for a "natural" animal repellent. See http://www.nimby.com.

19. See, for example, C. Piller, *The Fail-Safe Society: Community Defiance and the End of American Technological Optimism* (New York: Basic Books, 1991).

20. Roberta Crowell Barbalace, "Environmental Justice and the NIMBY Principle," *Environmental Chemistry.com,* http://environmentalchemistry.com/yogi/ hazmat/ articles/nimby.html.

21. See, for example, Vicki Been, "Compensated Siting Proposals: Is It Time to Pay Attention? *Fordham Urban Law Journal* 21 (Spring 1994): 787–826; Bradford C. Mank, "The Two-Headed Dragon of Siting and Cleaning Up Hazardous Waste Dumps: Can Economic Incentives or Mediation Slay the Monster?" *Boston College Environmental Affairs Law Review* 19 (Fall–Winter 1991): 239–85; Barak D. Richman, "Mandating Negotiations to Solve the NIMBY Problem: A Creative Regulatory Response," *UCLA Journal of Environmental Law and Policy* 20 (Winter 2002): 223–37.

22. See, for example, Peter S. Wenz, "Just Garbage," in *Faces of Environmental Racism: Confronting Issues of Global Justice,* ed. Laura Westra and Peter S. Wenz (Lanham, Md.: Rowman and Littlefield), 57–71; and Daniel C. Wigley and Kristin Shrader-Frechette, "Consent, Equity, and Environmental Justice: A Louisiana Case Study," in Westra and Wenz, *Faces of Environmental Racism,* 135–57.

23. Barry G. Rabe, *Beyond Nimby: Hazardous Waste Siting in Canada and the United States* (Washington, D.C.: Brookings Institution, 1994), 58.

24. The Alberta case is often put forward as a model of democratic hazardous waste siting. See, for example, Mazmanian and Morell, "The 'NIMBY' Syndrome," 242–44; Michael L. Poirier Elliott, "Improving Community Acceptance of Hazardous Waste Facilities through Alternative Systems of Mitigating and Managing Risk," *Hazardous Waste* 1 (1984): 397–410; and Frank Fischer, *Citizens, Experts, and the Environment: The Politics of Local Knowledge* (Durham: Duke University Press, 2000), 130–32.

25. Rabe, *Beyond Nimby,* 59–89.

26. Ibid., 86.

27. Luke W. Cole and Sheila R. Foster, *From the Ground Up: Environmental Racism and the Rise of the Environmental Justice Movement* (New York: New York University Press, 2001), 17.

28. Kevin Michael DuLuca, *Image Politics: The New Rhetoric of Environmental Activism* (New York: Guilford Press, 1999), 80.

29. Rik Scarce, *Eco-warriors: Understanding the Radical Environmental Movement* (Chicago: Noble Press, 1990), 57.

30. Ibid., 57.

31. Ibid., 49.

32. DeLuca, *Image Politics,* 1–2.

33. Ibid., 1–22.

34. Ibid., 15.

35. Ibid., 96.

36. William C. Gates, *The City of Hills and Kilns: Life and Work in East Liverpool, Ohio* (East Liverpool: East Liverpool Historical Society), 401.

37. Terri Swearingen, interview by the author, February 27, 2004.

38. T. C. Brown, "Incinerator Opponents Bring Concerns Home to Voinovich," *Cleveland Plain Dealer*, October 28, 1991, 2.

39. T. C. Brown, "Curbside 'Weenie Roast,' to Protest Waste Burner," *Cleveland Plain Dealer*, November 21, 1991, 3.

40. Press Release, "Weenie Wielding Women (and Men) Whack Voinovich on Waste," Greenpeace U.S.A., Great Lakes Regional Office, November 21, 1991, 1.

41. T. C. Brown, "Protest Roasts 'Weenie': Incinerator Foes Skewer Voinovich," *Plain-Dealer*, December 11, 1991, 4.

42. Ibid.

43. Swearingen interview, February 27, 2004.

44. Brown, "Protest Roasts 'Weenie.'"

45. Scott Powers, "Product-Labeling Law Would Required Warnings," *Columbus Dispatch*, November 1, 1992, 2F.

46. Ann Fisher, "Governor Flees," October 7, 1992. Opposition to the measure was fierce. Business groups spent considerable resources to ensure its defeat. Some chemical companies threatened to pull out of the state, threatening a loss of jobs. The measure, which purportedly had strong support early on, was handily defeated at the polls. Scott Powers, "Economic Fears Help Kill Chemical Labeling Law," *Columbus Dispatch*, November 4, 1992, 4D.

47 Mike Rutledge, "Weenie Protestors Disrupt Voinovich," *Steubenville Herald-Star*, October 7, 1992, 1.

48. *Akron Beacon Journal*, October 8, 1992, 2.

49. Robert E, Miller, *Wheeling Intelligencer*, October 7, 1992, 1.

50. Mike Rutledge, *Steubenville Herald Star*, October 7, 1992, 1.

51. "Ohio," *USA Today*, October 7, 1992, 4.

52. As Patrick Novotny notes, communities affected by toxics "have sought ways of collecting materials on the health of communities themselves and have a well-tempered distrust of health professionals and government agencies that work with environmental health." "Popular Epidemiology and the Struggle for Community Health in the Environmental Justice Movement," in *The Struggle for Ecological Democracy: Environmental Justice Movements in the United States,* ed. Daniel R. Faber (New York: Guilford Press, 1998), 141.

Frank Fischer has noted that the implementation of immense technical systems such as nuclear power plants and waste incineration has reversed the relationship between laboratory and society. "Whereas science typically seeks reliable knowledge through laboratory experiments, in the case of contemporary large-scale technologies, the process has been reversed. Before scientists can learn about the long-term risks of our mega-technologies, they have to first build and implement them in the society at large." This "reversal of normal scientific procedures" raises "basic ethical and epistemological questions . . . about the logic and conduct of research." Fischer, *Citizens, Experts, and the Environment*, 54.

53. Press Release, "Voinovich Will Not Draw the Blood of Ohio Valley Children: Health Study Proposal Based on 'Poor Science,'" December 30, 1991.

54. Ted Hill, letter to Peter Somani, December 6, 1991.

55. David Ozonoff, letter to Terri Swearingen, December 4, 1991.

56. Ibid.

57. Ibid.

58. Herbert L. Needleman, letter to Terri Swearingen, December 4, 1991.

59. Ibid.

60. Glenn Clark, "Health Risk Study Could Be Canceled," *Evening Review*, December 31, 1991, 1.

61. Press Release, "Children of East Liverpool Take Their Fears to the Governor: WTI Opponents Call Health Study a Sham," March 23, 1992.

62. Ulrich Beck, *Ecological Enlightenment: Essays on the Politics of the Risk Society*, trans. Mark Ritter (Amherst, N.Y.: Prometheus Books, 1991), 104–5.

63. Swearingen interview, February 27, 2004.

64. "The Governed Begin to Withhold Their Consent and 34 Are Arrested in Ohio," *Rachel's Hazardous Waste News no. 255*, October 16, 1991. The *Rachel's* article lists the number at the EPA meeting as 400, but Terri Swearingen states that the number as actually 700. Swearingen interview, February 27, 2004.

65. Linda Harris, "WTI Protestors Thwart Hearing: Comments Must Now Be Written," *Weirton Daily Times*, September 26, 1991, 1.

66. "Incinerator Trespassing Trials Begin," *Weirton Times*, February 12, 1992, 4.

67. John Mollo, "WTI Protest Trial Under Way," *Morning Journal*, February 12, 1992, 1A. Terri informed me that many other people had been willing and eager to hop the fence. But those that did so had been trained in techniques of nonviolence by Greenpeace. In fact, marshalls at the demonstration had to hold people back. When Greenpeace had first been asked to work with the activists there was some resistance, because some in the movement felt that the Greenpeacers were violent. Soon, however, it became clear that Greenpeace had clear principles of non-

violence, and they were serious about having them applied to any actions with which they were involved.

68. "Incinerator Trespassing Trials Begin," *Weirton Times.*

69. Glenn Clark, "Pivotal Pretrial Hearing Today," *Evening Review,* February 2, 1992, 1.

70. 14 Q.B.D. 273 (1884).

71. Quoted in John Kaplan, Robert Weisberg, and Guyora Binder, *Criminal Law: Cases and Materials,* 4th ed. (Gaithersburg, Md.: Aspen Law and Business, 2000), 641.

72. Ibid., 641.

73. Ibid., 655, quoting Supreme Court of Vermont, 410 A.2d 1000 (1980).

74. Ibid., 656.

75. "Incinerator Trespassing Trials Begin," *Weirton Times,* February 12, 1992, 4.

76. Dennis Wise, "Residents Have Their Say," *Evening Review,* February 12, 1992, 1.

77. Dennis Wise, "Residents Have Their Say: More than 300 Rally against WTI Plant," *Evening Review,* February 12, 1992, 1.

78. Dennis Wise, "Residents Have Their Say," 5.

79. John Mollo, "Media Are the Masses," *Morning Journal,* February 12, 1992, 1.

80. T. C. Brown, "Potential Juror Poses with Sheen," *Cleveland Plain Dealer,* Feburary 12, 1992, C1.

81. Glenn Clark, "WTI: Plant Should Not Be Target during Trial," *Evening Review,* February 12, 1992, 5.

82. Memorandum in Support of Defendant's Necessity Rights, *State of Ohio vs. Paul Connett, et al.,* Nos. 91CRB1304–1336, 91CRB1367–1368, 5.

83. Memorandum in Support of Defendants' Necessity Defense, 4.

84. Ohio Revised Code sec. 2911.21 (A) (1).

85. Ohio Revised Code sec. 2901.01 (L).

86. *State of Ohio v. Martin Sheen,* 5.

87. Glenn Clark, "King: Protest Was 'Exception' to Law," *Evening Review,* February 12, 1992.

88. John Mollo, "WTI Protest Trial under Way."

89. Don Hopey, "Jury Shown Tape of Actor Leading Activists at WTI Site," *Pittsburgh Press,* February 13, 1992, B4.

90. T. C. Brown, "Incinerator Site Called Shock to Health Experts," *Cleveland Plain-Dealer,* Feburary 13, 1992, 2C.

91. Hopey, "Jury Shown Tape."

92. John Mollo, "Prosecution Rests; Defense Argues Necessity of Protestors' Actions," *Morning Journal,* February 13, 1992, A8.

93. "Incinerator Permit Hit," *Pittsburgh Press,* February 14, 1992, 10.

94. John Mollo, "Witness Puts WTI, EPA on Trial," *Morning Journal,* 14 February 1992, 2.

95. T. C. Brown, "EPA Witness Cites Public Spill Costs," *Cleveland Plain Dealer,* February 14, 1992, 2C.

96. Gleen Clark, "Trial Testimony Continues," *Evening Review,* February 15, 1992, 1.

97. T. C. Brown, "Case Goes to Jury," *Cleveland Plain Dealer,* February 15, 1992, C1.

98. T. C. Brown, "Incinerator Site Called Shock to Health Experts."

99. Theresa Pudik Card, "A Momentous Victory, Sheen Says of Group's Acquittal," *Beaver Times,* February 16, 1992, A1.

100. Dennis Wise, "Case Closed: They're Innocent," *Evening Review,* February 15, 1992, 1.

101. T. C. Brown, "Jury Acquits WTI 29: Sheen, Others Cheer Verdict," *Cleveland Plain Dealer,* February 15, 1992, C1.

102. Dennis Wise, "Byers-Emmerling Defends Decision for Necessity Ruling," *Evening Review,* February 19, 1992, 1.

103. T. C. Brown, "Trespass Case Puts WTI on Trial," *Cleveland Plain Dealer,* February 18, 1992, C1.

104. Dennis Wise, "Kaufman Issues Challenge to WTI, EPA: 'Indict Me,'" *Evening Review,* February 22, 1992, 1.

105. "WTI: Verdict Won't Hinder Construction," *Morning Journal,* February 18, 1992, A1.

106. "Ohio," *USA Today,* February 18, 1992, A5.

107. Press Release, "Governor Voinovich 'In Bed' with Toxic Polluters: Citizens Hold Statehouse Protest against WTI," Terri Swearingen, et al., March 5, 1992.

108. Glenn Clark, "WTI Opponents Press Voinovich," *Evening Review,* March 6, 1992, 1.

109. T. C. Brown, "Incinerator Foes Stage Protest at Statehouse," *Cleveland Plain Dealer,* March 6, 1992, 1.

110. Scott Powers, "Incinerator Foes Vow Civil Disobedience," *Columbus Dispatch,* June 10, 1992, 5.

111. "Our Opinion: Protestors Showing Great Determination," *Weirton Daily Times,* June 13, 1992, 30.

112. Holly Yeager, "12 Incinerator Foes Arrested at EPA Sit-In," *Plain Dealer,* July 21, 1992, C1.

113. "Operations Plan, Environmental Protection Agency, Washington, D.C.," prepared by Lt. George L. Wood, Federal Protective Service, n.d.

114. Ibid.

115. Ibid., 1.

116. Later, Terri would also obtain a copy of the agenda that apparently belonged to an EPA official, "Item I. Welcome; Item II. Discussion of Issues; Item III. Other Issues." Under the last was a handwritten note, "GO TO JAIL—GO DIRECTLY TO JAIL—DO NOT PASS GO—DO NOT COLLECT $200.00. Signed, USEPA." Agenda, EPA Meeting with Ohio Valley Residents, July 20, 1992. Some in the EPA were apparently eager to see the activists punished for their activities.

117. Linda Harris, "WTI Protestors Recount D.C. Arrests," *Weirton Daily Times,* July 23, 1992, 1.

118. Ibid.

119. Press release, "Recording Star Richard Marx Visits East Liverpool to Support WTI Hunger Strike," Tri-State Environmental Council, July 22, 1992.

120. Debra Utterback, "Rocker Joins Incinerator Protesters," *Beaver County Times,* July 21, 1992, A1.

121. *The Evening Review,* July 23, 1992, A1, A2.

122. *Morning Journal,* July 23, 1992, A1.

123. John Mollo, "Singer Joins Chorus Against WTI," *Morning Journal,* July 23, 1992, A10.

124. Dennis Wise, "Pop Singer Raps Incinerator: Richard Marx Says Building WTI 'Just Feels Wrong,'" *Evening Review,* July 23, 1992, A2.

125. Dennis Wise, "450 Storm WTI," *Evening Review,* November 23, 1992, 1.

126. Dennis Wise, "Tear Gas Used to Control Angry Mob," *Evening Review,* November 23, 1992, 1.

127. Jay Brooks, "8 WTI Foes Arrested at the White House," *Morning Journal,* March 19, 1993, 1; "Failure to Quit: Guilty as Charged," flyer, n.d.; Don Hopey, "8 Arrested as They Make White House Sit-In Protest," *Pittsburgh Post-Gazette,* March 19, 1992, B1; Katherine Rizzo, "Protesters Arrested in White House," *Canton Repository,* March 19, 1993, E10; Ronald A. Taylor, "Protesters Arrested in White House," *Washington Times,* March 19, 1993, B3; "A WTI Sit-in at the White House: Activists Want Gore to Keep His Promise," *Cleveland Plain Dealer,* March 10, 1993, 1; Randy Wynn, "WTI Foes Arrested at the White House," *Review,* March 19, 1993, 1.

128. Press Release, Tri-State Environmental Council, July 14, 1993.

129. Harry Staffer, "22 WTI Protestors Arrested Near Swiss Embassy in D.C.," *Pittsburgh Post-Gazette,* July 15, 1993, 1B; Holly Yeager, "Protest Visits Swiss Embassy," *Cleveland Plain Dealer,* July 15, 1993; "23 Arrested at Embassy," *Weirton*

Daily Times, July 15, 1993, 1; "Twenty-three Arrested in D.C.," *Evening Review,*
July 15, 1993, 1; "WTI Opponents, Blockage Embassy," *Wheeling Intelligence,*
July 15, 1993, 1; "23 Incinerator Foes Arrested at Embassy Protest," *Columbiana
County Morning Journal,* July 15, 1993, 1.

130. Flyer, n.d.

131. Eric C. Webb, "WTI Foes Call Clinton a Chicken," *Review,* November 3,
1994, 1.

132. "Calling Bill a Chicken," *Pittsburgh Post Gazette,* November 2, 1994, 4;
"Why Is the Chicken Across the Road?" *Washington Times,* November 2, 1994, 5.

133. Jim Mackey, "Opponents: Clinton's a Chicken," *East Liverpool Review,*
October 31, 1994, 1A.

134. Tom Giambroni, "WTI Fires Back," *Morning Journal,* March 21, 1997, 1.

135. Ibid.

136. Answer and Counterclaim, *David Hager et al. v. Waste Technologies Industries et al.,* Case No. 97 CV 34, 8.

137. Ibid., 9.

138. Ibid., 10.

139. "Answer and Counterclaim," 10.

140. Ibid., 11.

141. Ibid., 12.

142. Both UBS and Credit Suisse eventually arrived at a settlement of $1.25
billion. "Swiss: Bank Settlement Will Cause Large Tax Loss," *Jerusalem Post,* August 20, 1998, 4.

143. 376 U.S. 254 (1964).

144. Notice to Take Deposition Duces Tecum, *David Hager et al. v. Waste Technologies Industries et al.,* In the Court of Common Pleas of Columbiana County,
Ohio, Case No. 97 CV 34.

145. Alonzo Spencer told me, with undisguised glee, that he and his close
friend Virgil Reynolds, also a long-term active opponent to the plant, had taken
his files out of his house and moved them into a storage area in Virgil's garage.
Personal interview, July 2004.

146. Swearingen interview, February 27, 2004.

147. Press Release, "Company Suspends Counterclaims: A Gesture of Good
Faith," VonRoll/WTI, March 24, 2000.

148. Ibid.

149. Tom Giambroni, "WTI Suspends Counterclaims Until Class Action Suit
Is Settled," *Morning Journal,* March 25, 2000, 1.

150. Summary Order, Gary Lutin v. Bruce A. Cassidy, et al., U.S Court of
Appeals, Second Circuit, Case No. 98-7692, 18 March 1999.

151. Gary Lutin, letter to Heinz Muller, October 30, 1995, 1.

5. Risky Business

1. Francis Bacon, *The New Atlantis and The Great Insaturation* (Wheeling: Harlan Davidson, 1989).

2. See, for example, John Dewey, *How We Think* (Lexington, Mass.: D. C. Heath, 1910); and Dewey, *Human Nature and Conduct: An Introduction to Social Psychology* (New York: Modern Library, 1922).

3. Abraham Kaplan, *The Conduct of Inquiry: Methodology of Behavioral Science* (New York: Chandler Publishing, 1964), 131.

4. See, for example, Paul Thomas Kuhn, *The Structure of Scientific Revolutions* (Chicago: University of Chicago Press, 1962); Karl Popper, *The Logic of Scientific Discovery* (New York: Harper and Row, 1959); Paul Feyerabend, *Against Method: Outline of an Anarchistic Theory of Knowledge* (Atlantic Highlands, N.J.: Humanities Press, 1975).

5. Ulrich Beck, *Risk Society: Towards a New Modernity* (London: Sage Publications, 1992), 21.

6. Ibid., 163.

7. Deborah Lupton, *Risk* (New York: Routledge, 1999), 6.

8. Ibid., 42–43.

9. Beck, *Risk Society,* 21.

10. As Lupton notes: "Science itself fails to respond to the large-scale indeterminate nature of contemporary hazards. Hypotheses about their safety cannot be tested empirically and science has little power to intervene in a context in which the world has become a laboratory for testing how hazards affect populations. Scientist have therefore lost their authority in relation to risk assessments" (64).

11. Frank Fischer, *Citizens, Experts, and the Environment: The Politics of Local Knowledge* (Durham: Duke University Press, 2000), 82.

12. Peter Montague, "Celebrating EPA's Birthday—Part 1: At 20, EPA Should Know Better," *Rachel's Hazardous Waste News,* November 27, 1990, 1.

13. See, for example, Mary Douglas and Aaron Wildavsky, *Risk and Culture: An Essay on the Selection of Technological and Environmental Dangers* (Berkeley: University of California Press, 1982).

14. Steven B. Katz and Carolyn Miller, "The Low-Level Radioactive Waste Siting Controversy in North Carolina: Toward a Rhetorical Model of Risk Communication," in *Green Culture: Environmental Rhetoric in Contemporary America,* ed. Carl G. Herndl and Stuart C. Brown (Madison: University of Wisconsin Press, 1996), 131.

15. Fischer, *Citizens, Experts, and the Environment,* 137–138.

16. M. A. Marty, "Hazardous Combustion Products from Municipal Waste Incineration," *Occupational Medicine* 8 (July–September 1993): 603–20.

17. Peter Montague, "Emissions into the Local Environment from a Hazardous Waste incinerator," *Rachel's Environment and Health News*, June 4, 1991, 1.

18. Ibid.

19. Neil Tangri, *Waste Incineration: A Dying Technology* (Berkeley: Global Anti-Incineration Alliance, 2003), 1.

20. Ibid., 23.

21. Harvey W. Rogers and Betty C. Willis, "Public Health Overview of Incineration as a Means to Destroy Hazardous Waste: Guidance to ATDSR Health Assessors," Agency for Toxic Substances and Disease Registry, February 1992, http://www.atsdr/cdc/gpv/HAC/hwincin.html/#contents.

22. Montague, "Emissions," 1.

23. Peter Montague, "Hazardous Waste Incinerators," *Rachel's Environment and Health News*, November 27, 1988, 1.

24. Peter Montague, "Study of Hazardous Waste Incinerators Reveals 'Widespread Deficiencies'—EPA," *Rachel's Environment and Health News*, June 11, 1991, 1.

25. Ibid., 1.

26. Tangri, *Waste Incineration*, 9.

27 Rogers and Willis, "Public Health Overview," 6.

28. Montague, "Emissions," 1.

29. Ibid., 1.

30. Center for Health, Environment, and Justice, *America's Choice: Children's Health or Corporate Profit; The American People's Dioxin Report; Technical Support Document*, Falls Church, Va., November 1999, http://www.rachel.org/library/getfile.cfm?ID=111.

31. Ibid., 7.

32. Ibid.

33. Science Advisory Board, "An SAB Report: A Second Look at Dioxin," EPA-SAB-EC-95-02 (Washington, D.C.: U.S. Environmental Protection Agency, 1995), esp. chap. 8.

34. Barry Commoner, "The Political History of Dioxin," *Synthesis/Regeneration* 7–8 (Summer 1995), http://www.greens.org/s-r/078/07-03.html.

35. L. L. Aylward et al., "Relative Susceptibility of Animals and Humans to the Cancer Hazard Caused by 2,3,7,8-tetrachlorodibenzeno-p-dioxin Using Internal Measures of Dose," *Environmental Science and Technology* 34 (March–April 1997): 1507–22.

36. Heiko Becher et al., "Quantitative Cancer Risk Assessment for Dioxins Using an Occupational Cohort," *Environmental Health Perspectives* 106 (April 1998): 663–70; David Mackie et al., "No Evidence of Dioxin Cancer Threshold," *Environmental Health Perspectives* 111 (July 2003): 1145–47; Kyle Steenland et al.,

"Risk Assessment for 2,3,7,8-Tetrachlorodibenzo-p-Dioxin (TCDD) Based on an Epidemiologic Study," *American Journal of Epidemiology* 154 (September 2001): 451–58.

37. U.S. EPA, "Volume Three: Risk Characterization," *Draft Dioxin Reassessment,* Washington, D.C., 1994.

38. U.S. EPA, *Draft Dioxin Reassessment,* September 2000, http://cfpub.epa .gov/ncea/cfm/recordisplay.cfm?deid=55265&CFID=2156180&CFTOKEN =62646359.

39. Tangri, *Waste Incineration,* 13.

40. Ibid.; U.S. EPA, *Dioxin: Summary of the Dioxin Reassessment Science,* 2000.

41. See, for example, Jeong-Eun Oh et al., "The Evaluation of PCDDs from Various Korean Incinerators," *Chemosphere* 38 (April 1999): 2097–2108, comparing stack releases of dioxin from small incinerators, municipal incinerators, and industrial waste incinerators. Small incinerators turned out to release the highest dioxin concentrations.

42. Tangri, *Waste Incineration,* 1.

43. Mark D. Cohen et al., "Modeling the Atmospheric Transport and Deposition of PCDD/F to the Great Lakes," *Environmental Science and Technology* 36 (November 2002): 4831–45.

44. Mick Corliss, "Dioxin: Levels High in Incinerator Happy Japan," *Japan Times Online,* May 7, 1999, http://www.japantimes.co.jp/cgi-bin/getarticle.pl5 ?nn19990507a4.htm; Peter Hadfield, "Dioxin Limits Split Japan's Pollution Gurus," *New Scientist* 154 (May 1997), 6.

45. Michelle Allsopp, Pat Costner, and Paul Johnston, *Incineration and Human Health* (Exeter, U.K.: Greenpeace Research Laboratories, 2001), 46.

46. Ibid., 47.

47. Shin-Ichi Sakai et al. tracked the formation of dioxin-like PCBs from a municipal waste incinerator and the deposition of dioxin-like PCB congeners in the area of Kyoto City, Japan. They found that dioxin-like PCB 81, 126, 169, and 189 were deposited in amounts similar to those released from the incineration process, but that for other congeners—105, 114, 118—there were higher deposition rates than would be expected from incineration, leading the researchers to conclude that the other congeners were primarily from industrial PCB processes. "Dioxin-like PCBs Released from Waste Incineration and Their Deposition Flux," *Environmental Science and Technology* 35 (September 2001): 3601–7. T. H. Keller et al. analyzed unwashed leaf samples over a twenty-year period and found increases in chlorine compounds correlated with bringing a waste incinerator online. "Beech Foliage as a Bioindicator of Pollution Near a Waste Incinerator," *Environmental Pollution* 85 (1994): 184–89.

48. A. A. Lovett et al., "PCB and PCDD/DF Congeners in Locally Grown Fruit and Vegetable Samples in Wales and England," *Chemosphere* 34 (March–April 1997): 1421–36.

49. A. A. Lovett et al., "PCB and PCDD Concentrations in Egg and Poultry Meat Samples from Known Urban and Rural Locations in Wales and England," *Chemosphere* 37 (October–November 1998): 1671–85.

50. J. H. Leem et al., "Health Survey on Workers and Residents Near the Municipal Waste and Industrial Waste Incinerator in Korea," *Industrial Health* 41 (July 2003): 181–88.

51. T. Takata, "Survey on the Health Effects of Chronic Exposure to Dioxins and Its Accumulation on Workers of a Municipal Solid Waste Incinerator; Rural Part of Osaka Prefecture, and the Results of Extended Survey Afterwards," *Industrial Health* 41 (July 2003): 189–96.

52. M. Schuhmacher et al., "Baseline Levels of PCDD/Fs in Soil and Herbage Samples Collected in the Vicinity of a New Hazardous Waste Incinerator in Catalonia, Spain," *Chemosphere* 46 (March 2002): 1343–50.

53. E. Deml, "Chlorinated Dibenzodioxins and Dibenzofurans (PCDD/F) in Blood and Human Milk of Non-occupationally Exposed Persons Living in the Vicinity of a Municipal Waste Incinerator," *Chemosphere* 22 (November 1996): 1941–50.

54. This conclusion is based on a study of the exposure of Turkish incinerator workers to a variety of harmful substances, including particulates, heavy metals, volatile organic compounds, and dioxins. Using an analysis of ambient air samples in different parts of the plant, researchers concluded that dioxin exposure was highest near the kiln. M. Bakoglu, "An Evaluation of the Occupational Health Risks to Workers in a Hazardous Waste Incinerator," *Journal of Occupational Health* 46 (March 2004): 156–64.

55. T. Nakao et al., "Survey of Human Exposure to PCDDs, PCDFs, and Coplanar PCBs Using Hair as an Indicator," *Archives of Environmental Contamination and Toxicology* 12 (April 2005): 124–30.

56. Shingi Kamagai et al., "Exposure Evaluation of Dioxins in Municipal Waste Incinerator Workers," *Industrial Health* (July 2003): 167–74.

57 Ibid.

58. K. Kitamura, "Health Effects of Chronic Exposure to Polychlorinated Dibenzo-P-Dioxins (PCDD), Dibensofurans (PCDD) and Coplanar PCB (Co-PCB) of Municipal Waste Incinerator Workers," *Journal of Epidemiology* 10 (September 2000): 262–70.

59. Ibid., 171.

60. S. Kumagai et al., "Relationships between Dioxin Concentrations in De-

posited Dust and Those in Serum of Workers at Municipal Waste Incineration Plants," *Sangyo Eiseigakyu* 46 (January 2004): 1–9.

61. Allsopp, Costner, and Johnston, *Incineration and Human Health,* 47.

62. J. M. Blais et al., "Assessment and Characterization of Polychlorinated Biphenyls Near a Hazardous Waste Incinerator: Analysis of Vegetation, Snow, and Sediments," *Environmental Toxicology and Chemistry* 22 (January 2003): 126–33.

63. Allsopp, Costner, and Johnston, *Incineration and Human Health,* 48.

64. J. Angerer, "Internal Exposure to Organic Substances in a Municipal Waste Incinerator," *International Archives of Occupational and Environmental Health* 64 (1992): 265–73.

65. Allsopp, Costner, and Johnston, *Incineration and Human Health,* 48.

66. Ibid., 46.

67. Ibid., 49.

68. R. Wrbitsky et al., "Internal Exposure of Waste Incineration Workers to Organic and Inorganic Substances," *International Archives of Occupational and Environmental Health* 68 (1995): 13–21.

69. D. W. Decker, "Worker Exposure to Organic Vapors at a Liquid Chemical Waste Incinerator," *American Industrial Hygiene Association Journal* 44 (April 1983): 296–300.

70. Tangri, *Waste Incineration,* 17.

71. Luciano Morselli, "The Environmental Fate of Heavy Metals Arising from a MSW Incineration Plant," *Waste Management* 22 (2002): 875–81. Investigators examined levels of heavy metals in soil and vegetation over both time and distance, discerning correlations with yearly fluctuations of emissions and distance from the plant.

72. Y. Feng, "Distributions of Lead and Cadmium in Dust in the Vicinity of a Sewage Sludge Incinerator," *Journal of Environmental Monitoring* 1 (April 1999): 169–76.

73. V. Fontana et al., "Epidemiologic Study of the Residents of the Southeastern Area of the Municipality of La Spieza," *Epidemiological Preview* 24 (July 200): 172–79.

74. R. M. Stedman et al., "The Evaluation of Stack Metal Emissions from Hazardous Waste Incinerators: Assessing Human Exposure through Noninhalation Pathways," *Environmental Health Perspectives* 102 suppl. 2 (June 1994): 105–12.

75. R. Malkin, "Blood Levels in Incinerator Workers," *Environmental Research* 59 (October 1992): 265–70.

76. R. S. Collett, "An Investigation of Environmental Levels of Cadmium and Lead in Airborne Matter and Surface Soils within the Locality of a Municipal

Waste Incinerator," *Science of the Total Environment* 209 (January 1998): 157–67.

77. Carl A. Bache, "Cadmium and Lead Concentration in Foliage Near a Municipal Refuse Incinerator," *Chemosphere* 24 (1992): 475–81.

78. S. M. Koblantz, "Impact of Assessment of Emissions from a Municipal Waste Incinerator," *Environmental Monitoring and Assessment* 45 (1997): 21–42.

79. Allsopp, Costner, and Johnston, *Incineration and Human Health,* 49.

80. Murray M. Holmes, "Assessment of Mercury Emissions Inventories in the Great Lakes States," *Environmental Resources* 95 (July 2004): 282–97.

81. Tangri, *Waste Incineration,* 16.

82. P. Kurttio et al., "Increased Mercury Exposure in Inhabitants Living in the Vicinity of a Hazardous Waste Incinerator: A Ten-Year Follow-Up," *Archives of Environmental Health* 53 (March–April 1998): 129–37.

83. S. Gombert, "Monitoring the Chlorine Pollution of a Refuse Incinerator Using Lichens and Sphagnum Mosses," *Ecologie* 28 (1997): 365–72; Anthony Carpi, "Bioaccumulation of Mercury and Sphagnum Moss Near a Municipal Solid Waste Incinerator," *Journal of Air and Waste Management Association* 44 (1994): 669–72.

84. Tangri, *Waste Incineration,* 16.

85. Allsopp, Costner, and Johnston, *Incineration and Human Health,* 51.

86. Ibid.

87. Tangri, *Waste Incineration,* 23.

88. Allsopp, Costner, and Johnson, *Incineration and Human Health,* 46.

89. A. H. Stern, "Potential Exposure Levels and Health Effects of Neighborhood Exposure to Municipal Incinerator Bottom Ash Landfill," *Archives of Environmental Health* 55 (January–February 1989): 40–48.

90. A. Biggeri et al., "Air Pollution and Lung Cancer in Trieste, Italy: Spatial Analysis of Risk as a Function of Distance from Source," *Environmental Health Perspectives* 104 (July 1996): 750–54. The researchers looked at lung cancer increases at four sources: an iron foundry, a steelworks, and incinerator, and a city center. The incinerator was associated with the highest rates, although there was a steep decline away from the source.

91. P. Elliott et al., "Cancer Incidence Near Municipal Solid Waste Incinerators in Great Britain," *British Journal of Cancer* 73 (1996): 702–10.

92. The study encompassed residents of 70 municipal incinerators, 307 hospital incinerators, and 460 toxic waste landfill sites in Britain. The authors found increased risk (2:1) of childhood cancer relative to the distance from incineration sites. E. Knox, "Childhood Cancers, Birthplaces, Incinerators, and Landfill Sites," *International Journal of Epidemiology* 29 (June 2000): 391–97.

93. Per Gustavsson et al., "Increased Risk of Esophageal Cancer among Work-

ers Exposed to Combustion Products," *Archives of Environmental Health* 48 (July–August 1993): 243–45.

94. Per Gustavsson, "Mortality among Workers at a Municipal Waste Incinerator," *American Journal of Industrial Medicine* 15 (1989): 245–53.

95. P. Michelozzi et al., "Small Area Study of Mortality among People Living Near Multiple Sources of Air Pollution," *Occupational and Environmental Medicine* 55 (September 1998): 611–15.

96. E. G. Knox and E. A. Gilman, "Hazard Proximities of Childhood Cancers in Grear Britain from 1953–1980," *Journal of Epidemiology and Community Health* 51 (April 1997): 161–69.

97. Allsopp, Costner, and Johnston, *Incineration and Human Health,* 29.

98. E. A. Bresnitz, "Morbidity among Municipal Waste Incinerator Workers," *American Journal of Industrial Medicine* 22 (1992): 363–78.

99. Allsopp, Costner, and Johnston, *Incineration and Human Health,* 32.

100. I. Mori et al., "The Sex Ratio in the Offspring of Municipal Solid Waste Incineration Workers," *Epidemiology* 15 (July 2004): S118–19.

101. N. Obi-Osius et al., "Twin Frequency and Industrial Pollution in Different Regions of Hesse, Germany," *Occupational Environmental Medicine* 61 (June 2004): 482–87. (The ratio of twins born near the incinerator was 1.4–1.6 per 100 versus a rate of .8 per 100 in the general population.)

102. Gavin W. Ten Tusscher et al., "Open Chemical Combustions Resulting in a Local Increased Incidence of Orofacial Clefts, " *Chemosphere* 40 (May–June 2000): 1263–70.

103. T. J. Dummer, H. O. Dickinson, and L. Parker, "Adverse Pregnancy Outcomes around Incinerators and Crematoriums in Cumbria, North West England," *Journal of Epidemiology and Community Health* 57 (June 2004): 456–61. Given the criticism that studies of incineration and human health have not always properly controlled for social class and other potentially intervening variables, this study was especially significant. Researchers controlled for class, birth order, birth year, and multiple births. The criticism regarding improper controls has been made forcefully in L. Rushton, "Health Hazards and Waste Management," *British Medical Bulletin* 68 (2003): 183–97.

104. T. Tango et al., "Risk Adverse Reproductive Outcomes Associated with Proximity to Municipal Solid Waste Incinerators with High Dioxin Emissions Levels in Japan," *Journal of Epidemiology* 14 (May 2004): 83–93.

105. S. Cordier et al., "Risk of Congenital Anomalies in the Vicinity of Municipal Solid Waste Incinerators," *Occupational Environmental Medicine* 61 (January 2004): 8–15.

106. See, for example, "Air Pollution and Daily Mortality in Rome Italy," *Occupational and Environmental Health* 55 (September 1998): 605–10.

107. ATSDR (Agency for Toxic Substances and Disease Registry), U.S. Department of Health and Human Services, *Study of Symptom and Disease Prevalence, Caldwell Systems, Inc. Hazardous Waste Incinerator, Caldwell County, North Carolina, Final Report*, ATSDR/HS-93/29, Atlanta, Georgia, 1993.

108. Martin S. Legator et al., found statistically significant higher levels of respiratory distress between those living near the kiln and those in a control group (p value = .002) even with a small sample size (58 and 54 in the test and control groups respectively). "The Health Effects of Living Near Cement Kilns: A Symptom Survey in Midlothian, Texas," *Toxicology and Industrial Health* 14 (November–December 1998): 829–43.

109. J. Y. Wang et al., "Bronchial Responsiveness in an Area of Air Pollution Resulting from Wire Reclamation," *Archives of Disease in Childhood* 67 (April 1992): 488–90.

110. M. J. Hazucha et al., "Characterization of Spirometric Function in Residents of Three Comparison Communities and of Three Communities Located Near Waste Incinerators in North Carolina," *Archives of Environmental Health* 57 (March–April 2002): 103–12.

111. C. M. Shy, "Do Waste Incinerators Induce Adverse Respiratory Effects? An Air Quality and Epidemiological Study of Six Communities," *Environmental Health Perspectives* 103 (July–August 1995): 714–24.

112. E. J. Gray et al., "Asthma Severity and Morbidity in a Population Sample of Sydney School Children: Part I—Prevalence and Effect of Air Pollution in Coastal Regions," *Australia and New Zealand Journal of Medicine* 24 (April 1994): 168–75.

113. T. J. Callendar, "Social and Economic Impact of Neurotoxicity in Hazardous Waste Workers in Lenoir, North Carolina," *Environmental Research* 73 (1997): 166–74.

114. M. Hours et al., "Morbidity among Municipal Waste Incinerator Workers: A Cross-Sectional Study," *International Archives of Occupation and Environmental Health* 76 (July 2003): 467–72.

115. J. M. Scarlett et al., "Urinary Mutagens in Municipal Refuse Incinerator Workers and Water Treatment Workers," *Journal of Toxicology and Environmental Health* 31 (1990): 11–28.

116. X. F. Ma et al., "Mutagens in Urine Sampled Repetitively from Muncipal Refuse Incinerator Workers and Water Treatment Workers," *Journal of Toxicology and Environmental Health* 37 (December 1992): 483–94.

117. Donggeun Sul et al. studied the impact of PAHs on two groups of workers: auto-emissions workers and workers in incineration plants. They found significant damage to T-cells, but some damage to B-lymphocytes and granulocytes as well, in both groups of workers. "DNA Damage in T- and B-lymphocytes and

Granulocytes in Emission Inspection and Incineration Workers Exposed to Poly-cyclic Aromatic Hydrocarbons," *Mutation Research/Genetic Toxicology and Environmental Mutagenesis* 538, nos. 1–2 (July 2003): 109–20.

118. G. Blanko et al., "Contamination with Nonessential Metals from a Solid-Waste Incinerator Correlates with Nutritional and Immunological Stress in Pre-fledgling Black Kites," *Environmental Research* 94 (January 2004): 94–101.

119. O. L. Lloyd et al., "Twinning in Human Populations and in Cattle Exposed to Air Pollution from Incinerators," *British Journal of Independent Medicine* 45 (August 1988): 556–60; Williams et al., "Low Sex Ratios of Births in Areas at Risk from Air Pollution from Incinerators as Shown by Geographical Analysis and 3-Dimensional Mapping," *International Journal of Epidemiology* 21 (April 1992): 311–19.

120. Allsopp, Costner, and Johnston, *Incineration and Human Health,* 34.

121. Tangri, *Waste Incineration,* 1.

122. Peter Montague, "Hazardous Waste Incinerators," *Rachel's Environment and Health News,* November 27, 1988, 1.

123. Tangri, *Waste Incineration,* 19

124. Ibid., 20. The other way that emissions are estimated is via trial burns. Trial burns are problematic, however, in that they are generally conducted under ideal conditions, so that the actual releases of dioxins and other substances are substantially underestimated (19).

125. Letter to Mr. Schregardus, "Summary Document: U.S. EPA Risk Assessment Regarding the WTI Facility," April 1998, 1.

126. Pat Costner, letter dated January 5, 1995, in U.S. EPA, *Risk Assessment for the Waste Technologies Industries (WTI) Hazardous Waste Incineration Facility (East Liverpool, Ohio). Volume I: Executive Summary,* EPA-905-R97-002a, May 1997, G-15.

127. Ashley C. Schannauer, "Issues in Environmental Law: The WTI Risk Assessments: The Need for Effective Public Participation," *Vermont Law Review* 24 (Fall 1999): 66.

128. Robert J. Martin, National Ombudsman, memorandum to Timothy Fields, Assistant Administrator, *Preliminary National Ombudsman Report—Waste Technologies Industries (WTI) East Liverpool, Ohio,* October 20, 2000, 21.

129. Ibid., 25.

130. Ibid., 26.

131. Steve Bennish and Ken McCall, "Scandal May Trail Voinovich: Feds Cast Wide Net in Corruption Hunt," *Dayton Daily News,* November 22, 1998, 1A.

132. Steven Bennish, "U.S. Judge Sentences 3 for Scam," *Dayton Daily News,* March 11, 2001, 1B.

133. Bennish and McCall, "Scandal May Trail Voinovich," 3A.

134. "Senator's Brother Accused of Kickbacks," *Associated Press,* March 29, 1999. 1.

135. William MacDowell, Chief AECAB, memorandum to Ivan Lieben, Assistant Regional Counsel, Re: Draft: Ohio Petition Review, North East District Office, December 28, 2000. A number of comments from the reviewer throughout the discussion of WTI reporting indicate the minimal or nonexistent character of much reporting (27, 28, 29, 30, 31, 32). There seems doubt that proper records were being kept through much of this period. Moreover, the evidence suggests that the Ohio EPA did its best to accommodate WTI when air pollution control regulations were violated, and reduced fines on the grounds of economic hardship, not taking into account the assets of the parent company (37).

136. Martin, *Preliminary National Ombudsman Report,* 27.

137. Ibid., 30.

138. Ibid., 31.

139. Robert J. Martin, National Ombudsman, letter to Christine Todd Whitman, Administrator U.S. EPA, Re: Resignation from Service, April 22, 2002.

140. Edward Walsh, "Ombudsman Resigns Over Transfer," *Washington Post,* April 23, 2002, A2.

141. "EPA Official Quits After Move," *New York Times,* April 23, 2002, B2.

142. Bryan Zima, memorandum to Karen Haight, Re: Investigation, April 8, 2003.

143. Quoted in "EPA Cannot Assure Citizens in the Tri-State Area that Von-Roll/WTI Poses No Risk to Human Health," *Greenlink,* June 19, 2003, http://www.greenlink.org/public/hotissues/wti7.html.

144. VOCs are volatile organic compounds, or organic compounds that evaporate easily, including substances such as toluene, methylene chloride, and methyl chloroform.

145. Polycyclic aromatic hydrocarbons are actually a group of ten thousand chemicals. These compounds are generally formed during processes of combustion. The U.S. Department of Health and Services has determined these substances to be carcinogenic when breathed or eaten, or when the skin is exposed. "ToxFAQs for Polycyclic Aromatic Hydrocarbons (PAHs)," Agency for Toxic Substances Disease Registry, September 1996, http://www.atsdr.cdc.gov/tfacts69.html#bookmark05.

146. "EPA Cannot Assure Citizens."

147. Zima memorandum, 3.

148. Geoff Dutton, "EPA Air-Quality Data Unaccounted for: Columbiana County Waste-Burning Site not Fully Monitored," *Columbus Dispatch,* June 21, 2003, 1C.

149. Ibid., 1C.

150. Ibid., 1C.

151. Eastern Research Group, *Report on the U.S. EPA Technical Workshop on WTI Incinerator Risk Assessment Issues,* U.S. EPA Risk Assessment Forum, May 2, 1996, 1–2.

152. Dated November 14, 1999. Ohio EPA, June 9, 2003, 9.

153. Dated March 15, 1995 and August 6, 1996. On the first occasion, the source of the release was never found. Ohio EPA, June 9, 2003, 5, 6.

154. Dated February 10, 1996, and December 9, 1998. Ohio EPA, June 9, 2003, 6.

155. Letter to Mr. Schregardus, *Summary Document: U.S. EPA Risk Assessment regarding the WTA Facility,* April 1998, 4.

156. *Trueblood v. Von Roll,* 2002-WPC-3 to 6, 2003-WPC-1 (*Administrative Law Judges, Decisions and Orders,* March 26, 2003), 2.

157. See U.S. EPA, "Chemical Specific Toxicity Values," http://risk.lsd.ornl.gov/tox/tox_values. shtml, January 2004.

158. Schannauer, "Issues in Environmental Law," 67.

159. Ibid., 67–68.

160. Ibid.

161. U.S. EPA, "The 1994 Dioxin Reassessment, Health Assessment, Volume III: Risk Characterization," Sec. 9.7, http://www.cqs.com/dioxh97.htm.

162. U.S. EPA, "The 1994 Dioxin Reassessment," Sec. 9.11.

163. Letter to Schregardus, 3.

164. Tom Webster, letter dated January 10, 1996, in U.S. EPA, *Risk Assessment,* G-17.

165. Schannauer, "Issues in Environmental Law," 80.

166. Joe Thornton, *Pandora's Poison: Chlorine, Health, and a New Environmental Strategy* (Cambridge: MIT Press, 2000), 52.

167. Schannauer, "Issues in Environmental Law," 45–46.

168. Tom Webster, letter dated January 10, 1996, U.S. EPA, G-17.

169. Ulrich Beck, "The Reinvention of Politics: Towards a Theory of Reflexive Modernization," in *Reflexive Modernization: Politics, Tradition and Aesthetics in the Modern Social Order,* ed. Ulrich Beck, Anthony Giddens, and Scott Lash (Palo Alto: Stanford University Press, 1994), 9.

Conclusion

1. Michael B. Gerrard, "Fear and Loathing in the Siting of Hazardous and Radioactive Waste Facilities: A Comprehensive Approach to a Misperceived Crisis," *Tulane Law Review* 68 (May 1994): 1170.

2. Peter Montague, "Hazardous Waste Incineration—Part 4: Real Alternatives to Incineration," *Rachel's Hazardous Waste News,* November 13, 1990.

3. Ibid.

4. Brad Lemley, "Anything into Oil," *Discover,* May 24, 2003.

5. Jerome Burne, "Life: Is This the Ultimate Recycler?" *Guardian,* May 22, 2003, 11.

6. Lemley, "Anything into Oil," 2, 5.

7. "Changing World Technologies Named to Scientific American 50," *PR Newswire,* December 8, 2003, http://www.prnewswire.com.

8. A. J. Carter, "The Ticker," *Newsday,* January 19, 2003, A25.

9. Zachary Coile, "Fat Energy Bill Seen as Laden with Pork," *San Francisco Chronicle,* November 21, 2003, A2.

10. "Changing World Technologies Responds to False Information Posted by U.S. PIRG," *PR Newswire Association,* November 19, 2003.

11. Joe Thornton, *Pandora's Poison: Chlorine, Health, and the New Environmental Strategy* (Cambridge: MIT Press, 2000), 364.

12. DDT is slated for eventual elimination, but its limited use for malaria control is recognized by the convention.

13. See Stockholm Convention on Presistent Organic Pollutants, http://www.pops.int/documents/convtext/convtext_en.pdf. Also see Peter Hough, "Poisons in the System: The Global Regulation of Hazardous Pesticides," *Global Environmental Politics,* May 2003, 11–21.

14. Hough, "Poisons in the System," 16.

15. "POPS Treaty Enacted," *Science News,* November 8, 2003, 30.

16. Kristin S. Schafer, "Global Toxics Treaty: U.S. Leadership Opportunity Slips Away," *Foreign Policy in Focus,* September 9, 2002, 1.

17. Paul Hawken, Amery Lovins, and L. Hunter Lovins, *Natural Capitalism: Creating the Next Industrial Revolution* (Back Bay Books, 2000), 127.

18. The information in this section, unless otherwise cited, comes from interviews that I conducted with Alonzo Spencer and Terri Swearingen, July 7 and 11, 2005, respectively.

19. Ohio Citizen Action, citing *Columbiana County Morning Journal,* January 27, 2004, http://www.ohiocitizen.org/campaigns/wti/wti.html.

20. Terri Swearingen to Gary Victorine, February 6, 2004.

21. Gary Victorine to Beverly Reynolds (Save Our County), February 6, 2004.

22. Terri Swearingen to Gary Victorine, February 12, 2004.

23. Gary Victorine to Terry Swearingen, February 12, 2004.

24. Fred Miller, "WTI Fireball Rattles Windows," *East Liverpool Review,* cited at Save Our County Web site, http://saveourcounty.homestead.com/soc_home.html.

25. Fred Miller, "EPA Proposes $600K Fine against WTI," *East Liverpool Review,* cited at http://saveourcounty.homestead.com/soc_home.html (italics mine).

26. U.S. EPA, *Hazardous Waste Combustors: Maximum Achievable Control Technology Standards,* June 2005, http://www.epa.gov/epaoswer/hazwaste/combust.

27. The analysis here was provided in a letter from Eric Schaeffer to Sandy Buchanan of Ohio Citizen Action. Schaeffer had been the EPA's director of regulatory enforcement for five years. He resigned his position in protest over what he viewed as the White House's determination to undermine enforcement of power plant air pollution regulations. See "Top EPA Official Resigns," *Grist Magazine,* March 2002, http://www.grist.org/news/muck/2002/03/01.

28. Fred Miller, "WTI Celebrates Wildlife Habitat Recertification," *Review Online,* July 8, 2005, http://www.reviewonline.com/business/story/078202005 _biz01 wticelebration.asp.

Index

Riady, James, 63
Riady, Mochtar, 63, 64
Richy, Sam, 179
risk assessment, 176, 178, 255n10;
   accident assessment; 148, ambient
   air analysis, 145–7, 169; as chain
   of uncertainties, 194; and citing
   decisions, 168; as cost-benefit
   analysis, 152, 193–94; and death,
   152, 193–94; and democracy, 195;
   and fear, 153; food chain analysis,
   145–47, 169–70; as fragmented,
   194; historical origins, 150 -151;
   as political, 153; and rationality,
   153; as wrong, 168. *See also* WTI
   risk assessment
risk-free society, 153
River Services company, 62
Rodfong, G. Thomas, 129, 130, 131
Rose Law Firm, 55, 56, 63, 64
Rosa Parks, vii
Rothblatt, Steve, 75
Ruckelshaus, William, 71
Rupert, John, 69
rust belt, ix

Saro-Wiwa, Ken, 205
Save Our County, 38, 76, 140, 207
Scafide, James, 130
Scarce, Rik, 116
Scarlett, J. M., 167
Schannauer, Ashley, 173, 190
Schneider, Keith, 4
Schregardus, Donald, 170
scientific method, 124; and citizen
   activism, 149, 250n52; and environ-
   mentalism, 150; and risk assess-
   ment, 151, 152, 165–66, 168, 194,
   n255
Sea around Us, The, 109

sex ratios, 166
Shank, Richard, 89
Sheen, Martin, 106, 125–26, 128, 130,
   131, 135, 147
Shell Oil Corporation, 205
Sigg, Fred, 108, 138–39, 141, 181,
   186–89
Silent Spring, 109
SLAPP suit, 143, 138–41; discovery
   process, 140–41
Solid Waste Disposal Act (SWDA), 46
sovereignty, 22–24
Spencer, Alonzo, 7–8, 9, 11, 52, 97, 98,
   10, 114, 119, 125, 133, 134, 169, 209,
   214, 245n53, biography, 76–79;
   lawsuit against, 138–41; optimism
   of, 210
State v. Warshaw, 127
Stein, Connie, 121
Stephens Inc., 62–63, 64
Stephens, Jackson, 20, 55, 56, 61,
   63–65, 219, 225
Stephens, Witt, 62, 64
St. Lawrence County, 146
St. Lawrence University, 145, 146
Stockholm Convention on Persistent
   Organic Pollutants. *See* POPs
   Treaty
"stopping up the toilet," 114–15
supergun, 18, 91–92
Superfund, 44, 45, 46, 58, 68, 177, 199.
   See also Comprehensive Environ-
   mental Response, Compensation,
   and Liability Act
Sussman, Robert, 4
sustainable business practices, x,
   202–6
Swan Hills hazardous waste facility,
   113–14, 161
SWDA. *See* Solid Waste Disposal Act

Thomas Shevory is professor of politics at Ithaca College, where he teaches courses in public law, public policy, and popular culture. He is the author of five books, including *Notorious H.I.V.: The Media Spectacle of Nushawn Williams* (Minnesota, 2004). He has been coordinator of the Ithaca College Environmental Studies Program and is codirector of the Finger Lakes Environmental Film Festival.